AF866009

VOLUME 7

THE COLLECTED WORKS OF ARTHUR SELDON

The IEA, the LSE, and the Influence of Ideas

THE COLLECTED WORKS OF ARTHUR SELDON

VOLUME 1 The Virtues of Capitalism

VOLUME 2 The State Is Rolling Back

VOLUME 3 Everyman's Dictionary of Economics

VOLUME 4 Introducing Market Forces into "Public" Services

VOLUME 5 Government Failure and Over-Government

VOLUME 6 The Welfare State: Pensions, Health, and Education

VOLUME 7 The IEA, the LSE, and the Influence of Ideas
(includes an index to the series)

Arthur Seldon

VOLUME 7

THE COLLECTED WORKS OF ARTHUR SELDON

The IEA, the LSE, and the Influence of Ideas

ARTHUR SELDON

Edited and with a New Introduction by Colin Robinson

LIBERTY FUND, Indianapolis

This book is published by Liberty Fund, Inc., a foundation established to encourage study of the ideal of a society of free and responsible individuals.

The cuneiform inscription that serves as our logo and as the design motif for our endpapers is the earliest-known written appearance of the word "freedom" (*amagi*), or "liberty." It is taken from a clay document written about 2300 B.C. in the Sumerian city-state of Lagash.

New Robinson Introduction © 2005 by Liberty Fund, Inc.
All rights reserved
Frontispiece photo courtesy of the Institute of Economic Affairs
"The Essence of the IEA" from *The Emerging Consensus? Essays on the Interplay Between Ideas, Interests and Circumstances in the First 25 Years of the IEA* © 1981 Institute of Economic Affairs and reprinted with permission.
"New Hope for Economic Policy in a Changing Polity" from *Agenda for Social Democracy* © 1983 Institute of Economic Affairs and reprinted with permission.
"Recollections: Before and After *The Road to Serfdom*" from *Hayek's "Serfdom" Revisited: Essays by Economists, Philosophers and Political Scientists on "The Road to Serfdom" After 40 Years* © 1984 Institute of Economic Affairs and reprinted with permission.
"Economic Scholarship and Political Interest: IEA Thinking and Government Policies" from *Ideas, Interests and Consequences* © 1989 Institute of Economic Affairs and reprinted with permission.
"From the LSE to the IEA" from *Economic Affairs* 18, no. 1 (March 1998) © 1998 Institute of Economic Affairs and reprinted with permission.
The Making of the Institute: A Selection of Arthur Seldon's Prefaces 1960–1992 © 2002 Arthur Seldon and reprinted with permission.

Printed in the United States of America
09 08 07 06 05 C 5 4 3 2 1
09 08 07 06 05 P 5 4 3 2 1

Library of Congress Cataloging-in-Publication Data

Seldon, Arthur.
The IEA, the LSE, and the influence of ideas/Arthur Seldon; edited and with a new introduction by Colin Robinson.
p. cm—(Collected works of Arthur Seldon; v. 7)
Includes bibliographical references and index.
ISBN-13: 978-0-86597-548-4 (alk. paper) ISBN-10: 0-86597-548-5 (alk. paper)
ISBN-13: 978-0-86597-556-9 (pbk.: alk. paper) ISBN-10: 0-86597-556-6 (pbk.: alk. paper)
1. Great Britain—Economic policy—20th century. 2. Economics—Great Britain—History—20th century. 3. Institute of Economic Affairs (Great Britain) 4. London School of Economics and Political Science. I. Title.

HC256.143 2005
338.941'009'045—dc22

2005045185

LIBERTY FUND, INC.
8335 Allison Pointe Trail, Suite 300
Indianapolis, Indiana 46250-1684

CONTENTS

INTRODUCTION

The seventh and final volume of *The Collected Works of Arthur Seldon* brings together six works in which Seldon discusses the role of the Institute of Economic Affairs (IEA), the London-based think tank where he spent most of his working life, and in which he explores his own relationship with the IEA. Seldon worked together with Ralph (later Lord) Harris from 1957, when the institute began operating after its founding in 1955, for about thirty years in a remarkably fruitful partnership that was of great significance in reviving classical liberal thinking and applying it to economic policy.[1] Many of the liberal market think tanks in the United States and other countries were established by Antony (later Sir Antony) Fisher, the founder of the IEA, and were modeled on and took their inspiration from the IEA. The regard with which the IEA and sister think tanks came to be held is clear from the following quotation from *The Economist* in December 1993: "Governments in search of advice looked to think tanks such as the Institute of Economic Affairs in Britain and the Heritage Foundation in the United States rather than to Oxford or Harvard."

F. A. Hayek, who regarded himself as partly responsible for the creation of the IEA (see page 84), was very much aware of its influence. For example, when the Cato Institute, now in Washington, D.C., was being formed in 1982, Hayek advised it to study the IEA's publications catalogue: "The IEA has become the most powerful maker of opinion in England. Bookshops have a special rack of IEA papers. Even people on the Left feel compelled to keep informed of its publications."[2] Seldon has always emphasized the power of ideas to change society, and the writings gathered here provide an insight into how he saw the place of the IEA, and his own role within the IEA, in

1. Further details are in the introduction to volume 1 of these Collected Works.

2. Arthur Seldon, *The Making of the Institute* (London: Economic and Literary Books, 2002), the final work in this volume, page 84.

the market for ideas in which he and Harris were complementary entrepreneurs.

In 1981 the IEA published a collection of essays titled *The Emerging Consensus*, in which a number of distinguished scholars discussed the Institute's work in the previous quarter century. Some were academics, not all completely sympathetic to classical liberal ideas, one was a senior civil servant, and another was an industrialist. Seldon wrote a preamble to the collection, "The Essence of the IEA," which sets out the Institute's "central approach" and reveals how he set about his task of commissioning and editing publications. It is the first work in this volume.

Seldon explains that dissatisfaction with the Keynesian and collectivist consensus led the IEA to muster and present "in modern dress the truths of classical political economy"—that government cannot possess the information required to produce the desired use of resources, that only individuals can derive such information, and that effective use of the information requires their "coming together as buyers and sellers in markets" (p. 4). The essence of the IEA approach, says Seldon, is to question the belief that "government could deal with any and every economic problem by regulation or direct management" (pp. 4–5), starting instead from the view that, except in some specific circumstances, such as where there are genuine "public goods,"[3] economic and social problems are best solved by individual, voluntary action. The Institute unleashed a barrage of papers that "refined and applied old truths to new subjects in contemporary circumstances" (p. 6). A feature of Seldon's editorship was his insistence that authors "apply economic analysis ruthlessly," paying no regard to the "administrative practicability" or the "political impossibility" (p. 6) that so often provides excuses for delay or inaction.

Seldon goes on to illustrate the IEA approach by reference to its publications, explaining, for example, the "indispensable role of price," before, in the final section of his preamble, coming to the vexed questions of whether ideas triumph over interests (as Keynes believed) or Marx was right in arguing that vested interests rule the world. The IEA's experience, argues Seldon, shows the power of ideas: the Institute's papers have clearly influenced thinking. Ideas, however, though necessary, are not sufficient to change policy. For that purpose, the "conspiring circumstances" identified by John Stuart Mill are required. The "battle of ideas is being won in the mind" be-

3. For an explanation of the public goods problem see the introduction to volume 1 of these Collected Works, note 3.

cause "IEA ideas increasingly synchronised with the developing disillusionment with the false wartime and post-war macro-economic consensus; they opened men's minds to new thinking, unconventional diagnoses and unfamiliar policies" (p. 14). The obstacles to reform are still formidable because of obstruction from vested interests, but, in the end, those interests will find it difficult to resist change. Despite its failings, Seldon says, "the market remains the best hope of mankind" (p. 16).

The second work in this volume consists of the opening chapter from a book, *Agenda for Social Democracy,* published by the IEA in 1983 (Hobart Paperback 15). Seldon's chapter is titled "New Hope for Economic Policy in a Changing Polity." The book was published at a time when a realignment in British politics appeared to be taking place. Some prominent members of the Labour Party had left the party to form the Social Democratic Party (SDP), which had then allied itself, for electoral purposes, with the Liberals. The intention of the book is to explore the meaning of "social democracy." Both Harris and Seldon contributed chapters, and there were seven other authors, mainly academic economists.

Seldon argues that the incipient realignment in British politics opens the way for new thinking on the scope for the market and other voluntary institutions. The new elements in the 1980s, he says, are the "questioning of [the] efficacy of the state by influential public men and women" (p. 22) who had previously accepted that efficacy, and the related view that prosperity requires the increased use of decentralized institutions. Seldon then poses ten questions that must be addressed if the maximum scope for voluntary market exchange is to be achieved, with government confined to its necessary functions and with a smooth transition to the new regime. He predicts a bright future for the British economy if, in contrast to the previous thirty-five years, it is governed by alternating political coalitions, "both of which accept the verdict of history that voluntary co-operation, in the market or outside it, is not only compatible with social equity but essential to achieve it" (p. 24). Both Britain's major political parties now accept the benefits of using markets (even if acceptance within the Labour Party is still somewhat grudging). The free market reforms of the Thatcher years are still mainly in place and the more flexible economy that has ensued has significantly enhanced economic performance relative to other European Union countries whose governments are reluctant to accept the central place of markets.

The following year, 1984, the IEA published a tribute to Hayek's *Road to Serfdom,* on the fortieth anniversary of its publication. The book, *Hayek's*

"Serfdom" Revisited (Hobart Paperback 18), contains six chapters by classical liberal scholars and an introductory piece by Seldon, "Recollections: Before and After *The Road to Serfdom.*" Seldon's paper is the third work in this volume of his Collected Works.

His recollections of Hayek are of particular interest, as Seldon is the only author in the IEA volume to have known Hayek personally. In his chapter he describes the influence Hayek had on him, first at the London School of Economics and Political Science (LSE) in the 1930s and later at the IEA. That influence began as a teacher-student relationship in 1934, when Seldon, as an undergraduate at the LSE, attended Hayek's lectures on industrial fluctuations. It continued at the LSE to 1941, when Seldon was a research assistant to the classical liberal Professor Arnold (later Sir Arnold) Plant. Many of the LSE staff were socialists, but Seldon drew his inspiration first from the leading classical liberal economist, Lionel (later Lord) Robbins, who brought Hayek to the LSE, and then from Hayek, who reintroduced Austrian economics to the LSE after it had "almost fallen out of sight" (p. 34).

Hayek's influence on Seldon and, in part through Seldon, on intellectual thought in Britain continued through a surprising combination of circumstances. Seldon describes (p. 34) how Fisher, who was concerned at the prevalence of government planning in early postwar Britain and was contemplating a career in politics, went to see Hayek after reading the *Reader's Digest* summary of *The Road to Serfdom.* Hayek advised Fisher against becoming a politician and suggested that Fisher find a means of appealing directly to intellectuals. Fisher, who did not then know Seldon, responded some years later by incorporating the IEA in 1955 and appointing Harris, one of the few economists of the time with strong promarket views, as general director. Harris worked with Seldon as editorial director,[4] providing Seldon with a platform from which to express, both in his own writings and in the works he edited, the Austrian ideas that Hayek had done so much to revive and that Seldon had absorbed from Hayek and LSE classical liberals such as Robbins and Plant in the 1930s. Seldon aptly describes his work in the post of editorial director of the IEA from 1957 onward as "the fulfilment of my post-graduate hopes of 1938–39" (p. 34). Moreover, in his IEA role he was able to collaborate productively with his intellectual mentors. Hayek wrote for the IEA and was helped by Seldon's editing to produce papers accessible

4. For further information on this period see the general introduction to these Collected Works.

to a wide audience that were one of the key elements in the revival of classical liberal ideas from the late 1970s onward.[5]

The fourth paper in this volume was written after Seldon had retired from his post as IEA editorial director, a year before *Capitalism* (volume 1 of these Collected Works) was published. In June 1989 the IEA held a symposium, supported by Liberty Fund, on the influence of ideas on policy. The six papers given at the symposium were published later in 1989 as *Ideas, Interests and Consequences,* IEA Readings 30, edited by Cento Veljanovski, the new research and editorial director of the IEA. Seldon's paper, reprinted here, is titled "Economic Scholarship and Political Interest." In this paper Seldon explores the impact on policy of ideas, interests, and circumstances, using the experience of the IEA over its (then) thirty years of existence and developing the views expressed in the first work in this volume. The IEA's approach to the application of economic principles to policymaking, according to Seldon, was "based on classical liberal political economy, refined, as I saw it, by developments in 'Austrian-Hayekian' market process, Buchanan-Tullock public choice, and, later, Muth-Minford 'rational expectations' (people learn from their mistakes)" (p. 44). Seldon sets out fourteen reflections on the theme of the influence of ideas. He argues, for example, that a change in the intellectual climate is a precondition for policy change and that whether particular ideas are "adopted or adapted" depends on "their confluence with interests, chance, and the accident of exceptional individuals" (p. 45). Ideas flourish better when there is "political competition for new solutions to unsolved problems," he says, and they have to "chime with public sentiment" if government is to adopt them (p. 45). Seldon advises scholars that they should beware of providing politicians with "dangerous toys"—academic advice should "reflect the motivations, feasibilities and limitations of the political process" (p. 46). He concludes that the main lesson from the previous thirty years, and especially from the previous ten, is that "ideas in the general public interest can be obstructed and emasculated by the interests of capital, the professions, or labour generated by corporatist policies" (p. 46). Seldon is particularly concerned about this kind of obstruction and pleads for more discussion among scholars of means of neutralizing the rent-seekers who delay change.

5. In *Denationalisation of Money—The Argument Refined,* published by the IEA in 1990, Hayek acknowledges Seldon's help both with that paper and with earlier IEA publications of his: Seldon's "beneficial care has already made much more readable some of my shorter essays published by that Institute."

One of the interesting issues Seldon addresses is how an organization such as the IEA can obtain finance. Given that "an idea requires support from the interests it would benefit," how can the dispersed interests that would gain from the greater use of markets be mobilized? Finance was a serious problem for the IEA in its early days. The Institute decided, on principle, to accept no funds from government or its agencies, and it also refused to be confined to recommending policies that appeared "politically possible." As a charity, it could offer no specific benefits in return for donations. It deliberately aimed for a relatively large number of small donations to avoid undue influence from particular organizations or individuals. Despite these handicaps, it eventually succeeded in convincing a sufficient number of donors that they had more to gain than to lose from the introduction of free markets.

Seldon concludes his chapter with the observation that the economic system has been unable to produce its best results because existing political processes produce governments that escape "close supervision by the citizen between elections" (p. 65). Economic liberals should attempt to devise disciplines that prevent government from overtaxing, overcentralizing, and oversubsidizing and from depreciating the value of money. Fundamental reform is required that replaces "political by market sovereignty for the common consumer" (p. 65).

The fifth work in this volume is a short paper published in *Economic Affairs,* the journal of the IEA, in March 1998, in which Seldon amplifies his reflections in earlier articles on the influence of the LSE on the IEA. The article, "From the LSE to the IEA," emphasizes that the intellectual origins of the Institute "lie in a merger of the classical British and Austrian schools of liberal political economy. They reinforced each other in the mind of the naturalised-British Austrian economist at the London School of Economics (LSE) in the 1930s, Friedrich Hayek" (p. 69). Seldon traces the British-Austrian link back to the time of Edwin Cannan (1861–1935) at the LSE, early in the twentieth century. Cannan was a liberal market economist admired by Hayek, whose views echoed those of Austrian Eugen von Böhm-Bawerk.[6] Cannan's influence was still evident in the teaching of economics at LSE, for instance by Robbins and Plant, when Seldon was a student there in the 1930s. Cannan, Seldon points out, had recognized the imperfections of the political process long before public choice theory had been formalized, and his

6. One of Böhm-Bawerk's classic works was *Macht oder Ökonomisches Gesetz* (Political power or economic law). It is frequently quoted in Seldon's writings.

former LSE students, such as Robbins and Plant, transmitted Cannan's skepticism about government action to their own students, including Seldon. When Seldon went to the IEA he imbued its publications with a similar skepticism, thus providing a link with the LSE of the 1930s and the eminent figures who were then members of its faculty.

Seldon contrasts the intellectual rigor of the LSE of his student days with the "tracts of intellectual desert over the Houghton Street buildings of the LSE in the 1990s," as many LSE teachers "sadly continue their hopes of politicised industry and welfare" (p. 74). Cannan would have been dismayed at the state of the LSE, says Seldon, though he would have approved of the IEA and the influence of 1930s LSE that lives on there.

The final work in this volume is a selection of Seldon's prefaces to IEA papers, published in 2002 by Economic and Literary Books in association with the IEA, under the title *The Making of the Institute.* Seldon begins the book with an introduction that explains, inter alia, his view of how he and Harris divided the task of running the IEA: Seldon recruited authors and edited their work, while Harris carried the free market message to the outside world and raised funds.

Included in the book are prefaces to books in three of the IEA's main series—fifty-six Hobart Papers, eight Hobart Paperbacks, and four Readings[7]—and, at the end, Seldon's well-known letter to *The Times* ("Socialism Has No Future") of August 6, 1980.[8]

Seldon's prefaces are much more than standard introductions to books that summarize the author's conclusions. They are works in their own right. Each one is a carefully considered and crafted attempt to place the book in the context of the main body of economic thought and, in particular, to show how it fits within free market thinking, cross-referencing it as necessary to other IEA publications. Seldon never assumes that readers of IEA papers are familiar with classical liberal thought—many of them are, after all, students just becoming acquainted with economic principles. Therefore he explains how and to what extent the text he is introducing is consistent with classical liberalism, how it helps to advance free market ideas, and what are its policy implications. The reader is left in no doubt that the book Seldon is introducing is part of a bigger publishing program designed to explain

7. The IEA's other series during the period of Seldon's editorship were Occasional Papers and Research Monographs. He plans to publish his prefaces to these series separately along with some further prefaces to Readings (p. 85 of *The Making of the Institute*).

8. See the general introduction to these Collected Works.

how markets work and how they can help to solve economic and social problems and raise living standards.

Reading these prefaces, intended as they are to introduce the work of others, provides a clear guide to Seldon's own thought as it developed over the thirty years from the late 1950s onward. The authors he so carefully selected to write IEA papers generally shed new light on some part of the economy or society, providing evidence of the problems caused by excessive government intervention and showing how greater use of markets would prove beneficial. As Seldon explains, in the last preface he wrote during his time as editorial director:

> In choosing authors for IEA Papers over 30 years, often with the assistance of the academic advisers, I sometimes felt like the manager of a cricket team putting the best players in to "bat" against the opposing sides. Historians will judge the effects of the long academic debate on public and political opinion, as seen in the intellectual and cultural revolution between the 1950s, when the market was anathema, and the 1980s, when it is being offered by every political party, old and new (p. 231).

Seldon, in his prefaces, seizes on the conclusions reached by his authors, demonstrates their significance, and places them in a wider context. In this way he reinforces their messages, emphasizing their consistency one with another and transforming individual texts into integral components of a formidable publishing enterprise that proved to be a major influence on government policies in many countries. That enterprise, in addition to his own books and articles, is one of his great legacies.

7 October 2003

THE ESSENCE OF THE IEA

The Essence of the IEA

This collection of essays, most by economists, historians of economic thought, economic and political historians and a sociologist of a wide range of philosophic sympathies, assesses the IEA and its work over 25 years against a background of changing economic thinking and public policy. An introduction to the essays may also serve as a short re-statement of the IEA's central approach, from which some IEA authors will differ.

The essays range over British history to consider the interactions between the influence of ideas, emphasised by J. M. Keynes as ruling the world, vested interests, singled out by Karl Marx as the dominant element, and "circumstances," identified by J. S. Mill as deciding which ideas would influence events. The classic illustration is Lenin who spent a lifetime of proselytizing before the First World War provided the "circumstances" for his ideas. (*Pace* Marx, "interests" were secondary or remote.) Four mainly historical chapters, by Professor T. W. Hutchison, Dr. Ian Bradley, Dr. Colin Clark and Professor Norman Gash, re-examine the past century for parallels with earlier efforts to educate by research and dissemination the general public and the men of ideas and of action who evolved and applied economic thinking. Professor Hutchison further discusses the IEA's dual emphasis on a general economic diagnosis with detailed proposals suited to the institutional conditions of the times.

Five essays analyse more closely and appraise the products of the IEA, with reservation as well as approval from Professors Denis O'Brien, Anthony Culyer and David Collard and Mr. Kenneth Judge, and with suggestions for further development from Professors J. M. Buchanan and Gordon Tullock. Two chapters judge the IEA's work as seen by Lord Croham from inside government and by Mr. Eric Sharp from inside industry. Mr. Graham Hutton, an early stalwart, discusses the pre- and post-war thinking on economics that dissatisfied the Founding Fathers of the IEA and induced them to examine its errors and consequences in industrial and public policy.

These essays are for readers to judge in the light of the IEA's work over 25 years. Any credit must go largely to the 300 economists, political scientists and other authors and to the advisers who were ready with suggested names of possible authors and subjects. Although the IEA staff have contributed to this published output, most of the Papers, etc., are the work of British economists in British universities. The IEA drew on a wide range of academic authority (and philosophic sympathy) without which it could not have maintained the flow of writing that has made it the largest source of concentrated but digestible economic expertise in Britain.

The IEA may perhaps claim to have created the post-war focus for the demonstration that market analysis was indispensable for understanding and solving economic tasks and problems. Its authors included economists sophisticated in mathematical macro-economic models of the economy as a whole (not least Colin Clark, who privately pioneered national income statistics), but IEA Papers showed that macro-economic analysis of national (or average) behaviour had to be explained by micro-economic analysis of individuals moved by changes at the margin of effort or reward. In particular, because we at the IEA were unconvinced from the outset by the Fabians, Keynes, Beveridge and Titmuss, we systematically mustered and presented in modern dress the truths of classical political economy: that government could not assemble the information required for the desired use of resources; that only individuals could derive the information from their local, voluntary, private lives; that they could reveal and apply the information only or most effectively by coming together as buyers and sellers in markets.

The New IEA Approach

This indeed was and is the essence of the IEA approach, and why it struck early observers as a fundamental break from the dominant but misguided post-war consensus (below). Although the approach has a noble intellectual lineage in the English and Scottish classical economists and philosophers from David Hume and Adam Smith, it had been overshadowed if not obliterated by the emphasis on national ("macro-economic") policy from the Great Depression of 1929–31 to the apparent effectiveness of Keynesian demand management in mastering unemployment before the Second World War and inflation after the war. From these apparent successes the belief developed that government could deal with any and every economic problem by regulation or direct management: not only in defence, law and order, and the supply of money but also in fuel and transport, education and medicine, housing and pensions, local services and everywhere else.

The IEA approach was very different. It began from the very opposite end of the economic pyramid: the large number of individuals organised in families, voluntary groups, co-operative organisations, one-man businesses, partnerships or firms. It recognised that some goods or services—the so-called "public goods"—had to be supplied by government, national or local, and financed by taxes or rates, because they could not be refused to people who refused to pay and who would otherwise batten on those who did pay by taking "free rides." But for the rest it opened up questions that had lain dormant for decades. Why should this or that service be supplied by government? Why could it not be supplied by people coming together in "markets" where those who wanted things could choose between those who offered them? If markets were not feasible, was that because choice for buyers or competition among suppliers was impracticable, or because government itself was putting legal or other obstacles in the way of individuals with goods or services to exchange?

If markets were impracticable, what other method of co-operation between buyers and suppliers was feasible? Was it better to construct state monopolies—as in fuel or transport, education or medicine—and try to arrange that they served buyers faithfully and efficiently? Or did such organisations have their own weaknesses of political and impersonal control, bureaucratic inflexibility, high taxation and restriction of choice between suppliers? If markets were practicable, how could the obstacles to them be removed?

In opening up these prospects the IEA released a shoal of questions that to many early observers seemed closed and settled. The very first Paper in 1957 asked not how the state could best finance its "national insurance" pensions but why pensions had to be supplied by, or rather through, the state at all: why should they not gradually move from the state to the market, where suppliers were developing a wide variety of schemes to suit individuals and firms with much more flexibility than the state could arrange? That the state may have considered it desirable, on the grounds of poverty in 1908 or the high cost of approved societies in 1925, to develop state pensions was no reason for continuing and enlarging them in 1957. Yet the Labour Party was proposing to extend state pensions in 1957 and the Conservatives extended them in 1961.

Some Fundamental Economic Truths

And so on in scores and hundreds of Papers on many more services and activities. A barrage of IEA Papers refined and applied old truths to new subjects in contemporary circumstances. Authors were asked to apply economic analysis ruthlessly, with recognition of current conditions but without regard for "administrative practicability," because that could not be ascertained except by practical trial, or for "political impossibility," because that could be a pretext developed by politicians or bureaucrats who resisted reform that did not suit them however good the argument, and in any event because reasoned ideas could themselves make the "impossible" possible.

In pursuing these new/old approaches to new subjects IEA Papers illustrated from contemporary events and developments the fundamental truths of economics that had been often lost in the preoccupation with post-war monetary or fiscal measures to control inflation or unemployment. Production takes place for consumption (derived from the Scot Adam Smith), not the other way round. Value is measured not as an average but at the margin (the Englishman W. S. Jevons, the Frenchman Leon Walras, and the Austrian Carl Menger). The cost of producing a commodity or service is not the labour required (the German Karl Marx) but the commodity or service thereby lost (the Austrian Friedrich von Wieser). The instinct of man is to "truck and barter" in markets (Adam Smith). He will find ways round, under, over or through restrictions created by government (the Austrian Eugen von Böhm-Bawerk). There is no such thing as absolute demand (for education, medicine or anything else) or supply (of labour or anything else) because both vary with price (the Englishmen Alfred Marshall, Lionel Robbins and many before and since). Not least, without the signalling device of price, man cannot spontaneously and voluntarily co-operate for prosperous co-existence (the Austrian Ludwig von Mises and the Austrian-born but voluntarily-British Friedrich Hayek).

Otherwise sophisticated laymen in government and industry often find difficulty with fundamental economic truths. Demand and supply are not absolute, fixed in amount; they can be elastic in response to changes in price and income—an increased demand for private education will eventually expand supply. Unemployment is not an immutable technical total; the lower the cost of labour the higher the demand for it would rise: and unemployment will fall. Cuts in government expenditure will impair government services; that is not a reason for not cutting: the economist asks whether the money would do more good elsewhere—its opportunity cost and marginal utility. Competition is the environment—the *only* environment—in which commodities or services can be judged by *comparison* with alternatives; if there is only one, how can it be judged? And competition is the *only* effective method of defending the consumer by making every seller his ally against every other seller.

The Indispensable Role of Price

The post-war ills of the British economy derive ultimately from the neglect of these and allied truths. Government is grossly inflated. Inefficient state monopolies hamper competitive private industry. Unnecessary growth in taxation discourages risk-taking and investment. Rampant trade unions resist the monetary mastery of inflation, the modernisation of industry, and the movement of men. Activities in which people spend other people's money and are unaccountable to them have multiplied. Unemployment is concealed by workers in the wrong jobs, in the wrong firms, in the wrong industries, in the wrong regions, because *relative* wages do not move to attract them to the right jobs, in the right firms, in the growing industries, in new regions.

The divorce of supply or demand from price in electricity, gas, rail, road, education, medicine, housing, a host of local government services, not least in labour by incomes policies, has produced massive, de-stabilising, simultaneous wastes of surpluses and shortages. The suppression or distortion of price in the public sector has annihilated the information on relative values and scarcities of resources in alternative employments without which rational or efficient use is unlikely or impossible. Government policy has fastened on the income effects and ignored the price (rationing) effects of its policies in taxation, nationalised industries, the public corporations, welfare and local government. For decades the British economy has been unhinged from the sources of grass-roots information. The repression of price is the genesis of the economic weakness, by concealing reality. Such is the case for restoring markets, where possible, in public as well as in private economic life. It is the argument for charging in public services where possible and taxing only where necessary.

Not least, the welfare state has developed, as IEA authors said in the early 1960s, into an uncontrollable monster with an insatiable appetite for tax finance and incestuous administrators. It denies choice. It substitutes incorrigible differences in cultural power which determine access in the state for corrigible differences in purchasing power which determine access in the market. It demands increasing coercion as incomes rise, as in the suppression of private education and medicine. And it is largely unaccountable and therefore irresponsible because it is run by men spending other men's money. Economists and sociologists who emphasise the external benefits of state welfare strangely overlook its external costs in tax disincentives, resistances to reform, diminished personal liberties, weakened family cohesion, and social conflict where political consensuses are enforced on minorities, groups or individuals.

The Challenge to the Economic Establishment

Many economists helped to build the IEA's reputation. Among others, Professor B. S. Yamey's (first) *Hobart Paper* on resale price maintenance in 1960 is generally thought to have prompted the debate that led to the Resale Prices Act of 1964. Colin Clark in 1961 showed the superficiality of "growthmanship." The *Choice in Welfare* surveys from 1963 went over the heads of politicians who said reform was "politically impossible" and revealed high and growing demand for choice in education and medical care. The late Professor F. G. Pennance's original study of making housing subsidies "mobile" followed in 1968. John Brunner destroyed the theoretical foundations of the 1965 National Plan. Research Monographs in 1967 rebutted the consensus on "universal" social benefits. Professor H. S. Ferns's 1968 Paper elaborated the unassailable argument for an independent university. In 1972 nine economists and historians rejected the Marxist link between capitalism and poverty. Two Papers by John Wood in 1972 and 1975 introduced price into the discussion of unemployment and revealed the micro-unrealities in the official macro-totals. Not least, market analysis was applied to unlikely products like blood, water, fire-risks, refuse removal, animal semen, employment exchanges, charity (10 authors), sport, and the family. And several studies examined methods of supplementing low incomes, the most recent by Colin Clark in 1977.

To list these few is to be conscious of omitting hundreds of other IEA authors. The IEA was first in Britain to publicise studies in the economics of politics, government and democracy or "public choice" (the American originators Professors Buchanan and Tullock, the British A. T. Peacock, Charles Rowley and Jack Wiseman) and of bureaucracy (Professor W. A. Niskanen). Two Papers challenged the plausible but vulnerable claim—now repeated in protests at cuts in government expenditure—that "external benefits" justify untold expenditure on unimpeachable causes but unidentifiable benefits, from opera and the universities to space research, by the simple device of ignoring the opportunity costs. And so on, and so on, and so on.

The IEA was a substantial going concern when it published the first of several Papers by Professor Hayek in 1968 and by Professor Milton Friedman in 1970 (a Wincott Lecture attended by Mr. James Callaghan) to emphasise the neglected monetary and "Austrian" analyses of inflation and unemployment.

Consensus by Common Interest, Not Compromise with Myopia

The perennial straining after "consensus" reflects the desire to base society on a sense of community without which it might otherwise disintegrate.

Men are consumers and producers. Their interests as consumers are general and long-term, as producers particular and immediate. The danger is that the immediate will prevail over the fundamental: that man looks through the wrong end of a telescope.

The market is the means of reconciling conflict and establishing a consensus from which all benefit. Adam Smith's propensity to "truck and barter" can be frustrated if government yields to pressure from organised groups of producers for protection against competition. If this shortsightedness were indulged, the economic system would end as a structure of warring groups organised as syndicates or corporations of producers protecting themselves from change. Sooner or later it would slow down and seize up. The only way to prevent this degeneration is to make the market the dominant form of organisation, so that men's interests as consumers prevail over their interests as producers. It is thus the common interest of all men to maintain the market. It is the consensus in which the long-term interest in maintaining open doors for innovation and change is shared by all as the only way to escape from stagnation and ensure progress. All other consensuses in Britain such as social contracts have required compromise with producer interests or government job creation or preservation that slowed down the adoption of improvement, retained resources in decaying industries, and prevented the rise in living standards that could have taken place, and that has taken place in the USA, Germany and Japan where men as producers have yielded to their interests as consumers in competitive markets.

The alternative is a medieval war of all against all among industrial barons, with the full panoply of restrictive practices, closed shops, demarcation, job protection, licences, permissions, permits, long patents, tariffs, quotas, and physical war, civil and international. In contrast with this world of divisiveness, the market offers co-operation by specialisation and exchange, a framework for industrial and international peacekeeping, with multi-lateral disarmament to mutual advantage. The political consensus sacrifices the long view to the short; it compromises with vested interests; it rests on the Irishism that lauds neutrality between right and wrong, good and evil. The market embodies the consensus that rests on common interests in a framework of society within which each man can do his own thing in using his talents to produce goods and services that will freely exchange for the products of his fellows.

Experience Confirmed the Market Approach

Experience of state economy is creating the readiness to learn what markets can achieve. The IEA was formed to address thinkers and doers in economic life, but since government virtually controls one-half of the economy and regulates the other half, economists must address politicians and their officials. It is evidently necessary for a people to suffer the consequences of suppressing markets before they are ready to see it as the most natural and civilised form of human co-operation. What the late Professor T. S. Ashton said in 1948 of the absence of industrialisation is still true today in the 1980s of countries which try to live without the markets that facilitate and follow industrial innovation:

> There are today on the plains of India and China men and women, plague-ridden and hungry, living lives little better, to outward appearance, than those of the cattle that toil with them by day and share their places of sleep by night. Such Asiatic standards, and such unmechanised horrors, are the lot of those who increase their numbers without passing through an industrial revolution.[1]

But since 1948 the people of China who left for Taiwan and who today escape to Hong Kong know that markets have saved them, but not their countrymen, from their former horrors. The people of India have yet to be saved. And the communist governments of Poland and Eastern Europe know that the market could save their peoples from famine and impoverishment but dare not tolerate it widely for fear it would destroy their precarious political

1. *The Industrial Revolution, 1760–1830,* Home University Library, OUP, 1948.

power. In Britain, after long suppression, markets are coming to be understood in all schools of thought as information-gatherers and distributors that enthrone the consumer, reward the responsible and responsive producers, and teach the outmoded to change course. It will emerge as the dominant instrument of economic policy when it divides people in all parties who understand it from those who cannot. Market-oriented governments will then alternate in Britain as state economy recedes in Russia, China and the rest of the world and the market oases spread to fertilise the desert of state economy.

Store of Ideas to Be Tested

So far not much has been done to re-introduce markets into the mass of British economic activity unnecessarily controlled by government or to encourage their stronger growth elsewhere by removing the obstacles to the technological innovation and *embourgeoisement* that would undermine monopoly in industry or trade unionism. There is thus a large store of ideas in IEA writings that no British government has yet applied—or tested by experiment. IEA Papers have argued that government could withdraw from many activities (perhaps two-thirds) that are not "public goods" and leave them to local, voluntary and private competitive activity in the market. There are large, hopeful, liberating, popular reforms in the British economy that could be made by a government of any party or coalition that explained how its policies could reach the objectives.

We can say this with some justification because the field researches sponsored by the IEA (and carried out by an independent organisation) uncovered trends in the real state of public preferences that throw doubt on much accepted prejudice. The characteristic case is public attitudes to the National Health Service. Conventional opinion polling since the war has repeatedly returned favourable opinions of 80 to 90 per cent. Such statistics have misled public men for 20 years or more. First-year economics students know it is meaningless to measure demand without reference to price. The IEA field studies introduced the price of the NHS and alternative health services. The results were very different. In all socio-occupational groups they found increasing *dis*approval of the NHS personal services—as a whole from 30 per cent in 1965 to 57 per cent in 1978 as measured by the readiness to pay for a choice of insurable private medicine by adding out of pocket to refunded taxation in the form of a voucher worth two-thirds of the insurance cost. For education the percentage rose from 30 to 51 per cent for a voucher worth two-thirds of day secondary school fees. (The results are analysed in detail in *Over-Ruled on Welfare*, 1979.)

Other findings indicated an increasing rejection of the state or its local agents in a widening range of the services it supplies as a bureaucratic monopoly in return for taxes: housing, pensions, and local welfare, and around 80 per cent in favour of allowing people who wished to contract out of state education and medicine.

These findings await a government that will heed the implications: that taxes can be substantially reduced, personal and family liberties strengthened, and the efficiency of welfare and other services improved by introducing consumer choice between competing suppliers.

The Outside from the Inside

The 12 Chapters have been written by "outsiders" concerned principally with ideas and their influence on thinking and policy. Since some also discuss the IEA as an institution, an "inside" interpretation of its beginnings is added, written by John Wood who draws on his recollections to reconstruct the early days vividly despite fragmentary documents and fading memories. Until a full history is written, his sketch, necessarily more personal than the body of the book, provides insights into the early financial and marketing tasks and how they were solved, not always fully to this day, in building the new organisation.

As seen from the production (editorial, etc.) side, there were parallel problems. It was rare chance that the early difficulty of discovering authors to work for an unknown, unfashionable institution made it necessary for Ralph Harris and me to work in intellectual and literary co-operation between two contrasting yet complementary minds, developing after some years into broad specialisation on production of Papers and development by fund-raising and dissemination. Commuting between two offices and dashes to clubs and restaurants by taxi to save time in the early years made the co-operation to build the embryonic fabric a breathless if exhilarating venture until a settled office and staff made possible a more systematic strategy.

The early hostility from critics and the indulgent scepticism about our prospects (the late Sir Andrew Shonfield in 1961 gave the infant IEA "six months") must have made us marvel that we had abandoned safe jobs for a speculative venture (against which I was warned by a friendly Sir John Benn about risking a young family), though it was a mission as well as a job. The gradual building of finances while maintaining independence in order to give authors power to say what they wished was a task in chicken-and-egg timing. The earliest sense of impact, when we drew blood from the late R. H. S. Crossman in 1963 (who wrote an apology in *The Guardian* after being misled by Professor Peter Townsend), left the feeling that David could still fell Goliath. And the reaction from Mrs. Shirley Williams on TV that the early welfare findings were "nonsense" indicated that the evidence had discomforted the political consensus.

The chicken-and-egg timing is crucial. The IEA raises fundamental issues and examines new, sometimes radical, policies, and it may have to be run by two people in harness (and in harmony on ultimate goals) sufficiently strong-minded for one to raise funds but properly attribute responsibility for their disbursement on publications to the other, concerned primarily for the independence of authors. The IEA's independence from outside pressure has also throughout been reinforced by resting on general rather than earmarked funds.

Increasing interest from principled politicians in all three Parties (not one, as Mr. Hugh Stephenson of *The Times*[2] and others suppose) removed the anxiety that we would tend to veer to one political side to gain influential hearing. The IEA thus avoided the error of the Fabian Society (analysed by Dr. Colin Clark in Chapter IX).

As the 1960s moved on, approaches were made by people in all walks of life, including Labour politicians and trade union leaders anxious about trends in public policy, one of whom said "it's the market or machine-gun." MPs from all three Parties addressed IEA seminars and putative leaders from all four Parties came to talk with IEA economists. Visits from former Conservative and Labour Prime Ministers encouraged the hope of competitive bidding for public support for policies based on economic reason. The fourth Party symbolises the movement in British public life away from state economy to the market.

The change from author reluctance to an increasing flow of unsolicited manuscripts (rarely used because the theme for almost all IEA Papers originates in the office) confirmed the growing sense of authority. And success in recruiting teachers, schools, libraries, universities as regular subscribers indicated the pedagogic-academic quality of IEA texts.

2. *Mrs. Thatcher's First Year,* Norman, 1980.

Sociology Back to Sanity

The IEA's latest inspiration is the formation in late 1980 of a Social Affairs Unit to re-examine conventional sociological thinking on industry, welfare, and the rôles of the state and the market. Its Director, Dr. Digby Anderson, lately from the University of Nottingham, was introduced to us by Professor Dennis Lees, an early IEA author and a constant friend, and the Assistant Director, David Marsland of Brunel University, shares the view that sociology has gone sadly astray. Since the faculties of sociology in British universities have produced men who have confused rational thinking, we look to these two relatively youthful pioneers, who remind us of the spirit of the early IEA days, to undo the damage and perhaps to help sociology to become part of the intellectual enlightenment.

Ideas Reign over Interests

After 25 years—for me the IEA began in 1956—my conclusion is that the combination of John Stuart Mill and J. M. Keynes was more profound than Karl Marx. The IEA sponsored, "produced," refined and timed the ideas; insofar as they have influenced thinking (the verdict is evidently yes) or policy (so far not much), Keynes is vindicated. But "vested interests" played no part at all in our production; nor would it have done them much good if they had: for a century market-oriented economists have been dismissed as the lackeys of the capitalists. Karl Marx stood truth on its head. Our authors drew their researches from a wide range of industrial and other sources which exerted no influence on the final published outcome because they were numerous, individually small, diverse and self-cancelling. So in the work of the IEA ideas prevailed over interests.

But if ideas were necessary, they have not proved sufficient. Mill's "conspiring circumstances" have to bring them to life with timely intellectual and public hearing. And down the years during the 1960s and 1970s, experience of other policies taught that reform was overdue in resale price maintenance, welfare and poverty, planning, trade unions, taxation, inflation and unemployment, discussed in the stream of IEA Papers. IEA ideas increasingly synchronised with the developing disillusionment with the false wartime and post-war macro-economic consensus; they opened men's minds to new thinking, unconventional diagnoses and unfamiliar policies.

Yet if the battle of ideas is being won in the mind, the obstacles to reform remain formidable. The suppression of markets for decades has created obstruction from the interests generated by decades of error which subsist on ideas without which they are vulnerable. The hope is that the interests will see that in resisting change and reform they are mistaking short-term gains for lasting advantage: not even bureaucrats or nationalised industry chairmen or trade unions can forever resist change in the conditions of supply and demand. But the obstructing institutions may require new techniques to dismantle, with the minimum of dislocation but not too slowly since the longer the process is delayed the more disruptive it will have to be. It is in demonstrating the techniques of removing the obstacles that the IEA's next phase may chiefly lie—whether in removing the legal props or impediments, or in constitutional rules that deprive government of the temptation to yield to the obstructors, or in buying out the obstructors' accumulated expectations of income legitimised by myopic government but destructive of economic order resting on public approval.

The ultimate safeguard remains in the realm of reason. Men of action who cannot enforce their will by coercion want to believe that the argument is on their side, like the Minister for Fuel who asked: "Do you really think we have a good case?"[3] The truth, as so often, was seen in the eighteenth century by David Hume:

> Though man be much governed by interests, yet even interest itself, and all human affairs, are entirely governed by opinion.

Above all the IEA was not deterred by the tired defences of established practices—"politically impossible," "administratively impracticable," "socially unacceptable." Its Founding Fathers saw behind the circular reasoning, for it is ideas that can make possible, practicable and acceptable what reason shows to be desirable, timely, overdue.

State or Market

And what is it that a century of critics have said is impossible, impracticable or unacceptable? We now see around the world the fruits of their intention—the use of political power to expand wealth-creation, regulate industry, administer social justice, abolish hardship. There are now enough comparisons and contrasts in all countries to contest the formerly un-

3. The policy discussed was the denationalisation of gas.

checked claims for the state. Little wonder that where people are free to choose—in Britain, America, Australia, France, Germany, the smaller countries of Europe, Asia and Africa—they do not choose the state.

It is now less difficult to see why, when all is said, the market, where it works by opening doors to new supplies and new demands, humbles the mighty, destroys privilege, enables David to fell Goliath, equalises rewards, enfranchises the inarticulate, emancipates the proletarian. Because money is the irresistible leveller, the market is more democratic, more disrespectful of persons, more moral and more just than the state, which bows to and thus incites influence, faction and conspiracy to control it. By aggrandising man as consumer, the market saves society from degenerating into impoverishment by parochial syndicalism or aggressive corporatism. That is why, despite its tendency to thicken into monopoly, to generate high incomes as temporary signals of scarcities, and its slow solutions to alienation and externalities, which preoccupy some technical economists, the market remains the best hope of mankind.

NEW HOPE FOR ECONOMIC POLICY IN A CHANGING POLITY

New Hope for Economic Policy in a Changing Polity

The IEA has for many years been interested not only in the analysis of economic thought but also in the processes which decide whether and how economic thinking is translated into policy. This is the purpose for which the *Hobart Paperbacks* were established in 1971. The first volume was written by the distinguished British economist, Professor W. H. Hutt, under the title *Politically Impossible . . . ?*, to set the tone for the whole series. Since the Institute had found in its early years that promising new thinking had been pre-judged and prematurely discouraged by the assurance of "practical men" that it was "politically impossible," the determination to pursue economic thinking rigorously to its logical conclusions has pervaded the work of the IEA since its foundation in 1957.

This attitude—that the duty of economists was to stick to their last and not to think as politicians—has been amply vindicated by events. Some of the ideas in early IEA Papers that seemed to have little chance of adoption when first analysed have lately become the currency not only of economic debate but also of political discussion in Parliament and in the media. Some have been incorporated in policy, for example in the abolition of exchange control, the shift to floating exchange rates and the abandonment of incomes policies. Others have at last breached conventional thinking, not least on education, health, housing, pensions and income maintenance. The objection "politically impossible" has now become particularly irrelevant in the last two or three years.

The long-delayed re-orientation within the British political parties began with the Labour Party, continued through the Alliance between the Social Democratic and Liberal Parties and may proceed to the Conservative Party. The result has been to open up new readiness to consider as potential public policy economic thinking on the scope for the market, quasi-market and other voluntary institutions that has too long lain dormant, despised and rejected by public men who did not understand its wide and deep implications for equity and harmony as well as efficiency. I discuss these implications and the scope for new policies below.

Economic Aspects of Public Policy

The essays assembled in *Hobart Paperback 15* under the title *Agenda for Social Democracy* were written on seven main policies by independent professional economists. They follow a review by Lord Harris of the post-war economic scene and the all-party policies that failed to solve its dilemmas, not least to combine efficiency with humanity.

The essays are addressed to people in public, academic, industrial and other activities, not as members of political parties but as people who wish to combine what have hitherto seemed to be, or at least have been said to be, irreconcilable objectives—dominantly, economic freedom and social equity. All the contributors are interested in showing what the specialist expertise in their subject can contribute to the discussion—Geoffrey Wood on inflation and the labour market, Professor A. R. Prest on taxation, Professor Michael Beenstock on social policy, Professor S. C. Littlechild on competition, Dr. Ljubo Sirc on employee participation, Professor A. I. MacBean on international policy, and, not least, and in a sense fundamental to all, Professor C. K. Rowley on the formation of economic policy as seen through the school of public choice economists who analyse the working of government and its motivations as economists have long analysed industry.

The economists are therefore all interested in discussing economic policy for social democracy as a policy, not necessarily of one Party. Some show a measure of sympathy for SDP and Alliance thinking and prospects in particular, but they write primarily as scholars and their main aim is to discern conflicts between analysis and policy, economic means and economic ends. Thus, Professor Littlechild agrees with much of the SDP approach to the maintenance of competition, but suggests that its current thinking could with advantage be revised to make its objective more certain.

As always the main purpose of the Institute is to show the light that economic analysis can shed on current thought and policy in all schools and parties in the realm. It is not concerned with the direction from which practical or Parliamentary interest is forthcoming, but has persevered with its function of following economic analysis wherever it leads and making its work available to all who wish to explore below surface rhetoric or rise above popular sentiment.

These essays are timely because the contemporary political re-alignment—the emergence in Britain of "social democracy" in the overt form of a new political party and its alliance with an older party—is significant for economic policy and the contribution to it of economic science. For it indicates a candid recognition of past errors in policy by statesmen and politicians and in economic thinking by academics. It therefore promises a more ready approach to underlying truth than in the years of Conservative-Labour "duopoly" when it was concealed by over-expectations from the power of myopic government and under-estimation of the beneficent power of market forces in shaping the economy and society.

The Meaning of "Social Democracy"

The term "social democracy" can be understood in several senses. For economists, interest lies in its expression of a desire to combine the strengths of four elements in evolving the good society: first, the decentralised market, with all it implies in local, voluntary or mutual co-operation in private activity and enterprise; second, profit as the reward of entrepreneurship; third, pricing as the method of rationing scarce resources between alternative uses; and, not least, fourth, the "social justice" of common access to the means of civilised living. "Social democracy" with these ingredients thus hopes to reconcile the economic efficiency necessary for high living standards with the sense of equity and humanity desirable for communal harmony.

In this sense "social democracy" is not new to British public life or political institutions. For part of British history in the nineteenth century, the critics of liberal capitalism said that efficiency was given precedence over equality or humanity: living standards rose rapidly but not uniformly, so that wealth co-existed with wide inequalities and poverty. Between the two world wars, wealth advanced further despite the early restrictions on markets and "the great depression," but poverty, conspicuous inequalities and insecurity in sickness, unemployment and old age persisted.

Productivity, Equality, Equity

Concern about the "social" consequences of rapid change in the nineteenth- and early twentieth-century conditions of supply and demand and of the 10-year "trade cycle" were the common property of public men in all the historical political parties—Conservative, Labour and Liberal—

whether their reactions or motivations were emotional, intellectual or predominantly electoral—or a mixture of all three. Since "social justice" was furthered by increases in production as a prelude to re-distribution, they differed in their judgement of the extent to which technological change and social advance could be retarded in order to minimise inequalities without prejudicing the general progress of the economy and the rise in the living standards of all, even if shared unequally. But the desire to reconcile progress with humanity has moved British public men and government of all political parties and scholars of all schools because it expresses national sentiment over two centuries. It is not a new development in the 1980s, but a new turn in national concern by the more fortunate for the less fortunate and a readiness to contemplate new and more effective methods of reconciling progress with liberty and liberty with humanity.

What is new in the thinking in all parties and schools is the change in the understanding of the economic institutions required to attain the optimum combination of economic advance and "social justice." For 200 years the classical British liberal thinking has been that the open society was, with unhampered access to resources and scientific method in free or quasi markets, the best vehicle for productivity and the removal of poverty. For 100 years since the 1880s the Fabians have taught that government, national and municipal, is the essential instrument of both efficiency and humanity. For 50 years the self-styled followers of J. M. Keynes have taught that government can ensure high output through full employment without inflation by "managing" the national demand for goods and services. For 40 years the followers of Beveridge and Titmuss have taught that only government can reduce or remove the inequalities, injustices and poverty accompanying economic freedom even where it produces progress.

Thus the significant new element in the 1980s is the questioning of this efficacy of the state by influential public men and women who had accepted it for 30 or 40 years of political activity or power in government. Without abandoning their emphasis on equity or humanity, more leaders and thinkers in all parties, Conservative, Liberal, Social Democratic and, to a larger degree than is made public, Labour, now believe it cannot be assured by the centralising state, that government has been allowed too much control of economic life to the point of endangering both prosperity and liberty. So much for the "consensus" on the limitations of government. But, perhaps more unexpectedly, yet for that reason more hopefully, there is increasing assertion that the prosperity required to sustain humanity and abolish poverty requires increased use of decentralised institutions based on individual, group, local initiatives, voluntary, mutual, competitive or commercial, that reflect better knowledge of local circumstances, family preferences and individual aspirations. This change in emphasis is heard most from some leaders, academics and rank-and-file in the Conservative and Social Democratic Parties.

A New Enlightenment: State and Market

In this attitude to the requirements for maximum production and optimal re-distribution, the pursuit of prosperity and equality, the reconciliation of efficiency and humanity, and consequently the relative rôles of the state and the market, economists who see virtue in the market and other voluntary decentralised institutions may re-appraise and re-assert their relevance and scope in answering questions that must be answered in what may now be hoped will be a new enlightenment following disillusionment with the state and its far-reaching agencies in nationalised industry, transport, fuel and welfare, and in local authority jurisdiction over much of private and family life.

1. What is the combination of the necessary functions of government and the maximum scope for voluntary exchange in the market or in co-operative or mutual activity that will promote the optimal reconciliation of efficiency and equity?
2. How far has equality been pursued at the expense of progress and without benefit to the relatively poor? And, as a corollary: How far do the still relatively poor prefer equality or less poverty?
3. How far may it be easier to remove by re-distributed taxation or other measures differences in income or wealth that decide access to goods and services in the open market than to remove by political activism or "participation" differences in cultural, occupational or political power that decide access to services supplied by the state?
4. How far can equalisation of opportunity be achieved indirectly by removing obstacles to mobility, exchange and co-operation as well as by direct re-distribution of income?
5. How much inequality and even inequity is the necessary price that has to be paid for progress in a dynamic, innovative, flexible economy? What are the lessons of East as well as West Europe?

6. How far can government, central or local, relax the dispensable control of economic activity beyond the supply of joint, collective "public" goods?
7. Is it sufficient to decentralise government politically to regional or local authorities elected in the ballot box, or must it proceed further to enable individuals or groups to control producers more effectively by the power to withhold their purchasing power in the market?
8. How much of the British economy can be controlled by government or must be left to the market or other independent institutions in an increasingly interdependent world linked by trade and investment? If 60 per cent is too large, how soon can it be reduced to 50 per cent? How urgent is it to reach 40 per cent?
9. How can the cultural attachment to "security," embodied and crystallised in the welfare state, be reconciled with the necessity to adapt British institutions to a continually evolving world with accelerating technical innovation and social advance?
10. Not least, how can the transition, where desirable, from the state to the market and voluntary institutions be made with least dislocation and most harmony by removing the power of politicians, officials and trade unions to obstruct reform in central and local government?

Exchange in the Market or Mutual Aid outside It

These are among the main questions, addressed in brief to the contributors to this book, that will be faced in the 1980s and 1990s by politicians in all parties who have in recent years increasingly recognised the essential rôles of decentralised markets and other voluntary organisations in reconciling high productivity with spreading opportunities, efficiency with humanity—Messrs. Roy Jenkins, David Owen, William Rodgers, Dick Taverne, John Horam and others among the Social Democrats, Messrs. Jo Grimond, John Pardoe, Richard Wainwright and others among the Liberals, Mrs. Margaret Thatcher, Sir Keith Joseph, Sir Geoffrey Howe, Messrs. Norman Tebbit, David Howell, Nigel Lawson and others among the Conservatives. In this sense they are all "social democrats." And if it comes to pass that the British Government to the end of the century and beyond alternates between two political coalitions, both of which accept the verdict of history that voluntary co-operation, in the market or outside it, is not only compatible with social equity but essential to achieve it, the British economy may re-emerge to rejoin the industrial leaders of the world in whose countries there has been both more rapid economic progress and increasing equality of opportunity and income in thriving decentralised and spontaneous economic activity.

The essays in this collection are intended as a contribution to re-thinking among men and women in British public life. They are addressed to "social democrats" in all parties, to teachers and students of economics who will be a major influence in the ferment of policy reform until the end of the century and beyond, and to people in all walks of life concerned with the translation of ideas into policy in their lifetimes.

RECOLLECTIONS: BEFORE AND AFTER *THE ROAD TO SERFDOM*

Recollections: Before and After *The Road to Serfdom*

The continuity of Hayek's thought is generally if not universally recognised. The reaction to his teaching and writings has varied, at least in the short run. And their influence has fluctuated, with a doldrum in the middle period, and a crescendo in the last decade. These personal sketches recollect Hayek's LSE from 1934 to 1939 when he produced *Collectivist Economic Planning* (1935) nine years before *The Road to Serfdom* and episodes following *The Constitution of Liberty* (1960) 16 years after.

I

It is evidence of Hayek's resurgent influence in academia that the six essayists in this collection, two economists, two political scientists, and two philosophers, were born after *The Road to Serfdom* was published in 1944. The IEA is marking the 40th anniversary with essays that examine the relevance of Hayek's warning for the 1980s and beyond. The world can judge how far his apprehensions have been vindicated. We in Britain, in July 1984, can see the symptoms, not least in the rise of the culturally adroit to the top of a politicised society, even one with a liberal tradition, that responds to decibels rather than to demos.[1]

When I first knew Hayek 10 years before *The Road to Serfdom,* in October 1934 as an undergraduate taking notes from his lectures on "Industrial Fluctuations," and from 1937 to 1939 as a near-neighbour working in R. F. Fowler's room,[2] the intellectual atmosphere ranged from scepticism to hostility, not least from his colleagues,[3] even some in the economics faculty. Young academics, even economists, were enveloped in the seductions of collectivism,

1. Below, p. 39.
2. Below, p. 32.
3. H. J. Laski was in his heyday: a committed socialist who was angered by Lionel Robbins's

lately proclaimed by Sidney and Beatrice Webb as "a new civilisation" (1935), and of Keynesianism, proclaimed by its author (1936) as displacing the classical capitalist world of unemployment. Hayek has regretted omitting to controvert *The General Theory of Employment, Interest and Money* for fear that Keynes would change his mind, as indeed he did over his *Treatise on Money* (1931):

> I had undertaken to review for *Economica* his *Treatise on Money* . . . and I put a great deal of work into two long articles on it . . . I felt that I had largely demolished his theoretical scheme . . . Great was my disappointment when all this effort seemed wasted because . . . he [Keynes] told me that he had . . . changed his mind and no longer believed what he had said . . .
>
> This was one of the reasons why I did not return to the attack when he published his now famous *General Theory* . . . for which I later much blamed myself. But I feared that before I had completed my analysis he would again have changed his mind.[4]

But he did not have to regret omitting to controvert the claims for collectivism which were not similarly let off lightly by benign neglect.

The notion that collectivism could emulate the efficiency of competitive markets in capitalism was being canvassed by English (and American) economists, and Hayek must have felt it was time to nip the new heresies in the bud. Maurice Dobb had (*Economic Journal*, 1933), so he thought, disposed of the argument, mounted forcefully by Mises in 1920, that "rational" calculation in socialism without markets was not feasible, by declaring that it was

---

use of Shakespeare to describe his conclusion on socialism: "Lilies that fester smell far worse than weeds." (*Economic Planning and International Order*, 1937.)

Herman Finer, a Fabian, who later wrote an angry reply to *The Road to Serfdom* in *Road to Reaction* (1945), had written *Municipal Trading* (1941), and asked Arnold Plant for a young economist to run over the economic argument in his MS. I had reservations, and proposed that he anticipate criticism by amplifying his Preface to recognise the advantages of competition in local government, then a rare notion. The Preface was roundly condemned by W. A. Robson, another Fabian.

4. Hayek, "Personal Recollections of Keynes and the 'Keynesian Revolution,'" *The Oriental Economist*, January 1966, reprinted in F. A. Hayek, *A Tiger by the Tail—The Keynesian Legacy of Inflation*, subtitled "A 40-years' running commentary on Keynesianism by Hayek," compiled and introduced by Sudha R. Shenoy, and edited by A. Seldon, Hobart Paperback 4, IEA, 1972 (2nd edn. 1978), p. 100.

dispensable simply by ignoring consumer preferences! But other economists in England and the USA, lagging after social scientists on the Continent (Max Weber 1921, Jacob Marshak 1924, Boris Brutzkus 1921–2, and others), were discussing schemes for market socialism—F. M. Taylor (1929), H. D. Dickinson (1930), Barbara Wootton (1934), and A. P. Lerner (1934). E. F. M. Durbin, B. E. Lippincott and others came later, although their unpublished thinking was being discussed informally. (Sir) Arthur Lewis, who graduated with me in 1937, was voicing his tentative sympathy in Arnold Plant's seminars.

Apart from *Prices and Production* (1931) and *Monetary Theory and the Trade Cycle* (1933 in England), *Collectivist Economic Planning*, with essays by N. G. Pierson, L. von Mises, G. Halm and E. Barone assembled by Hayek (who also wrote two of its five chapters), was his most explicit contribution to the raging economic debates of the pre-war years. Nor was it "a 1930s book": it ran through six impressions in the 30 years to 1963.

In the celebrated final chapter, "The Present State of the Debate," Hayek drew on two LSE economists with whom I worked closely when appointed Research Assistant to Arnold Plant (1937). There Hayek argued that markets were not feasible under socialism, not least because the plant managers who were to be instructed on pricing to ensure the efficient use of resources did not own them. The origins and rationale of private property had been revealed by David Hume in his *Enquiry concerning the Principles of Morals:* Book III, "Of Justice" (1740), to which Hayek's attention had been drawn by Plant. (It was regretted by Plant's colleagues and students that he did not complete his life's work in a treatise on property.) Plant, in turn, acknowledged Hayek's influence on his thinking on intellectual and industrial property.[5] Hayek in private occasionally voiced appreciation of Plant's work, which unfortunately was not easily accessible because mostly dispersed in specialist technical journals. Encouraged by Lionel Robbins, and with the support of Ralph Harris, I edited a selection of his work in *Economic Essays and Addresses* (1974).[6] Plant's teaching was mainly handed down verbally through the works of his students, notably the three Ronalds (Coase, Fowler, and Edwards), Arthur Lewis, and others.

5. Arnold Plant, "A Tribute to Hayek—the Rational Persuader," *Economic Age*, January–February 1970.

6. Routledge & Kegan Paul for the IEA, 1974.

Hayek's reference to R. F. Fowler in "The Present State of the Debate" was to his book, *The Depreciation of Capital* (1934), on which Hayek drew to re-inforce the argument that the often ingenious attempts to simulate competition under socialism, by making (public) monopolies charge competitive prices, had all necessarily failed. The reason was clear from the arbitrary regulation of prices in (so-called) "public utilities." Fowler, said Hayek, had demonstrated that the attempts at simulation were bound to fail because interest and depreciation on fixed plant could be determined only *after* the price obtainable for their product (transport, fuel, etc.) was known. It is true that fixed costs are (or can be) ignored when setting prices in the short run, and the socialist-inclined economists argued that they could also be ignored in socialist markets. But in the long run when capital has to be replaced, no costs are fixed, all are marginal, and prices have to reflect all costs. "To make a monopolist charge the price that would rule under competition, or at a price that is equal to the necessary cost, is impossible," concluded Hayek, "because the competitive or necessary cost cannot be known until there is competition." And since there was no real competition in socialism without private property, socialism could not reproduce the efficiency of markets in capitalism.

The circular reasoning, question-begging and pre-judgements in the case for market socialism revealed by Hayek in these and other searching counter-arguments, and developed in later writings, have never been refuted by market socialists (below, p. 39). They have finally, if reluctantly, been accepted by socialist economists like Professor Alec Nove,[7] who was also an LSE undergraduate at the time. Re-inforced by the teachings of T. E. Gregory and younger dons like Frederic Benham (whose elementary textbook *Economics* appeared in 1938) and Gilbert Ponsonby,[8] Hayek's intellectual assault on the economics of collectivism fortified five post-graduates in 1938–39 to form a small group to discuss ways of refuting collectivist economic heresies. The war prevented it from evolving into an embryo IEA-type organisation of liberals: L. M. Lachmann, who developed into a foremost exponent of "Austrian" economics; A. A. Shenfield, who had arrived after a brilliant record at Birmingham University, later added law to economics, and became

7. *The Economics of Feasible Socialism*, George Allen & Unwin, London, 1983.

8. And with knowledge of non-LSE economists like F. H. Knight, Knut Wicksell, Philip Wicksteed, Bertil Ohlin, Gottfried Haberler, not least W. H. Hutt, whose *Economists and the Public* had appeared in 1936; I should add Walter Lippmann, whose *The Good Society* (1938) acknowledged Hayek's influence.

President of the Mont Pélèrin Society (1972–74); A. M. Neuman, a Polish economist; I. P. Andren, a Swede; with me, a raw graduate, as the youngest member. The perch on the LSE research staff had brought me into physical proximity, several yards away, to Hayek, Robbins, Plant, Paish and, for a time as a refugee from Cambridge, D. H. Robertson. It could not have been a surprise to any of the post-graduate group of five (I cannot recall that we could find others in a student body influenced more by the socialist political scientists like H. J. Laski than by the liberal economists) that Hayek followed *Collectivist Economic Planning* by *The Road to Serfdom.* (Some essays in this IEA collection trace the evolving links.) I imagine the group would also have expected the further step to *The Constitution of Liberty* (1960).

My seven years at the LSE to 1941, when Hitler supervened, had led me to absorb the "Austrian" flavour of economics as favoured by Robbins, the leading light of the economics faculty, and admired by Plant. The LSE connection and influence continued for a further 20 years when, in 1946, Plant, perhaps because he thought me "unburdened" by the latest econometric sophistications,[9] proposed me to Robbins as a tutor for external commerce students and later as an examiner for internal economics students. Later, the "Austrian" teaching on marginalism, subjectivism, opportunity cost (Wieser), and the dynamic nature of competition led me to apply it in the IEA, as in the early books on advertising and the welfare state, later in the *Hobart Papers* by Lachmann on the micro-economic foundations of macro-economics (1973) and Littlechild (1978) on the implications of Austrian economics for contemporary British economic policy, the Kirzner Seminar on entrepreneurship (1980) and, most recently, in the IEA journal, *Economic Affairs,* which emphasises public choice and "Austrian" economics[10] as well as the Minford (Muth, 1961) "new classical economics." The public choice approach was a powerful re-inforcement, resting ultimately on classical insights. Both "Austrian" and public-choice elements at the IEA continued alongside, and were not submerged by, the Friedmanite counter-revolution against Keynes "sponsored" at the IEA from the late 1960s.

9. In retrospect it was probably Plant's lectures on the economics of industry and business administration that fortified my resistance to the abstract constructions and the economic geometry of Robinson and Chamberlin, a time-wasting parody of real-world "kaleidoscopic" (Shackle, 1965) competition. In writing books on advertising (1959, 1962) our exchanges of ideas and drafts led Ralph Harris to write in lines on imperfections as the frictions necessary to give the economic structure stability. (*Advertising and the Public,* 1962, pp. 84–85.)

10. The "Austrian" flavour also appeared in *Everyman's Dictionary of Economics,* designed to redress the over-Keynesian imbalance of other such texts for newcomers to economics.

II

Of Hayek's influence in the early years at the LSE, Plant has provided ample testimony.

> I can testify from personal experience to the immense stimulus and direction which Hayek's migration to this country gave to economic research in the 1930s, not only in London and economics faculties throughout the United Kingdom, but also in the international world of scholarship.
>
> The focus was Robbins's Economics seminar at LSE, which became the forum for timeless discussion of Hayek's ideas on monetary influences on the structure of production and industrial fluctuations, and their many-sided implications throughout economic, social and political policy.[11]

The Austrian school had almost fallen out of sight until Hayek introduced it into the LSE. Much more is written of Hayek's activities and influence in Chicago and the USA from 1951 to 1964 than about his work and influence at the LSE and beyond from 1931 to 1950.

Of Hayek's external benefits, one was the direct link between *The Road to Serfdom* and the IEA. Antony Fisher has told the story of his visit to Hayek at the LSE after reading a summary of *The Road to Serfdom* in *The Reader's Digest* in 1945, the advice to eschew political for intellectual influence, and how it led him to incorporate the Institute in 1955,[12] run from 1957 by Ralph Harris as General Director and me as Editorial Director. For me it was the fulfilment of my post-graduate hopes of 1938–39. Although its early publications reflected the influence of Hayek on us both, four years followed before the IEA acted explicitly on Hayek's work. *The Constitution of Liberty* led us to invite 10 authors—six economists (Frederic Benham, the 1930s LSE colleague, Michael Fogarty, Graham Hutton, who had advised on *The Constitution of Liberty*, Victor Morgan, Eric Nash, Arthur Shenfield), two philosophers (H. B. Acton, J. W. N. Watkins), a labour lawyer (Sir Henry Slesser) and an historian (John Lincoln)—to assess Hayek's biggest book so far. They produced an assortment of praise and criticism in the IEA book, *Agenda for a Free Society* (1961).

Hayek had left Britain for the USA in 1951 and had produced two main works abroad—*The Sensory Order* and *The Counter-Revolution of Science* (both 1952), although the first was also published in Britain. My impression

11. Plant, *op. cit.*
12. Antony Fisher, *Must History Repeat Itself?*, Churchill Press, London, 1974.

was that in Britain knowledge of his work had fallen away. I found the wide sweep of *The Constitution of Liberty* magisterial and profound, its scholarship massive and its insights brilliant, and I ventured to say in the Introduction to the *Agenda* that, while "it would be folly to assess [its] influence on the second half of the 20th century," in its "conception, intellectual insight and execution it could be compared with *The Wealth of Nations.*" This claim was too much for the anonymous reviewer in *The Economist* (25 November 1961). He referred to Hayek's "massive tome" as "undoubtedly important," but thought my claim "somewhat exaggerated"; to class *The Constitution of Liberty* with *The Wealth of Nations* was "silly," because "there is no sign of it becoming a general seminal work," and it did not advance far beyond Adam Smith or Mill. "The value of Professor Hayek's work is in the application of libertarian and neo-*laissez faire* ideas to contemporary society rather than in any striking originality of thought." Since he added that "the role of the intelligence [*sic*], especially in political affairs, is to assess the possible" (which he accused Hayek of failing to do), I took his judgement with a bucketful of salt. The superstition of "political impossibility" has no place in a scholar's intellectual equipment, and Hayek has rightly emphasised in recent writings that the task of politics is to make possible that which is desirable but thought impossible—or, I would add, what are politicians for?[13]

That was the qualified and modest pat on the back *The Constitution of Liberty* received from the reviewer chosen by *The Economist* in 1961. Hayek's work in the 24 years since *The Constitution of Liberty,* refined in *Philosophy, Politics and Economics* (1967), *Law, Legislation and Liberty* (1973, 1976, 1979) and *New Studies in Philosophy, Politics, Economics and the History of Ideas* (1978), and shorter texts, has evidently impressed the later generation more than *The Economist* reviewer expected. The Oxford philosopher John Gray (who contributes to this collection), says in his new book, *Hayek on Liberty* (1984):

> Hayek's work comprises a system of ideas, fully as ambitious as the systems of Mill and Marx, but far less vulnerable to criticism than theirs because it is grounded on a philosophically defensible view of the scope and limits of human reason.

13. ". . . what I have often had occasion to explain but may never have stated in writing, that I strongly feel the chief task of the economic theorist or political philosopher should be to operate on public opinion to make politically possible what today may be politically impossible . . ." (Hayek, *Denationalisation of Money—The Argument Refined,* Hobart Paper 70, IEA, 2nd edn. 1978: from the author's "Note to the Second Edition," p. 17.)

> . . . we find in Hayek a restatement of classical liberalism in which it is purified of errors—specifically, the errors of abstract individualism and uncritical rationalism—which inform the work of even the greatest of the classical liberals . . .[14]

If Dr. Gray is right, Hayek has advanced beyond Adam Smith. (And that is no reflection on the Great Master, writing two centuries earlier.)

III

The "sequel" to the 1935 argument of *Collectivist Economic Planning* came in 1982 with a letter from Hayek (below).

For varied reasons, the political attractions of state or government (euphemistically labelled "public" or "common") ownership of resources had overwhelmed the economic demonstration that socialism in practice, even if it tolerated or used "markets," could not reproduce the efficiency of capitalism and private ownership. The theoretical pretence rumbles on. And East European communist/socialist countries claim to decentralise economic authority or initiative to state-owned plants, as in Yugoslav worker self-management. If for no other reason, this attempted reproduction of the benefits of decentralisation is no solution, for it is ultimately at the discretion and mercy of the central political control, to which it is a standing threat, and which is not likely to tolerate it when economic decentralisation arouses interest in local autonomy, civil liberties and cultural independence from state control,[15] as they seem to have done in Poland. If markets in Hungary bring something of Western living standards, it is insofar as they rest on private ownership.

But the theorists of market socialism wearyingly insist after 40 years that markets can work with state ownership under socialism. Hayek's letter in 1982 said he was

> particularly indignant about the steadily repeated silly talk of [Oskar] Lange having refuted Mises . . . ,

and he was enclosing a text of 3,500 words that he thought might make an IEA *Paper.* I replied it was too short and suggested expansion. He responded

14. John Gray, *Hayek on Liberty,* Basil Blackwell, Oxford, 1984, p. viii.

15. The argument is developed in Brian Crozier and Arthur Seldon, *Socialism Explained,* Sherwood Press, 1984.

he would have to put it aside for later attention. So I proposed it go into the IEA's journal *Economic Affairs*. He readily agreed.

The article bore the intriguing title "Two Pages of Fiction: The Impossibility of Socialist Calculation." The two pages were from Oskar Lange's essay of 1936 reprinted in *On the Economic Theory of Socialism* (edited by B. E. Lippincott), which Hayek said had given birth to "endless repetition" of the claim that Lange in 1936 had refuted the contention advanced in 1920 by Ludwig von Mises that "economic calculation is impossible in a socialist society."[16] In it Hayek was fairly aggressive, certainly more so than in his younger or middle years. He laid about him with verbal exuberance. He referred to Lange's "most extraordinary 'solution,'" his "brazen assertion" for which he "offers no evidence or justification." Lange "has the audacity to blame Mises for the very mistake he himself is committing." Robert Heilbroner, a pupil of Lange, had, in his *Between Capitalism and Socialism* (1980), made "the even more fantastic assertion that a central planning board 'would receive exactly the same information from a socialist economic system as did the entrepreneurs under the market system.'" This, said Hayek (at 83), was "a blatant untruth, an assertion so absurd that it is difficult to understand how an intelligent person could ever honestly make it." Hayek attacked even Schumpeter who, "like so many mathematical economists, appears to have been seduced . . . to believe that the relevant facts that the theorist must *assume* to exist are actually *known* to any one mind" (my italics). Moreover, Schumpeter had made a "most startling assertion" about economic rationality in the real world: it was "sheer nonsense." K. J. Arrow and L. Hurwicz in *Studies in Resource Allocation Processes* (1977) had dealt "irresponsibly" with fictitious "data." Hayek accused Lange and others of the "negligence and carelessness with which words have been used throughout [the 40 years of] this whole, long discussion" (on economic calculation). The assertion that the planning authority would possess a complete inventory of all relevant materials and instruments of production was "a somewhat comic fiction." And the notion that the planning authority could enable the plant managers to do their job by fixing uniform prices was "the crowning foolery of the whole farce."

The urbane economist whose thinking has been assailed and denigrated over 50 years, but who throughout remained courteous to his critics, has at last come out of his corner fighting, at least verbally.

16. The article can be read in full in the April 1982 issue of the IEA journal.

In her *Freedom under Planning* (1945), which must have been written quickly in reply to *The Road to Serfdom,* Barbara (later Lady) Wootton wrote:

> Intellectual controversy on serious practical and political issues is not always conducted in an atmosphere of personal goodwill. It is on that account the greater pleasure to express here my appreciation and reciprocation of the unchanging friendliness of Professor Hayek's attitude. (p. 5)

Hayek, she said, had given her "an early view of his *Road to Serfdom.* Much of what I have written is devoted to criticism of the views put forward by Professor Hayek in this and other books" (*Freedom under Planning,* p. 5). She repaid his kindness by a book that, despite her continuing attachment to "planning" and adoption, *inter alia,* of the fashionable deficit financing cure for unemployment, was more respectful of Hayek and more scholarly in tone than other critiques by "planners"/socialists in the 40 years after 1944. Socialists in our day would be sobered by re-reading the concessions in *Freedom under Planning,* not least that Hayek could, after all, be right. And she invited Hayek to

> write another book elaborating [the] constructive aspects of his thesis . . . that the defects of a system in which economic priorities are not consciously determined . . . could be overcome by . . . measures . . . well within our grasp. (p. 62)

She had his response in *The Constitution of Liberty.*

IV

A basic insight of *The Road to Serfdom* is vividly illustrated for Hayek's British compatriots by recent developments in economic policy—the attempts by the new ("Whig") Conservatives since 1979 to bring the British economy closer to the underlying realities of supply and demand from which post-war governments have separated it for 40 years by subsidies to decaying industries, privileges for organised trade union and other interests, acquiescence in restrictive practices, vindictive taxation, a welfare state that is increasingly seen as benefiting the relatively rich at the expense of the relatively poor.

In 1944, in the Introduction to *The Road to Serfdom,* Hayek said:

> The problem is . . . to determine the circumstances which during the last 70 years have made possible the progressive growth and the ultimate vic-

> tory of a particular set of ideas, and why in the end this victory has brought the most vicious elements . . . to the top.

And Chapter X is entitled "Why the Worst Get on Top."

Even Barbara Wootton, who disputed *The Road to Serfdom* (and who interpreted Hayek's "the worst" as "the scum" (*Freedom under Planning*, p. 142)), conceded:

> . . . there is a challenge here that the constructive planner would do well to meet with care and courage. (p. 142)

(She defined "planning" as "the conscious choice of economic priorities by public authority," distinct from public production or socialism.) Her admonition is unheeded by many who still call themselves planners or socialists in the Britain of 1984. "The problem," she concluded, was

> an open one, capable of better or worse solution according as we are successful, or unsuccessful, in creating the conditions which favour the rise to power of the wise and public-spirited and the preservation of their wisdom and public spirit against the corruptions of office. (p. 144)

Collectivists of the world, whether "planners" of priorities or socialisers of production, are united in their faith in "public spirit," which to the liberal begs the essential question of motive and maximand in politics raised (and answered) by the economics of public choice. The development of socialism in the post-war world does not vindicate the hope that "wisdom and public spirit" would generally prevail over "corruption." Nor, to us in Britain, is the solution "the wise selection of the men and women at the top" (p. 150), nor "the politically active citizen of the future" (p. 152) who serves on "one or other of the executive, advisory, or judicial organs of an active democracy" (p. 154). This is the voice of the politically active who see society run by the politically active, not by the generality of citizen-consumers. It epitomises the élitism that underlies collectivist theorising. Equality of status as consumer, if not equality of income or wealth, is best approached in the market.

The British economy now displays the paternalist naiveté of Fabian and Tory theorists who envisage that government can be run by "benevolent autocrats." In Britain there are still "public-spirited," able, upright men and women who want to serve their fellow-countrymen through government. It is no less true that, by deploying enormous power of life or death, prosperity or penury, on industry and individuals, government has become a pit of power that attracts men and women who can do better for themselves in politics than they could by producing goods or services for consumers in the market. People who would not be entrusted with the hundreds of pounds of pensioners' savings (or the thousands of professional investors) can, in local as well as central government, aspire to control over the millions and billions of taxpayers' and ratepayers' money. Their qualification is not that they can anticipate consumer preferences but that they can deploy the arts of political organisation and manipulation by skills at conferences, on committees and in "representative" assemblies that Abraham Lincoln would turn in his grave to hear dignified as government of the people, by the people, for the people.

"Representative" government, increasingly a misnomer, responds to pressure from the herd: the marchers, the slogan shouters; the meek and the mild have to take to the streets to be heard, or risk being ignored—like parents who want to escape from bad schools, or patients from bad doctors, where, for 95 per cent of British people, the market escape by exit has been suppressed and almost destroyed. Professor A. O. Hirschmann's "voice" is unheeded unless it carries the sanction of "exit."[17] The "representation" and "accountability" now emphasised by advocates of state economy are ineffective if the "represented" cannot escape from misuse of power and corruption by the "representatives." Constitutional reform and entrenched clauses may not be enough without competition in open markets whenever and wherever possible.

By 1978, 33 years after her reply to *The Road to Serfdom,* Lady Wootton was reduced to a double negative. In an article, "Can we still be Democratic Socialists?",[18] her case for planning/socialism had changed from confident assertion to tortuous defence. Because collectivism had not so far in history been found compatible with freedom (an acceptance that Hayek had been right), it did not follow that it never would be. The case is now turned on its head: history is not proof that planning/socialism cannot produce what it has not yet produced.

Human behaviour is at its best, because most corrigible, in the market; at its worst, because least corrigible, in politics. It is not the least of his services to mankind that Hayek has focussed attention on the political and philosophic as well as economic reasons for urgency in rebuilding the liberal society.

17. A. O. Hirschmann, *Exit, Voice, and Loyalty,* Harvard University Press, 1970.
18. *New Statesman,* 8 December 1978.

ECONOMIC SCHOLARSHIP AND POLITICAL INTEREST

IEA THINKING AND GOVERNMENT POLICIES

Economic Scholarship and Political Interest

IEA Thinking and Government Policies

I. Introduction

Dr. Veljanovski's invitation was to present "reflections on the past 30 years of trying to influence events through the propagation of ideas." The IEA, he said, had promoted the thinking of economic liberalism "with a ruthless disregard for popularity or political acceptability." Keynes's dictum on the supremacy of ideas over interests, echoing Hume and Dicey, had reversed Marx's emphasis on the dominance of interest in the determination of power relationships, and was qualified by J. S. Mill's judgement that the influence of ideas waited on "conspiring" circumstances.

With a flavour of the Chicago prescription for the empirical testing of hypotheses, Dr. Veljanovski suggested that economists and political scientists had developed theories (explanations) of the influence on events of vested interests but they had not shed much light on the influence of intellectual ideas. The purpose of the seminar was to explore the evidence on the power of ideas, if any, in the context of the recent apparent ascendancy of liberal political theory.

II. The Power and Limitations of Ideas

To search for evidence on the influence of ideas on events is to examine their interactions with interests and "circumstances." To these three influences the most recent events suggest the addition of a fourth—the influence in history of exceptional individuals emphasised by Bertrand Russell (as we are reminded by Professor Gamble in *The Free Economy and the Strong*

I have to thank Ralph Harris for reading an early draft and suggesting clarifications; remaining obscurities are private property and a public good (or bad).

State).[1] The relative influence on public policy of academic thinking and established interests, and their dependence on predisposing chance developments, are accordingly discussed here from the experience of the IEA over its first 30 years from 1957, illustrated by the activities of governments from the corporatist-inclined Conservatives of the late 1950s to the liberal Conservatives of the first three Thatcher Governments in the 1980s.

The origins and *rationale* of the long-term IEA strategy to influence academic and, indirectly, public *thinking* (rather than, or as a preliminary to, changing *policy* and *events*) is reviewed. The IEA as a charity may not aim at the direct influence on political reform; but initial IEA thinking also rested on the view that intellectual error in the 1950s was too deep-rooted to yield to early treatment: it set out on a long voyage of discovery by research into and re-education in the role of the long-neglected market as superior to the over-used state.

The IEA approach to the application of economics to industrial and government policy was based on classical liberal political economy, refined, as I saw it, by developments in "Austrian-Hayekian" market process, Buchanan-Tullock public choice, and, later, Muth-Minford "rational expectations" (people learn from their mistakes). They combined to induce scepticism on the power of government to over-ride the market, on the beneficence of the political process, and on its capacity to heal itself.

It is still too soon after the events of the last 10 unprecedented years to draw conclusions that are much more than tentative. The Institute of Contemporary British History (ICBH) is encouraging the scholarly study of recent events from oral as well as documentary evidence. These reflections on the (indirect) influence of the IEA on political thinking and policies could be checked against the diverse assessments in the ICBH journal, *Contemporary Record*, as seen from the ivory castles of the universities and the day-to-day cockpit of politics.

The Impact of Ideas on Government

The main reflections are briefly stated under 14 main heads. They are illustrated, where feasible, below (Section VI).

1. A change in the intellectual climate is a pre-condition for a change in political policies and events.
2. The decisive circumstances in the fate of ideas—whether adopted or

1. Andrew Gamble, *The Free Economy and the Strong State*, London: Macmillan, 1988, p. v.

ignored, and, if adopted, the *rate* at which and the *form* in which they are applied—are their confluence with interests, chance, and the accident of exceptional individuals.

3. Ideas go through a political process or "filter" of approval and adaptation. They are adopted or adapted in a wide range of forms from "pure" to tempered or emasculated, according to current *political* judgement of public acceptability and party interest.
4. Ideas fare better in political competition for new solutions to unsolved problems than in the political monopsony of a sole interested political party. The IEA was originally confronted by a monopsony of Conservatives, now replaced by competition between four of the five political parties that have embraced markets—Conservative, Social Democrat, Labour and Communist. (The historical irony is that the Liberals were until recently unregenerate corporatists.)
5. Ideas may be adapted at a cost in political support, at least in the short run. Governments make rational choices. Intellectual conviction is more likely to give birth to policies with a proportionately small than with a proportionately large risk of loss of political approval and power.
6. Ideas have to chime with public sentiment to induce government to adopt them. The division of labour between scholars and politicians in the explanation of policies to the public has not been clearly demarcated. Politicians have a more material interest in the public acceptance of ideas than academics, but there has been an imbalance of advocacy against liberal capitalism: in the first 30 years of the IEA, liberal scholars have become less reticent but the collectivists are still more tenacious in writing, teaching and preaching. There are exceptions: Hayek the supreme scholar has been a tireless advocate.
7. Academic reinforcement is, perhaps subconsciously by liberal but more overtly by socialist politicians, desired by people in government to validate or rationalise policies, whether inspired by the inclination to yield to rent-seeking vested interests or by the hope of serving the public interest.
8. Political self-interest, in achieving or maintaining power, is not necessarily in conflict with the underlying, long-run public interest.
9. It is unrealistic to expect politicians to pay much attention to very distant externalities of current policies, except when under pressure from vocal single-issue pressure groups.

10. Policies in conflict with underlying conditions of supply or demand ("market forces" reflecting the myriad decisions of the millions) cannot be maintained forever: they provoke evasion or require coercion. The indestructibility of the "black" free market is a monument to political conceit in capitalist as well as communist countries.
11. Ideas for measures in the public interest based on reasoned argument and empirical evidence can be kept at bay for long periods by political value-judgements, bureaucratic self-interest, or producer resistance.
12. Scholarship must surmount the *desiderata* of politics because politicians are not disinterested judges of the "politically possible," bureaucrats of the "administratively practicable," or government advisers of the "socially desirable."
13. The Buchanan/Tullock analysis of the economics of politics has added a refinement to the academic development of solutions. Economists and political scientists who dissect the micro-economics of politics have learnt that ideas cannot be developed and presented without regard for the realities of political behaviour. Academic advice must reflect the motivations, feasibilities and limitations of the political process. Scholars must ask themselves whether they have handed politicians dangerous toys.
14. The main lesson from the 30 years, especially from the last 10, is that ideas in the general public interest can be obstructed and emasculated by the interests of capital, the professions, or labour generated by corporatist policies. In 1822 David Ricardo complained that the House of Commons had been "tormented . . . with constant solicitations to sacrifice the public good to particular interests."[2] In 1986 Douglas Hurd was reported in the press as warning "Members of Parliament and Ministers . . . to shake themselves free from the embrace of pressure and interest groups . . . serpents constantly emerging from the sea to strangle Laocoon and his sons in their coils."

Government has not yet evolved procedures for removing or neutralising the "rent-seekers" who attempt to extract from the political process what they have failed to earn in the market process. A fruitful outcome of the seminar would be discussion, and if possible agreement, by scholars of diverse schools of thought on methods of neutralising the interests.

2. David Ricardo, in *Hansard,* May 1822.

III. Over-Simplifications in the Influences on Policy

The propositions of Keynes on the power of ideas, of Marx on the dominance of interests, and of Mill on the necessity of conspiring circumstances are sometimes over-simplified.

First, Keynes's emphasis on the power of ideas in the familiar dictum that "the world is ruled by little else" contained a time limitation. It appeared in his *magnum opus, The General Theory,* which provided an outstanding example of a lesson in public choice, examined by Professor J. M. Buchanan in an IEA Paper in 1978 (below).[3]

In discussing the prospects for his proposals in *The General Theory,* and whether "these ideas" were a "visionary hope," Keynes referred tangentially to the political process, the power of interests, and the state of public opinion. He asked specifically (a) whether his ideas had "sufficient roots in the motives which govern the evolution of political society" and (b) whether "the interests they will thwart [were] stronger and more obvious than those they will serve." He also referred subtly (c) to the importance of the long, or at least not short, run, in which evidently we were not all dead: apart from "this contemporary mood [in which] people are unusually expectant of a more fundamental diagnosis" (presumably the socialism being widely urged by academics in the 1930s based on the example of the USSR), "the *gradual* encroachment of ideas" would prevail over the power of vested interests, not immediately but *after a certain interval* because "not many" people over 25 or 30 were influenced by new ideas (my italics). His "soon or late, it is ideas, not vested interests, which are dangerous for good or evil" was mangled English (dangerous for good?), but these were the concluding words in the book, by a supposed master of the English language, that supplied the outstanding example in our times of the dangerous toy of deficit financing and unbalanced budgets.

The General Theory embodied the fallacy of giving politicians a respectable reason for their disposition, understandable in four/five-year periods of office, to take short views. Their temptation to overspend by unbalancing budgets triumphed for 20 years into the 1960s over the general interest by generating the stagflation Keynes did not foresee in 1936. And Keynesian politicians, Conservative as well as Labour, were "rationally" induced by the

3. J. M. Buchanan, R. E. Wagner and J. Burton, *The Consequences of Mr. Keynes,* Hobart Paper 78, London: IEA, 1978.

political process to ignore the damaging post-war economic consequences of the supposed budgetary solution for inter-war unemployment.

Keynes said that ideas prevailed over interests in the *longer* or *long* run. *Ergo*, in the *shorter* or *short* run interests could or would prevail over new ideas. But politicians were *always* influenced by ideas; Keynes's objection was that they were usually out of date. Politicians tend to regurgitate the predominant thinking of their undergraduate or early years. In the 1950s, when the IEA was created, politicians of all parties were reflecting the war-time consensus on the solutions for the pre-war politico-economic *malaise* of unemployment, industrial inefficiency and social insecurity. Politicians who had advocated outdated or falsified policies could not easily change their minds and confess error. Yet there are evidently exceptions. The interesting question is whether the economic liberalism that informed the change in policies after 1979 required a Keith Joseph to change his mind in 1975 (aged 57) from his earlier persuasion by consensus thinkers like Andrew Shonfield and Rudolf Klein and a Margaret Thatcher (aged 50) to assert her instincts after having to tolerate the consensus under Edward Heath.

Marx's Vested Interests — the Ambivalence of Capitalists

Second, Marxist emphasis on the supremacy rather than strong influence of vested interest also has to be re-interpreted. The intriguing reflection must be that the Marxist *idea* that interest was more influential than ideas has had more influence on politico-economic thinking over a century than any other despite its self-contradiction.

The Marxist interpretation of the interests of the capitalist "class" does not explain the ambivalence of capitalists to the market economy described as "capitalism." The post-war industrialists, mostly organised in the CBI, inspired and connived in the two decades of corporatist alliance with politicians, Conservative and Labour, and the trade unions from the early 1960s to the late 1970s. They supported policies and principles hostile to capitalism—over-expansion of the state far beyond the boundaries of public goods and collusion with trade unions in monopolistic and restrictive practices; and they displayed their occupational predilection for protectionism.

The corporatist influence may have been partly ideas: the illusions of growth targets, incomes policies, physical rather than priced financial controls, and the indicative planning of benevolent government *à la française*, culminating in George Brown's grandiose folly of national planning. And the National Plan collapsed after a year, perhaps expedited partly by the intellectual ridicule in John Brunner's IEA Paper in 1965, described by *The Economist* as "corrosive," which brought the IEA the first attention of a Labour Minister eight years after its formation.[4]

But the capitalist caprice for corporatism reflected a deep-lying, though logical, dichotomy; the rational capitalist welcomes the competitive market for his purchases, including labour, but dislikes the free market for the sale of his products in competition with other producers. This love-hate relationship of the capitalists (often salaried executives as well as equity-owning entrepreneurs) with the capitalist system created a dilemma in the financing of the IEA (the solution is discussed below). The conclusion remains that the interests (of labour and of the professions as well as of divided capital) are influential, and political democracy allows them too much influence, but they are not the ultimate arbiter in the control of a market society if government is enabled to resist their pressures and importunities, perhaps by the constitutional or market reforms that the school of public choice is refining. The ground is reviewed in two 1988 Hobart Papers: Professor William C. Mitchell's *Government As It Is* (the title is taken from Alfred Marshall) and Professor Norman Barry's *The Invisible Hand in Economics and Politics.*

Mill's "Conspiring Circumstances"...

Third, Mill's "conspiring circumstances" suggest humility among economists. Ideas by themselves may hang on the vine for season after season if they serve no interest. T. W. Hutchison quotes Leslie Stephen on the abolition of the Corn Laws in a manner which suggests that interests prevailed over ideas: "Did it mark a triumph of logic, or was it that the class which wanted cheap bread was politically stronger than the class which wanted dear bread?"[5] And he implies that Disraeli, in his 1875 trade union Act which outbid Gladstone's 1871 Act, anticipated Professor Gordon Tullock's analysis of the competitive bidding for votes.[6]

Hutchison suggests that Hayek may also have neglected the electoral gains from the widening franchise in acting on the view, developed by Edgeworth and others in the 1890s, that the notion of diminishing marginal util-

4. J. Brunner, *The National Plan: A Preliminary Assessment,* Eaton Paper 4, London: IEA, 1965 (3rd edn. 1969).

5. T. W. Hutchison, *Markets and the Franchise,* Occasional Paper 10, London: IEA, 1966, reprinted in *The Politics and Philosophy of Economics,* Oxford: Basil Blackwell, 1981.

6. Gordon Tullock, *Entrepreneurial Politics,* Research Monograph No. 5, Thomas Jefferson Center for Political Economy, University of Virginia, 1962.

ity of income justified progressive taxation, adopted by Dalton and others as the Labour Party's fiscal policy, later rejected by Robbins and others as requiring unfounded inter-personal comparison of utilities. Yet Hayek's criticism of Edgeworth and his successors reinforces the public choice analysis of the politics of budgeting by J. M. Buchanan, Robert Tollison, Charles Rowley and others for taking the same unrealistic, romantic view as Keynes on the (rational) proclivities of politicians by incautiously furnishing them with the plausible but dangerous economic toy of progressive taxation with which they have wreaked havoc with the economic structure of incentives.

Electoral advantage is included by Hutchison in Mill's "conspiring circumstances" but here again time is of the essence. Mill said ideas had no "*very rapid or immediate*" efficacy unless "outward" circumstances conspired with them.[7] "Outward" is ambiguous, but the clear implication is that in the *long* run new ideas may be able to prevail over material interests.

. . . and Bertrand Russell's Exceptional Individuals

Fourth, the Bertrand Russell element of exceptional individuals in history has to be disentangled from the other circumstances that explain the historic change in the Conservative Party from corporatist to liberal in the 1970s. The corporatist consensus had failed: any determined leader who led a revolt against it might have succeeded Edward Heath in 1975. Yet the historian has to accept as empirical evidence that the 1975 palace revolution in the Conservative Party and the economic revolution in government policy it engineered after 1979 required a politician of conviction, and/or of the upbringing that emphasised good husbandry, and/or of the strength of character to defeat the corporatist High Tories; and only Mrs. Thatcher seemed to satisfy the requirements. Heath promised change, but his philosophic roots were shallow. (His one visit to the IEA indicated that he was not "one of us.") Whatever the "unknowns" of history, historians will have to record, political scientists to explain, and philosophers to clarify that in the event the metamorphosis was accomplished, uncharacteristically and unpredictably, by an exceptional woman, of *petit bourgeois* origin, of independent temperament, who defied the high priests of her party, the bureaucracy, the trade unions, the professions, the intelligentsia, the *literati,* and the church. Either she is an extra-ordinary individual, or the political leadership re-

7. J. S. Mill, "The Claims of Labour," *Edinburgh Review,* April 1845 (my italics).

quired to induce the Conservative Party, as Lord Blake argues,[8] to return to its liberal past did not require an extra-ordinary individual. If it could not have been accomplished by an ordinary politician, the inference that Mrs. Thatcher is extra-ordinary seems more plausible. It is tempting to conclude that the economic liberalism taught by the IEA required a stubborn Mrs. Thatcher as much as (she said at the IEA's 30th Birthday Dinner in 1987) she required it.

Mrs. Thatcher was the first Prime Minister, and the first Conservative leader, since the IEA was founded in 1957, who seemed to understand its analysis of the state and the market as alternative economic prime movers. The conduit between economic scholarship and political implementation was the male scholar-politician, Lord (then Sir Keith) Joseph, but it was the female political unconservative radical who translated it into reality.

The frictions of which she was accused were the legacy of the male Prime Ministers who for decades had failed to adapt the economy to changing supply and demand; and the frictions would have become more intense the longer her belated reforms were delayed in deference to the political and industrial vested interests.

There can be little doubt that exceptional political individuals played a decisive role in translating the idea of economic liberty from the textbook to the statute book.

IV. Ideas, Interests, and Chance in the Formation of the IEA

The delayed, and still varying, influence of the IEA, and the 350 authors whose work it mobilised with the growing advice and co-operation of around 1,000 academics, individuals in industry, writers and journalists, reflects its unusual origins and structure. It was the product of an idea, outward circumstances, and unusual individuals, but not interests.

In the beginning there was a conspiring circumstance, reinforced by further conspiring circumstances. The genesis lay with Mill's deciding element of chance in the timing of the influences on events. (The origins will be related in the projected Macmillan history of the IEA and its times.)

The initiating element was an idea, or perhaps rather an inspiration, or an inchoate anxiety to do good. An RAF pilot who wanted the civil life of peace

8. "Cast in the Mould of Peel," *The Times*, 17 April 1989.

to be different from the military life of war sought advice from an academic, not well known, who advised abstention from party politics in favour of re-education based on research. The pilot chanced to meet a young Cambridge graduate with similar sentiments. They discussed the formation of an office. The Cambridge man chanced to meet an LSE graduate. The office was established.

A lesson of history is that an idea requires support from the interests it would benefit. The subsequent stage of resisting their sensitivities when they conflict with the general interest was the essence of the IEA enterprise. The interests that would gain from the IEA were difficult to mobilise. In principle, its purpose, reflected in the positive and normative aspects of its studies, was to discover how far the neglected market process could and should where desirable and possible be rehabilitated in place of the political process in economic society. The IEA could offer a better understanding of the very long-term advantages of an open economic society—an *ambience* favourable to innovation, enterprise, initiative, with prospects of gain in return for taking risks—but no identifiable, individual, material benefits.

In the absence of active interests to finance its activities, two sources of support from interests that gain from the operations of the free market were conceivable in principle: the general interest of final consumers and the special interest of industrial buyers of intermediate goods and labour services. The general interest of final consumers is too dispersed to exert coherent group pressure; their prospective gains are low in return relatively to the outlay required to reap them, and difficult to quantify. And industries or firms are organised as producers and sellers, as in the CBI, rather than as buyers of one another's products. The radical capitalists who see their long-run interests in free markets have yet to organise themselves as industrial buyers and consumers.

The financing of the IEA was the initial conundrum that the early founders had to solve. The solution was made especially difficult by three factors. First, the early decision, taken in order to avoid political influence from any quarter, was to accept no "public" funds from the state or its agencies. Second, since research and dissemination are in part non-excludable and non-rival public goods, free-riding capitalists would not subscribe without special persuasion. Third, capitalists who supported the IEA financially without material benefits could not expect personal preferment from support of a political party.

The task was solved by applying the principle of inquiry, the market. The market for scholarship reconciled support from interests for economic research into the industrial market with the possible loss they might incur from the resulting influence, if any, on government policy. An early loss was a subscriber with a well-known name who was disaffected by Professor Basil Yamey's Hobart Paper No. 1 in 1960 on resale price maintenance.[9] No. 1 set the tone for 100 Hobart Papers and 250 other Papers on the imperfections of the market as it had been allowed to develop under the political process operated by governments of both parties. Offended subscribers were offset by approval from academics led by Professor David Collard who in a Fabian Tract in 1968 conceded the "consistent and honourable attempt" to identify monopoly and other imperfections of capitalism.[10] (He coined the term "The New Right.")

The task was thus to persuade the interests that they stood to gain in particular more as buyers in the free market for their purchases than they lost as sellers in freer markets for their products, and in general from the better public understanding of the market and the advantages for consumers of competition.

The task was more difficult in the late 1950s and early 1960s than it has become in the 1980s, with the general acceptance of the market in all schools of thought (except part of the Marxist), in all British political parties (except the old Liberals), and in almost all socialist/communist as well as capitalist countries. The task in the early days of the IEA was eased by the decision to use the principle of the competitive market, that atomistic competition prevented a single seller from influencing the price of his product: subscriptions were to be small, so that no single subscriber could influence the analysis and conclusions of the authors. By the 1970s the number of subscribers rose to some 350 firms and industrial charities, with average contributions of 0.3 per cent of the annual revenue, and exerting no influence; a loss of several a year had no substantive effect on operations. The market had neutralised the power of subscribers to influence the work of independent scholarship.

Even so, the task was not made easy by the decision to avoid the distractions of the "politically possible." In conformity with the intention to avoid political influence, and the advice of Sir Sidney Caine to avoid entanglement with civil servants and their monopoly of information, authors were urged to follow their analysis wherever it led, not excluding conclusions that they

9. B. S. Yamey, *Resale Price Maintenance and Shoppers' Choice,* Hobart Paper 1, London: IEA, 1960 (4th edn. 1964).

10. David Collard, *The New Right: A Critique,* Fabian Tract No. 387, London: Fabian Society, 1968, p. 3.

might judge unlikely to be adopted by government or that subscribers might find unpalatable or untimely. The IEA tradition of examining solutions that politicians might consider politically impossible, the bureaucracy reject as administratively impracticable, or sociologists condemn as socially reprehensible was evolved from the very early years.

The new think-tanks allied to political parties, and without the financial independence of the IEA, would serve their clients best by pursuing this "anti-political" approach. The question is whether it is feasible with financial dependence on a small number of political sources. The Labour Party's Centre for Public Policy Research, financed by a small number of large donations from wealthy trade unions, has, surprisingly from a generally shrewd observer of the political scene, been urged by the usually undoctrinaire John Lloyd, former Editor of *The New Statesman,* to keep close to political realities and avoid seers and visionaries. This is precisely the myopic doctrine of "political possibility" which would have prevented the IEA from examining in the late 1950s and early 1960s solutions 25 or 30 years before they were applied in the 1980s. The Social Market Foundation of the Social Democratic Party has begun well with a scholarly Paper on *The Social Market* by Professor Robert Skidelsky most of which economic liberals would accept, especially its use of "social" as a prefix for market on the ground that the market serves the general "social" purpose.

The IEA strategy of "ruthless" pursuit of the politically impossible was based on the nature of politics that it requires popular as well as desirable politics and on the empirical evidence that policies can be made politically possible by demonstration that they are economically desirable. The IEA has in this way helped to break the vicious circle in which the occupational myopia and bias of party politics in dismissing new thinking as "politically impossible" were themselves the instruments that made it politically unlikely.

The replacement of the political monopsony of the 1950s–60s by new competition of the 1970s–80s in refining the politically most attractive market policies, and the consequent removal of the notion that the market is "politically impossible," enables economists to offer the competing political contenders alternative solutions between which they can make a political judgement. Professor W. H. Hutt proposed that academics could offer two alternatives: the politically easier and the politically more difficult to "sell" to the electorate.[11] But their power to influence policy lies in the competitive

11. W. H. Hutt, *Politically Impossible . . . ?*, Hobart Paperback 1, London: IEA, 1971.

political market. Lionel Robbins said he would talk to anyone who would listen. Scholars, especially liberals, are weak and risk their authority if there is only one listener.

V. In Place of the IEA?

If the IEA had not been established in 1957, the failure of the post-war Fabian-Keynesian-Beveridge collectivist consensus would no doubt have produced a liberal counter-revolution in different organisational form.

The intellectual heritage of political and economic liberalism over 200 years since David Hume would hardly have lain dormant for much longer in the face of the growing Leviathan. The Liberty Fund's reissue of the classics from Adam Smith through Acton to Buchanan and Hayek, at prices within the means of everyman, will enable students to compare them with the classics of socialism from Marx and Engels to Hobsbawm and E. P. Thompson.

The Mont Pélèrin Society, founded by Hayek in 1947, with the then giants of academic liberalism, operated for too long as a private debating society. With Hayek from England came Robbins, John Jewkes, Karl Popper, S. R. Dennison and the historian Veronica Wedgwood; from the USA, Frank Knight, Fritz Machlup, Aaron Director, Allen Wallis, George Stigler, the young Milton Friedman; from Germany, Walter Eucken, Wilhelm Röpke, Karl Boehm; from France, Bertrand de Jouvenel; from Austria, Ludwig von Mises; from Switzerland, William Rappard and Friedrich Lutz; from Norway, Trygve Hof; from Denmark, Carl Iverson. Few were known outside their ivory castles as embattled advocates of liberalism. Under the influence of younger scholars anxious to respond to the collectivist intellectual establishment, the MPS might gradually have developed as a "liberal international." Isolated liberal academics, though not many, were openly and courageously expressing unease, depite severe criticism from the academics of the incumbent consensus like Titmuss, Abel-Smith and Townsend, at the continuing dominance of the state over economic, political and civic life.

Yet it required an organisation prepared to translate scholarship into plain English, to show its relevance for the times, and philosophically combative individuals to harness the historic heritage and embolden the academic liberals as effectively as the Fabian Society had done for socialists a century earlier in the 1880s. The late Colin Clark, a former Fabian of massive intellect, and an early stalwart, referred to the IEA as the new "Fabian" Society. But the long-lasting failure of the liberal idea to resist the post-war political consensus for several decades owes much to the congenital tendency of the socialist intellectual to be more energetic in the propagation of his message.

In the mid- and late 1950s the post-war settlement on the potency of the state in mastering unemployment and inflation, the socialisation of industry, and the welfare state was still very new. A not uncommon response was "It has had only 10/12/15 years. Give it time." Preparations were made at the IEA for a long intellectual siege of Conservative/Labour/Liberal socialism, although in the event the impact on thinking and even events, although undesigned, came sooner than expected.

The Graveyard of the Political Filter

The validity of the decision to scout the *politician's* judgement of the politically possible is seen from the subjects of early studies. No party in the late 1950s or 1960s—when they were still locked in the unholy wedlock of the corporatist embrace—would have subjected to market criteria the structure of state pensions, the privileges of the trade unions, the National Health Service, home rent controls, broadcasting, wage regulation, the distribution of profits to shareholders, the coal monopoly, farming, transport, state education, steel, Third World aid, the professions, the restrictive practices of the building industry, roads and car-parking, the financing of water, fire protection, and other national or local government services. All these "politically impossible" subjects were analysed in IEA Papers in the first half of the 1960s.

A round dozen to a score followed each year. The prevention of environmental pollution, the "privatisation" of money, charging for local government services, the systematic treatment of poverty by topping up low incomes, student loans, the defects of workers' management, the building society cartel, the risks of European Monetary Union, the delusions of trust-busting, and more "political impossibilities" were analysed in the second half of the 1970s.

In varying degree, many radical reforms were found to be politically possible after 1979. If the IEA had limited itself to subjects and proposals thought by the *politicians* to be politically possible, the political agenda of the years since 1979 might have been very different. That is the view of Conservative Ministers who know what paternalistic or corporatist *nostra* the Conservative Central Office might have concocted. After the second Conservative election defeat in 1974, Sir Keith Joseph came to ask how the projected Centre for Policy Studies "could take over where the IEA left off" (I quote from memory). The sequence was right: the IEA was concerned with the "what" that had gone wrong and the "why" it had to be changed, but not with the legislative "how." But the "what" and the "why" were not always followed by legislating the "how."

And where early IEA analyses are not yet politically possible as we approach the 1990s, they are becoming urgent in the public interest. No proposal would have seemed politically more impossible than Hayek's for the privatisation of money in 1976.[12] Men with feet on their ground, who knew the ways of the world, and whose judgement of affairs is outstanding, would have thought the proposal unworldly. A former Governor of the Bank of England observed indulgently "That is for the day after tomorrow." But in 1988 a further IEA Paper by a young economist at Sheffield University, Kevin Dowd,[13] and a massive study by Professor George Selgin,[14] a product of the fertile Institute of Humane Studies at George Mason University, argued that the government monopoly was the ultimate pre-condition of inflation; no other remedy would suffice than competition in currencies between private banks or other suppliers who would suffer bankruptcy if the value of their money became unacceptable because it was over-supplied. Selgin went on to the University of Hong Kong, where the less conservative institutions of the Far East may take the improbable idea of competition in currency as seriously and as profitably as they have competition in almost everything else. It is not so long ago that Adam Smith's notion of money as a public good was accepted by the most liberal of economists. Experience of the political process, with its failures in serving the public interest since the end of the gold standard and other disciplines on national governments, is enforcing agonising reappraisal in the most unlikely quarters.

The period of germination of ideas into action is shortening. Hayek said it took 30 years for an idea to influence policy. In the decades since then, the application of micro-economics to the dissection of representative government and the sobering experience of the political process in practice, both in the supply of public goods and in its attempts to correct real or supposed market failure, must by now have reduced the 30-year time-lag to 20 or 10 years. The evidence seems clear—in the misplaced effort to improve the structure of industry by trust-busting legislation, in the failure to discipline

12. F. A. Hayek, *Denationalisation of Money—The Argument Refined,* Hobart Paper 70, London: IEA, 1976 (2nd edn. 1978).

13. Kevin Dowd, *Private Money: The Path to Monetary Stability,* Hobart Paper 112, London: IEA, 1988.

14. George Selgin, *The Theory of Free Banking—Money Supply Under Competitive Note Issue,* New Jersey: Rowman & Littlefield with the Cato Institute, 1988.

the so-called public utilities by regulation, in the ironic redistribution of income in favour of the middle classes by government welfare services, in enabling the trade union hegemony to favour the higher-paid employed against the unemployed, in minimum wage legislation or other measures that put the young, the female and the coloured out of work by disregarding the price-effect of income manipulation, in the economic futility of "job-creation," and in the indifferent control of environmental pollution by administrative prohibitions. Scholars who pursue the politically "impossible," which in practice transpires as the anticipation of the public interest, may find their rewards in earlier public recognition. They may be hailed as public benefactors with the intellectual impetus and courage to speak out before the politicians.

The pursuit of the politically "impossible" may thus prove to be the more politically realistic procedure for purveyors of economic ideas than the concentration on stratagems seen by politicians as timely and rewarding. The academic must remain the inspirer rather than the technical aide of the politician. However high the writ of politics, scholarship must rise above it.

The philosophic orientation of the IEA founders was liberal and (former) Fabian as well as conservative. The outlook that informed its approach was an amalgam of conservatism in the principles of the good society with liberal-radicalism in rigorously reforming the institutions that preserve the principles in periods of rapid change in the conditions of supply and demand. These were the conditions in the 1950s and 1960s after the War—rapid technological change and social advance. Here we could agree with our Lord North Street neighbour who spoke of the "white-hot heat of the technological revolution," but not when he proposed to nurture it by an unholy alliance of government, capitalists, and trade union leaders that would smother it. These changing economic conditions were not met by the Fabian-Keynesian-Beveridge thinking based on the conditions of the inter-war years of the 1920s and 1930s. If the IEA had to be labelled, it was radical, non-conformist, decentralist, individualist.

VI. Ideas and Events

The events of the 30 years can suggest how far ideas affect politicians, how long the process of re-education requires, and whether the ideas survive the political filter or are emasculated by political myopia or expediency.

1. *The intellectual climate.* If politicians will not learn error until their third or fourth decade, and the young require a 30-year coaching, the

IEA or some other liberal "think-tank" would have had to sow the seeds of doubt about *étatisme* in the 1950s to produce results in the 1980s. If liberal teaching had been absent, the Conservatives might have relapsed into more corporatist policies than those since 1979, which some present and recent Cabinet Ministers apparently still believe necessary.

2. *Action in the 1980s.* By the late 1970s the required confluence of the four elements had emerged: the most essential "conspiring circumstance" was disillusionment with the failed post-war consensus. The ideas were in place: the long-range intellectual artillery of the IEA had been reinforced by the David Hume Institute and complemented by the short-range infantry of the Centre for Policy Studies and the Adam Smith Institute (and, to continue the military metaphor, the IEA had beaten part of its artillery into anti-tank guns by lowering their sights and dealing with medium-term problems looming ahead); and the required political individuals, Mrs. Thatcher and Keith Joseph, with Howe, Tebbit, Lawson, Ridley, and Young, had arrived.

3. *The political filter.* The ideas emerged in varied form. Three examples illustrate the wide range. The central theme of desocialisation in numerous IEA Papers had become privatisation, which was pursued with a consistency generally unanticipated by IEA economists. The motive may have been partly to augment the government finances to facilitate tax reductions, yet the importance for the public was not motives but results.

   The Miller-Wood *Research Monograph* in June 1979 argued for the abolition of exchange control;[15] Hayek had described it as the core of economic nationalism. The intention may have been in the mind of the incoming Chancellor, but, as with gas policy earlier, the academic analysis added reinforcement (a financial writer said it "may well have changed the course of our financial and economic history"). But, perhaps on civil service advice, the administrative machinery was retained for a time.

   The "half-way" houses of opting out from state welfare by schools and hospitals will, as suggested by public choice analysis, develop barnacles of vested interests that will obstruct the further reform of

15. Robert Miller and John B. Wood, *Exchange Control for Ever?*, Research Monograph 33, London: IEA, 1979.

opting out by consumers; the "half-way houses" may become final resting-places. "Opting-out" by *suppliers* in education and medicine is an emasculated form of the opting out by *consumers* argued by Friedman, Peacock and Wiseman and other liberal economists who had anticipated that the economics of politics would create vested interests of school and hospital governors and staff reluctant to lose their new-found power based on riches beyond the dreams of routinised managers. The "half-way" houses put schools and hospitals into the political process, with its tyrannies of majorities, lobbying, log-rolling and the familiar paraphernalia of "politics" decided by the politically active, instead of into the market-place where politically passive individuals are sovereign.

4. *Political competition for ideas.* In 1966 a future Conservative Minister showed no interest in the reverse (negative) income tax as the means to top-up low incomes. Shortly thereafter, when Douglas Houghton, the Minister for Social Services, spoke of a minimum income guarantee, the Conservative inquired: "How did you say that idea would work?" (Houghton later became an IEA author and associate.)

   A second market-oriented party might have galvanised the Conservative faint-hearts into more enthusiastic support for Mrs. Thatcher. In 1983 Dr. David Owen outlined his proposals in the IEA journal, *Economic Affairs,*[16] for a competitive as well as "compassionate" society. In 1969 the late Professor Fred. Pennance proposed a portable Council house subsidy, *inter alia* to encourage mobility.[17] In 1989 Dr. Owen advocated a "tenant portable discount voucher." In six years the Conservatives have sold one in six Council homes to their tenants; the remainder will require 35 more years until A.D. 2025. Portable housing subsidies are long overdue.

5. *Fruitful ideas and political risk.* Some IEA ideas may have risked political loss of support, at least in the short run. The abolition of resale price maintenance by Edward Heath in 1963, following the political discussion aroused by Hobart Paper No. 1 in 1960, is said to have lost the General Election (narrowly) for his party in 1964 by alienating Conservative small shopkeepers organised in Chambers

16. David Owen, "Agenda for Competitiveness with Compassion," *Economic Affairs,* Vol. 4, No. 1, October 1983, pp. 26–33.

17. F. G. Pennance, *Housing Market Analysis and Policy,* Hobart Paper 48, London: IEA, 1969.

of Commerce. The lower prices for the much larger number of shoppers with votes came too late after the General Election. The political filter is the graveyard of many promising policies whose initial discomforts precede, and ultimate benefits follow, General Elections.

The germination period of tax rebates or earmarked vouchers for private school fees and health insurance may be several years before the supply-side effect of increased places in expanded or new schools and increased numbers of beds in enlarged or new hospitals could be expected. But opportunities were missed, not least to encourage expeditious commercial ventures to replace the slow-moving "non-profit" organisations. Politicians have yet to learn there may be more votes in speed than in (non-profit) sanctity. The professions that man the private welfare services—the doctors, teachers, actuaries, accountants, architects—often reveal a sense of mission but little sense of urgency because competition is sluggish. It may still be sacrilege to say that welfare could gain as much as consumer goods from the commercial spur of profit and the penalty of loss.

6. *Ideas require advertising.* Academics are producers of ideas ("theories," explanations, proposals, stratagems). If politicians cannot move without public support, it is their role to "sell" the ideas to the public. Here the collectivists have had long practice, aided by academics who have been more adept at writing for and speaking to the masses. The equity and common sense of the argument for charging for individual local government services would have been easier to explain than the notion of a uniform, collective charge for a bundle of services many of which—swimming pools by the over-80s—taxpayers would not use.

7. *Intellectual validation.* Although Keynes's "practical men" may scoff at "mere theory," they often want the comfort of knowing that they are on good academic ground to meet the rebuttals of better-endowed political critics. The Minister in the early 1970s engaged in reconstructing the gas industry who asked "Do you really think we have a good case?" was gathering theoretical reinforcement from mere academics.

8. *Political interest and the public.* Self-interest in the market, if it is competitive, generally makes for the public weal. In the political process it can damage the public weal, as by the inflation that

Conservative and Labour Chancellors of the Exchequer have engineered before General Elections. It does not follow that acts of political advantage to the government in power necessarily damage the public weal. Many ideas floated in IEA Papers would have served the God of public weal as well as the Mammon of private interests. The desocialisation of coal would have reduced industrial costs and benefited the consumer—and earned votes. The demunicipalisation of road transport has improved bus services and reduced fares.

If we are to wait until every reform earns as much in votes in the political process as it does in money in the market, we shall have to forgo much improvement in the lives of the people. The next step is to see how to remove the political obstacles to social advance.

If representative government finds difficulty in resisting the importunities of pressure groups, it may welcome a higher authority that denies it the powers to do what it would prefer to avoid. The establishment of the EEC enabled Conservative governments to withstand requests from industry for tariffs and other protectionist devices. A House of Lords transformed for some purposes into a Supreme Court that debarred government from taking in taxes more than 25 per cent of national income would help to remove the political displeasure of over-taxed citizens.

9. *Politicians and unintended externalities.* Taxes are raised if it is embarrassing to run budget deficits and their borrowing "requirement" too long (or too large) for public tolerance. But in the long run high taxes fertilise the economic underground. No Chancellor in the IEA's 30 years has acknowledged the encouragement to illegality and law-breaking as a reason for keeping taxes low. There could be a conspiracy of silence in the freemasonry of the Houses of Parliament. Professor Friedrich Schneider of Linz showed the fiscal consequences of party politics in *Economic Affairs.*[18]

10. *Political power and economic "law."* Böhm-Bawerk enunciated a proposition in 1913 (Macht oder Ökonomisches Gesetz) that is still ignored 75 years later. *Politicians may huff and puff, but they cannot blow the market down at will.* The disaster of rent restriction (de-

18. Friedrich Schneider and Markus Hofreither, "Measuring the Size of the Shadow Economy—Can the Obstacles Be Overcome?," *Economic Affairs*, Vol. 7, No. 2, December-January 1987, pp. 18–23.

nounced by Norman Macrae in Hobart Paper 2, 1960),[19] imposed two years after Böhm-Bawerk, has still not been ended because the fear of the loss of votes from incumbent Council tenants is stronger than the hope of gain from unknown younger owner-occupiers. Again the political process may require reform.

11. *Good ideas and bad bureaucrats.* New ideas may threaten the quiet life of officials. When an IEA author who had argued for prescription charges to be the same for all incomes in order to gain the advantages of their price-effects, without exemptions but with supplements to low incomes, was invited in 1971 to put his argument to the bureaucrats, the Minister heard them object that low charges would bring less revenue than the costs of collection and high charges disrupt household budgets. Other good arguments have been kept at bay by unquantifiable claims of untold externalities in higher education, the arts, museums and art galleries . . . The bureaucrats' monopoly of information, apparently impregnable, must be undermined by pluralisation and de-socialisation.

12. *Scholars and the judges who are juries.* Academics must suspect the objections of politicians, bureaucrats and advisers. Many IEA ideas lie fallow because the objectors have exclusive access to the information they quote in evidence, which they may have compiled themselves.

13. *Scholarship and the dangerous toy.* The role of academics is not simply to refine the best solutions and then wash their hands like Pontius Pilates. Beveridge was conscience-stricken not long after he had handed to the Coalition Government his proposal for a funded national insurance scheme for state pensions. (He also saw, too late, the danger for the friendly societies, and wrote a book in their defence,[20] but they were effectively destroyed.)

    The IEA's first Paper, in 1957, revealed the dangers of state-controlled pensions.[21] To Titmuss's question whether the nation's pensioners wanted to be at the mercy of "a vast commercial" system, the Paper asked whether they preferred a "vast political system." When we talked to Beveridge at the Reform Club in October 1961 he

19. Norman Macrae, *To Let?*, Hobart Paper 2, London: IEA, 1960.
20. W. H. Beveridge, *Voluntary Action*, London: Allen & Unwin, 1949.
21. Arthur Seldon, *Pensions in a Free Society*, London: IEA, 1957.

expressed his anxieties. The post-war Government had not taken his advice to wait 20 years so that the fund could be accumulated to pay the pensions. Even as upright a politician as Hugh Gaitskell had to explain that it was expedient to pay the pension in full earlier because other categories were not being asked to wait. It has never been funded but is paid mainly out of current taxes. It is inequitable and wasteful, and has accumulated horrendous budgetary liabilities. IEA Paper No. 1 has been ignored by all parties, but it is vindicated by events. The warning is still ignored because the politicians fear that the basic pension, still dispensed to rich and poor, is sacrosanct.

14. *The politicisation of scholarship.* Scholars must not take the word of politicians about what is politically possible, but they might present solutions with built-in safeguards against political myopia. To merge Keynes with Shakespeare, politicians are dead in the long run, but the citizen survives to suffer the evil they bequeath after them. And to maul Pigou, the externalities of politics over the generations are incapable of compensation.

If the thinking of scholars has too often been put at the mercy of politicians, politicians too often allow themselves to act as if at the mercy of the vested interests that obstruct the reform of outdated institutions. In 1966 the IEA sponsored Professor D. S. Lees's *Research Monograph* on the professions, which argued that they should be scrutinised no less than trade unions for objectionable practices.[22] Since then more IEA Papers have demonstrated the anti-social habits of lawyers, doctors, and other privileged people. The middle classes are probably doing more damage than the working classes: the doctors more than the dockers. The latest probes of the professions were Dr. David Green's *Which Doctor?* in 1985 and *Should Doctors Advertise?*, in 1989.[23] The lawyers and doctors are launching unprofessional assaults on the Government for attempting to reduce their restrictive practices.

The political process has not yet learned to develop counter-strategies to prevent the sectional interests from stopping it serving the general interest. This is a task that may require the combined talents of academic economists, political scientists, philosophers, lawyers and historians of all schools of thought.

22. D. S. Lees, *Economic Consequences of the Professions,* Research Monograph 2, London: IEA, 1966.

23. D. G. Green, *Which Doctor?,* Research Monograph 40, London: IEA, 1985; *Should Doctors Advertise?,* IEA Health Unit Paper 6, 1989.

VII. "Ruthless" for Truth

The main lesson of the last 30 years in the effort to provide the nation with the best economic thinking is that the economic system has been unable to yield its best results in living standards combined with wide freedom of choice between alternative suppliers because the political process produces government that escapes close supervision by the citizen between elections. Infrequent ballot-box voting for packages of 57 varieties could be supplemented by more frequent plebiscites and where possible replaced by voting with money in the market for individual purchases.

A supreme task for liberal economists and political scientists at the IEA and elsewhere remains to devise, first, politico-economic disciplines on government to prevent over-taxation, over-inflation, over-subsidisation, over-centralisation, and other excesses that have disfigured the competition for power in the democratic market-place and, second, and even more fundamentally, the replacement of political by market sovereignty for the common consumer. Scholars may take heart from the austere judgement of the most considerable intellect among the politicians of our day:

> No account of . . . the exploration of the market mechanism in the Conservative Party with widening enthusiasm from the 1950s on . . . would be well balanced which underestimated the effectiveness of the work of the Institute of Economic Affairs and its proselytizing influence . . .[24]

24. J. Enoch Powell in Dennis Kavanagh and Anthony Seldon (eds.), *The Thatcher Effect,* Oxford: Clarendon Press, 1989.

FROM THE LSE TO THE IEA

From the LSE to the IEA

The intellectual origins of the Institute of Economic Affairs (IEA) lie in a merger of the classical British and Austrian schools of liberal political economy. They reinforced each other in the mind of the naturalised-British Austrian economist at the London School of Economics (LSE) in the 1930s, Friedrich Hayek.

At the University of Vienna in the 1920s he had inherited the work of the Austrian school established by Carl Menger from the 1870s. And at the LSE in the 1930s he refined the British school of classical liberalism originated by the Englishman John Locke in the seventeenth century and the Scots David Hume and Adam Smith in the eighteenth.

When still at the University of Vienna in the 1920s Hayek had admired the writings of a little-known LSE economist whom he contrasted favourably with the famous Keynes at Cambridge. This was another Scot, Edwin Cannan, whose main writings have only now been made easily accessible by an American political scientist, Dr. Alan Ebenstein. They show Cannan's profound influence on his students, who later largely formed the economics faculty at the LSE in the 1930s.[1]

The British-Austrian link began even earlier. From the early twentieth century, Cannan at the LSE had taught the potential supremacy of the benevolent market over national government that thwarted rather than facilitated it. This theme echoed a classical 1914 monograph by the Austrian economist Eugen von Böhm-Bawerk, *Macht oder Ökonomisches Gesetz* (political power or economic law). And it became the fundamental principle of the relationship between politics and economic life I saw vindicated in the real world after the Second World War. Its latest manifestation was in Octo-

1. A. Ebenstein (1997) *The Collected Works of Edwin Cannan*, 8 volumes, with assessments by 30 economists and historians; London: Routledge-Thoemmes. This article is adapted from the foreword.

ber 1997 when the international market of private savers and investors, expressing the decisions of millions, prevailed over governments run by their political representatives.

The underlying contrast between the wisdom of the market and the errors of governments was the theme that emerged in Cannan's influence on the economics taught by his former students at the LSE in the 1930s. This thinking is now especially timely with the advent of a new British government that promises policies of both free markets and government controls.

My recollections of LSE teaching have been assisted by the notes I wrote from lectures in 1934–37 by liberal and socialist-inclined economists, many of striking originality, who later emerged as distinguished scholars or government advisers, several as Nobel Laureates: R. G. D. Allen, H. L. Beales, R. H. Coase, E. F. M. Durbin, R. F. Fowler, T. E. Gregory, F. A. Hayek, J. R. Hicks, Nicholas Kaldor, F. W. Paish, Arnold Plant, Lionel Robbins, G. L. Schwartz, W. T. Stephenson, Brinley Thomas.

Twenty years later, from the mid-1950s onwards, the teaching of the liberal school was selectively transmitted to the London Institute of Economic Affairs.[2]

I was introduced to Cannan's thinking in his *Wealth,* the first textbook I encountered in the school that taught economics, when it was still rare, at the early age of 16. The Cannan influence continued throughout my 32-year link with the LSE (with the interval of war) from 1934–66.

The LSE's liberal influence reached out to part-time students in the 1950s and 1960s. Lionel Robbins wrote guidance on the new insights that could be learned from economics in the evening and correspondence courses devised by tutors whom I joined at the London University Commerce Degree Bureau run by Arnold Plant, head of the LSE Commerce faculty.

Economics was still in the 1950s considered an advanced subject. A wider knowledge of even its elementary propositions could have helped to discipline error by post-war politicians commanding massive resources in government.

The general public might have been made acutely alert to political pretence if it had been taught the simple principles of supply and demand. Adults who, as consumers, understand Milton Friedman's microeconomic "There's no such thing as a free lunch" could have learned as voters that there is no such thing as "demand" without a price, that demand is elastic in re-

2. The transmission is described in "The Influence of Classical Liberalism at the Institute of Economic Affairs," in Frank Cass (1996) *Ideas and Think-tanks in Contemporary Britain.*

sponse to changes in price and incomes, and that the market is more effective than the political process in satisfying "demands" (misnamed "needs"). Some understanding of opportunity costs—as alternatives sacrificed—could have prompted public questioning of the political promises of "free" education, the tragically impossible "best medical care for all," "decent" housing for six million, "fair" pay for a "fair" day's work, "public" (meaning "political") control of industry, or the other question-begging vocabulary of party politics.

The Austrian influence on LSE students came early in the 1930s. Robbins' first reference for reading by new undergraduates was *Macht oder Ökonomisches Gesetz.* Earlier, Hayek from Vienna had thought well of Cannan's 1914–26 essays, published as *An Economist's Protest,* in a 1929 review in the *Zeitschrift für Nationalökonomie.* And Cannan had early commended the Austrians in his writings.

The intellectual solidarity of Cannan's students had been bequeathed to the school in its teachers, headed by Robbins and Plant, and later in their students, not least R. H. Coase (a recent Nobel Laureate) and R. F. Fowler, and in turn their students, W. Arthur Lewis (another Nobel Laureate) and others among whom I modestly place myself.

Early demonstration of Cannan's influence came in emphatic form. He had retired in 1926. While he was still actively writing, his students remembered his sustained critique of politicised economic life and economic nationalism when they launched in 1931 a sustained assault on the desertion of nineteenth- and twentieth-century free trade. Their target was the economists misled by J. M. Keynes into arguing for "protection" against imports, as well as the politicians in the National Government elected in 1931 to succeed the Labour Government after the collapse of the gold standard and the onset of the Great Depression.

Cannan's students, now lecturers, readers, and professors, did not mince their words in their final verdict on Keynes that moved me as a new undergraduate:

> . . . we should all think it a disaster if the free trade which has served Britain so well materially, as through her it has [inspired] all who have worked for good understanding among nations, were today to be sacrificed to ignorance or panic or jealousy or specious calculation of a moment's gain.

The then renowned director of the LSE, Sir William Beveridge, gathered eight liberal academics to judge "protection" in *Tariffs; The Case Examined,* a text written in plain English and directed to the general public as well as economists which still has lessons for today. F. C. Benham (a Cannan student) later wrote a textbook, *Economics*, that students used for over 30 years. A. L. Bowley was the gentle distinguished statistician. T. E. Gregory (another Cannan student) was the combative monetary economist who had crossed swords with Keynes on the 1929–31 Macmillan Committee on Finance and Industry. J. R. (later Sir John) Hicks was the Nobel Laureate (jointly with K. J. Arrow) in 1972. W. T. Layton was the Liberal newspaper owner/editor. Arnold Plant had recently returned from the University of Capetown, where he vacated the Chair of Economics to his assistant W. H. Hutt (yet another Cannan student). L. C. Robbins was the lion-hearted academic advocate of classical liberalism who had brought Hayek to the LSE. And G. L. Schwartz was the witty lecturer in risk and insurance who became a well-known journalist spreading the gospel.

They combined in *Tariffs* to acknowledge the inspiration of Cannan. Some of the writing was graphic, even lyrical, rare in present-day macroeconomic jargon. They applied the Cannan theme: civilised society was based on the principle that people should be allowed to do what they liked until reason showed the contrary; the argument that *laissez-faire* was defective was not enough to justify state control of economic life.

Beveridge and Hicks warned that the protectionist Imperial Preference enacted at Ottawa in 1932 could endanger good relations between countries. They also warned: "People with imagination to value the British Empire as a free association knit by blood or speech or institutions or ideals may well shudder at that prospect."

Robbins on fiscal protection for agriculture anticipated a future CAP. Even if the economic arguments were valid, he asserted, they could be satisfied by subsidies rather than by tariffs. But "if the advocate of protectionism claimed he was giving effect to the decisions of democracy by subsidy, he [was] bamboozling the electorate."

The economics of politics later refined by Buchanan and Tullock was also anticipated by Plant and Benham in rejecting the political naivety of A. C. Pigou's argument on taxes and subsidies for industries with "externalities." "Between the refinements of tariff theory and the crudities of tariff practice there is a great gulf." By examining the practices of the Tariff Boards in South Africa and Australia they warned against political pretence. The British Cabinet's proposals would be subject to "the play of party, regional and industrial forces"—Gordon Tullock's "rent-seekers."

The later-distinguished young Hicks was no less analytical but firmly dismissive of tariffs. The economic effect would be to conceal the disadvantages for consumers. And the maintenance of peaceable international relations would be at risk when the livelihood of many was endangered by cross-national disputes on import quotas.

Benham, a gentle scholar, was robustly unequivocal with arguments that echo mid-1990s disputes. The difficulties of generating exports to pay for imports were the rigidity of internal prices, especially wage-rates, and the political desire to remain on the gold standard. "Remove either of these and the problem vanishes. Remove the first, and it is solved by reducing money costs. Remove the second, and it is removed by a free exchange rate."

These early reactions in the classical liberal distrust of the political process, inherited from Cannan and taught by his former students at the LSE, were largely overlooked by the "political" economists at Cambridge. At the LSE the liberals were revealing their innate scepticism of the powers of politicians to enact the public good. The LSE was, through its young economists, carrying the torch of David Hume, Adam Smith, Mill in his middle years, Acton, Dicey, Marshall and Cannan. At Cambridge (USA as well as England) the post-war economists, with a few honourable exceptions, assumed that policy could be left to political benevolence.

Cannan had taught the instinctive sense of the classical economists—that the political process embraced faults which demanded scepticism or suspicion rather than gratuitous hope that people elected as politicians would miraculously be transformed into public benefactors. It required the post-war awakening to "government failure" to spread the understanding that imperfect markets were more remediable by the very operation of new demands and supplies than by chronically imperfect monopolistic government.

This was the same scepticism about government control of economic life which was applied to studies at the IEA from the very first years in the 1950s. Young authors were found to apply the same clinical surgery to the *non-sequitur*—"market-failure-therefore-state-control"—of the post-war political scientists and sociologists in Britain and abroad.

Almost every activity of government was found by IEA authors to have "failed." There were three groups. First, the most sacred, the main welfare services of education, medical care, housing, pensions and insurance for sickness, unemployment and retirement were found severely inefficient and increasingly superfluous. Second, the so-called "public" (more correctly, politicised) "utilities"—from energy and transport, telecommunications including broadcasting, to water, fire and refuse services—were found to be better privatised into competitive markets more responsive to consumers.

Third, the supposed historic "public goods," too lightly accepted as necessarily supplied by government, and even some aspects of law and order such as police protection against assault and theft, were re-examined for transfer to private suppliers.

The British public had never before seen such a relentless flow of confident, uncompromising, scholarly assault on the failed faith in the state. Twenty years later, in 1979 and forty years later in 1997, some of this revolutionary thinking has at last begun to be applied by both political parties. The new government of 1997 has yet to be judged on whether its crucial instinct is to liberate or to regulate.

The strategy at the IEA of winning public and political attention by earning the respect of the press and other "media" interpreters of liberal economic analysis reflected the spirit of the scholarly, uncompromising Cannanite authors of *Tariffs* in 1931. Hayek, a little later (from 1935) after his early work on the trade cycle, monetary policy and the structure of industry, took over from Robbins the leadership of the LSE classical liberal powerhouse.

Yet still damaging to the post-war liberal society are the post-war sociologists, some at the LSE, who emerged as professors and readers of "Public Administration" and taught the necessity of the state without examining the nineteenth-century growth of spontaneous voluntary services that made the welfare state outdated long before it was enlarged in 1946.

Cannan would have been dismayed by the blunting of the economic cutting-edge of LSE scholarship by the sociologists. They replaced rigorous economic analysis by subjective compassion which obscured the apparatus of market economics—supply and demand, costs and prices, income- and price-elasticity, and the distinction between impact and incidence—by a wilderness of immeasurable criteria which attempted to replace the Austrian Wieser's conception of value, popularised by Robbins, as measured by the sacrifice of scarce resources with alternative uses.

Eminent LSE economists continued the association with the IEA as authors or advisers into the post-war years: Hayek, Robbins, Plant, Hicks, Coase, Frank Paish, Harry Johnson, Alan Peacock, Alan Prest, Basil Yamey, not least a Director, Sydney Caine, and some younger scholars.

Regrettably there has been a relapse. Cannan would now see tracts of intellectual desert over the Houghton Street buildings of the LSE in the 1990s. Former socialist economies in every continent are seeking refuge in the market. But LSE teachers sadly continue their hopes of politicised industry and welfare. Its *Annual Review, 1995* reveals that it still provides a home for intellectual cul-de-sacs. Brian Abel-Smith proudly reviews his state-enhancing work as adviser on welfare services to the British Labour Party, the Social Affairs Commissioner of the European Union, and the World Health Organisation. Will Hutton, a former journalist now editor of a (non-classical) "liberal" newspaper, and described as a governor of the LSE, writes "if the scale of poverty and inequity was known and the dynamics of capitalism exposed, no right-thinking person could gainsay the case for economic and social change . . . for reviving the great spirit that gave birth to the LSE." That spirit was the Webbs' 1883 Fabian illusion on the power of benevolent government to enrich economic life. And Professor Peter Self writes of the "baleful influence" of the study of public choice and its application of microeconomics to politics. He rejects its "narrow view of bureaucrats as simply self-serving individualists" at a time when public choice theory, anticipated by LSE economists in the 1930s, has increasingly demonstrated the defects of government in democracy.

Cannan would finally have approved of the IEA, and the influence of the 1930s LSE that lives on, not least because he was an early exponent of Friedman and Stigler for their Chicago "empirical testing" in his concern that economic theory should be applied to the everyday working of industry.

Cannan's students must have imbibed enough of the common-sense Austrian conception of the market to see it as self-recuperative, curing its own imperfections, if the state allowed supply and demand the freedom and time to encourage the emergence of new demands and new supplies. And that may be the lasting tribute to Cannan's common-sense economics that, through his influence at the LSE, he left to the IEA.

THE MAKING OF THE INSTITUTE

A SELECTION OF ARTHUR SELDON'S
PREFACES TO IEA PAPERS,
1960–1996

THE IEA PAPERS: SUBJECTS AND AUTHORS

I. The Hobart Papers

Subject	*Author*	*University, etc.*
Resale Price Maintenance (2/60)	Prof. Basil S. Yamey	LSE
Rents (3/60)	Norman Macrae	The Economist
Purchase Tax (1/61)	Prof. Alan R. Prest	Cambridge
Growthmanship (3/61)	Colin Clark	Oxford
Health through Choice (10/61)	Prof. D. S. Lees	Keele University
Common Market (4/62)	Prof. J. E. Meade	Cambridge
Wage-Fixing (6/62)	Henry Smith	Oxford
Rate-Paying (3/63)	A. R. Ilersic	Bedford College, London
Primary Producer Prices (10/63)	Sir Sydney Caine	LSE
Education (2/64)	Prof. Alan Peacock & Prof. Jack Wiseman	University of York University of York
Taxation (7/64)	Colin Clark	Oxford
Vacant Possession (7/64)	John Carmichael	
Incomes Policy (9/64)	Prof. F. W. Paish & J. Hennessy	LSE
Land in the Market (12/64)	Dr. Donald Denman	Cambridge
International Money (2/65)	Prof. Gottfried Haberler	Harvard
Inheritance Taxing (3/65)	Prof. C. T. Sandford	University of Bath
Privatise Telephones (6/66)	Michael Canes	University of Chicago
Companies, Shareholders and Growth (8/66)	F. R. Jervis	
Monetary Policy (2/67)	Dr. N. J. Gibson	University of Manchester
Housing and Town Planning (8/67)	Prof. F. G. Pennance	College of Estate Management, Reading
The Price of Blood (3/68)	M. H. Cooper & A. J. Culyer	University of Exeter University of Exeter

Subject	*Author*	*University, etc.*
Education (6/68)	Prof. E. G. West	Carleton University, Canada
Paying for TV (7/68)	Sir Sydney Caine	LSE
Money (1/69)	Prof. A. A. Walters	LSE
UK and Floating Exchanges (5/69)	Prof. Harry G. Johnson & John E. Nash	LSE
Incomes Policy (6/69)	Prof. F. W. Paish	LSE
Housing Market (8/69)	Prof. F. G. Pennance & Prof. W. A. West	College of Estate Management, Reading
Industrial Mergers (7/70)	Dr. Brian Hindley	LSE
Competition in Banking (12/70)	Brian Griffiths	LSE
Housing and Whitehall (3/71)	Dr. Robert McKie	Cambridge
Macromancy (4/73)	Douglas Rimmer	University of Birmingham
Macro-thinking (8/73)	Prof. L. M. Lachmann	University of Hull
Aircraft (2/74)	Keith Hartley	University of York
The Price of Prosperity (3/74)	Prof. G. C. Allen & Prof. Chiaki Nishiyama	formerly University of London International University, Japan
Energy Crisis (7/74)	Prof. Colin Robinson	University of Surrey
Theft in Markets (10/74)	Prof. R. L. Carter	University of Nottingham
Participation without Politics (4/75)	Sir Samuel Brittan	The Financial Times
Choice in Education (10/75)	Prof. Alan Maynard	University of York
Pricing for Pollution (12/75)	Prof. Wilfred Beckerman	Oxford
British Disease (5/76)	Prof. G. C. Allen	formerly University of London
Too Much Money? (6/76)	Gordon Pepper & Prof. Geoffrey Wood	Greenwell City University
Gold or Paper? (9/76)	Prof. E. Victor Morgan & Ann D. Morgan	University of Wales
The Mixed Economy (6/78)	Prof. S. C. Littlechild	University of Birmingham
How Japan Competes (7/78)	Prof. G. C. Allen	formerly University of London
The Myth of Social Cost (10/78)	Prof. Steven N. S. Cheung	University of Washington
Protectionism (12/79)	David Greenaway & Christopher Milner	University of Buckingham University of Loughborough
Sport in the Market (4/80)	Prof. Peter Sloane	University of Stirling
For Love or Money? (7/80)	Dr. Ivy Papps	University of Newcastle, England
1980s Unemployment and the Unions (7/80)	Prof. F. A. Hayek	Universities in USA and Europe
Monopoly of Money (7/81)	Prof. H. G. Brennan & Prof. J. M. Buchanan	George Mason University

Subject	*Author*	*University, etc.*
Future for British Coal? (6/81)	Prof. Colin Robinson & Eileen Marshall	University of Surrey
Unemployment (2/82)	Robert Miller	IEA
	& John B. Wood	IEA
Land and Heritage: Public Interest in Personal Ownership (4/82)	Dr. Barry Bracewell-Milnes	
Will China Go Capitalist? (4/82)	Prof. Steven N. S. Cheung	University of Washington
Government As It Is (2/88)	Prof. William C. Mitchell	University of Oregon
Invisible Hand in Economics and Politics (8/88)	Prof. Norman P. Barry	University of Buckingham

II. The Hobart Paperbacks

Subject	*Author*	*University, etc.*
Politically Impossible? (5/71)	Prof. W. H. Hutt	
Government and the Market Economy (5/71)	Sir Samuel Brittan	The Financial Times
A Tiger by the Tail (1/72)	Prof. F. A. Hayek	Universities in USA and Europe
	Dr. Sudha R. Shenoy	University of Newcastle, Australia
Bureaucracy: Servant or Master? (9/73)	Prof. William A. Niskanen	University of California
The Cambridge Revolution (10/74)	Prof. Mark Blaug	University of London
The Vote Motive (7/76)	Prof. Gordon Tullock	Virginia Polytechnic Institute
	Dr. Morris Perlman	LSE
Keynes v. the Keynesians (7/77)	Prof. T. W. Hutchison	formerly University of Birmingham
Choice in Education (10/84)	Prof. S. R. Dennison	formerly University of Cambridge

III. The IEA Readings

Subject	*Author*	*University, etc.*
The Long Debate on Poverty (9/72)	Prof. R. M. Hartwell	Oxford, Nuffield
	Prof. G. E. Mingay	University of Kent
	Dr. Rhodes Boyson	University of Manchester and LSE
	Prof. Norman McCord	University of Newcastle
	Dr. C. G. Hanson	University of Newcastle

Subject	*Author*	*University, etc.*
The Long Debate on Poverty (9/72) (continued)	Prof. A. W. Coats	University of Nottingham
	Dr. W. H. Chaloner	University of Manchester
	Dr. W. O. Henderson	University of Manchester
	J. M. Jefferson	Economist in Industry
The Economics of Charity (8/73)	Prof. Armen Alchian	University of California, Los Angeles
	William Allen	retired
	Prof. Gordon Tullock	George Mason University
	Prof. Anthony Culyer	University of York
	Prof. Thomas Ireland	University of Missouri, St. Louis
	Prof. David Johnson	Louisiana State University
	Prof. James Koch	University of York
	Prof. Marilyn J. Ireland	University of York
	Michael Cooper	University of Exeter
	A. J. Salsbury	Brompton Hospital, London
The Economics of Politics (9/78)	Prof. James Buchanan	George Mason University
	Prof. C. K. Rowley	George Mason University
	Prof. Albert Breton	University of Toronto
	Prof. Jack Wiseman	University of York
	Prof. Bruno Frey	University of Zurich and Basle
	Prof. A. T. Peacock	University of York
	Jo Grimond	
	Prof. W. A. Niskanen	University of California, Berkeley
	Prof. Martin Ricketts	University of Buckingham
Reprivatising Welfare: After the Lost Century (10/96)	Prof. E. G. West	Carleton University, Canada
	Dr. David Green	IEA
	Prof. Martin Ricketts	University of Buckingham
	Prof. Michael Beenstock	City University, Business School, London
	Dr. Charles Hanson	University of Newcastle
	Prof. George Yarrow	Oxford
	Dr. Dennis O'Keeffe	University of North London
	Prof. Nigel Ashford	University of Staffordshire

INTRODUCTION

"George Bernard Shaw, (1856–1950)," says *The Oxford Companion to English Literature,* "was an indefatigable worker, writing over 50 plays . . . published with lengthy prefaces in which he clearly expresses his views as . . . a champion of the thinking man"[1] who was generally expected to conclude that for the good of the people socialism was superior to capitalism.

This book assembles the Prefaces to the papers, written over 30 years for the Institute of Economic Affairs[2] mainly by British, American and European university economists, from 1960 to around 1990, which present the argument and historical evidence for the view that capitalism is superior to socialism.[3]

The Making of the IEA

The thinking I developed at the IEA from 1960 was based on the teaching at the LSE in the mid-1930s. It was fundamentally derived from the understanding that had been refined during the late eighteenth century and the early nineteenth century from Adam Smith: that individual men and women best escape from poverty and inadequacy by exchanging in free markets the products of the skills they acquired by concentrating on their individual faculties.

This was the origin of the markets they had been developing from the mid-eighteenth century into the nineteenth, twentieth and now the twenty-

1. I am indebted for tracing Shaw's dictum to Lt. Col. Stuart Waterhouse with whom, since we met at the London School of Economics, I have shared our thinking on classical Liberalism.

2. The foundation of the IEA in 1955 is recorded by Gerald Frost in his biography of Antony Fisher, Profile Books, London, 2002.

3. To avoid repetition the Prefaces have omitted the opening statement on the historic superiority of markets over politics and the closing formal disclaimer of the IEA on the argument of the authors.

first century. The power and necessity of markets has been neglected by politicians in recent years. This book recalls their value and necessity.

My free market thinking was strengthened at the LSE by Professor Arnold Plant from 1934, by Professor Lionel Robbins and Friedrich Hayek and the younger Ronald Coase, and continued after the 1939–45 war as a tutor and LSE staff examiner for 20 years, 1946 to 1966, when I became increasingly involved with the IEA.

My LSE teachers in the 1930s numbered around 20, and ranged from the "Liberals" named above to the (mainly) Labour-inclined Hugh Dalton and Evan Durbin who understood markets and were sceptical of Keynes and respected Hayek.

The Harris-Seldon Division of Labour

The IEA was built by what economists since Adam Smith have analysed as the "division of labour" between specialists with complementary abilities.

My task was to "recruit" the best economists in the world to analyse the activities of industry in the British economy and overseas, to identify the most efficient in serving the population of consumers at the lowest prices and best qualities.

Ralph Harris, a Cambridge graduate in economics and history, carried the "liberal" market message to journalists, university students, and politicians, raised funds, and introduced IEA Papers at press launches.

Individual Freedom and the Size of Government

In December, 1982, the newly-formed Cato Institute in Washington asked Professor Hayek: "What role can a public policy Institute, like Cato, play to limit the size of government and increase individual freedom?"

Hayek replied: "One Institution I have watched from the beginning, and for the existence of which I am in some sense responsible, is the Institute of Economic Affairs in London.

"What I insisted, and was strictly followed, was not to appeal to the large numbers but to the intellectuals—the journalists, teachers, and so on.

"The IEA has become the most powerful maker of opinion in England. Bookshops have a special rack of IEA papers. Even people on the Left feel compelled to keep informed of its publications. If you are looking for a program in the United States you can do no better than study its publications catalogue."

Dedication

This collection of writings and discussions is dedicated to the 350 world scholars in economics who built the IEA by responding patiently to my requests over the years that they magnify their strongest arguments and clarify their most subtle reasoning for newcomers to economic liberalism.

The power of reason has been best revealed by two English economists:

> . . . The ideas of economists and political philosophers, both when they are right and when they are wrong, are more powerful than is commonly understood. The world is ruled by little else. Practical men, who believe themselves to be quite exempt from any intellectual influences, are usually the slaves of some defunct economist.
>
> . . . Soon or late, it is ideas, not vested interests, which are dangerous for good or evil. —*J. M. Keynes* (1936)

But Keynes lost sight of this view for the rest of his life, except in his last days. He was corrected by a younger colleague.

> I do not want the economist to mount the pulpit or expect him to fit himself to handle the keys of Heaven and Hell. I want him to be rather brave and rather persistent in hammering in those results achieved within his own domain about which he feels reasonably confident, not too readily reduced to silence by the plea that this, that or the other is ruled out of court by custom, or justice, or the temper of the age . . .
>
> —*Sir Dennis Robertson* (1949)
> Cambridge/London Universities

A Future Volume

The present volume comprises the Prefaces to 56 Hobart Papers, mostly by single authors, with several by two authors; eight Hobart Paperbacks, mostly by single authors, two by pairs of authors; and four IEA Readings, mostly by eight or more authors who assembled as a group or contributed their statements for symposia: in all there are around 215 authors.

A future volume would comprise the prefaces to three series: Occasional Papers, Readings and Research Monographs.

G. B. Shaw's 50 Prefaces in praise of socialism would confront some 250 Prefaces in favour of capitalism.

Acknowledgements

To Marjorie Seldon:

for her steadfast encouragement and the original suggestions I have incorporated.

To Peter and Anthony Seldon:

for covering most of the costs of a book they welcomed.

To Martin Anderson:

graduate of St. Andrews University for echoing Adam Smith in sub-editing IEA publications.

To Julian Gilchrist:

patient publisher and designer and prompt provider of proofs.

To Barbara FitzGerald:

for transforming hurried longhand into agreeable typeface, whose intelligent handling of drafts maintained a formidable timetable.

PART I

Prefaces to Hobart Papers

Hobart Paper 1
February 1960

Basil S. Yamey

Resale Price Maintenance and Shoppers' Choice

Representative government, as Tom Paine hoped, can draw on the wisdom of all sections of the community; but at its worst it impoverishes and enfeebles the community by concession and capitulation to sectionalism and short-sightedness. Much so-called "economic policy" can be explained only in terms of pressure from organised producers—in trade associations, trade unions or other groups. Too often politicians with meagre understanding of the free society succumb to the temptation to subordinate the interests of man as consumer to his interests as producer. Politicians would be well advised to reconsider their customary compromises on policy in which expediency has too much weight and principle too little.

The common assumption underlying the *Hobart Papers* is that rising incomes are creating scope for policies based on long-term consumer interests that require wider freedom in personal and business life. These policies become not only economically advantageous but also politically feasible when employers and employees are prepared to abandon the defence of established interest and to welcome the creation of new opportunities in trade and work. The economic is not the only criterion by which the success of policy may be judged; but, even where policy is shaped mainly by political or social purposes, the judgement cannot be made without measuring and counting the cost of diverting resources from their most economic employment.

It is in this spirit that the Institute invited Professor B. S. Yamey to review public policy on resale price maintenance. His closely-reasoned discussion of its consequences for the British consumer suggests that it inflates costs and prices, restricts choice, and obstructs technical progress in retailing. Unless Professor Yamey's arguments are rebutted, it must be accepted that the community would gain from the abolition of r.p.m., that substantial economies would follow the transfer of labour and capital to more efficient shops or other industries.

This discussion raises anew the question whether there is sufficient awareness of the need to save or insure against the risks of a dynamic economy.

And this provokes the further question whether compensation is desirable or practicable in order to remove not only individual hardship but also resistance to change, not least when governments are withdrawing privileges they (or their predecessors) have conferred on favoured groups.

In any event, change must be seen not as the working of "blind market forces" but as the result of the community's right to choose between alternative ways of supplying its needs. There is nothing blind about the shopper's preference for lower prices or time-saving shopping. Those who want personal service in the shop "at the corner" with flexible hours should be free to buy it, but so also should those who want standardised service and cheapness. The free market system, if allowed to work, induces suppliers to acknowledge the consumer's sovereignty; those who complain of its imperfections should produce a better method of enthroning him.

These reflections are prompted by Professor Yamey's formidable array of analysis and evidence. Although the Institute is not committed to his diagnosis or conclusions, it commends them for urgent public discussion and decision.

Third Edition, 1964

The first of the *Hobart Papers* published in February 1960 has proved to be distinguished and perhaps influential. In examining the arguments for and against resale price maintenance Professor Yamey accumulated a formidable array of argument and evidence which, despite the exceptional circumstances claimed for particular commodities and trades, left the independent observer with little doubt that on balance the effect on the economy was to debilitate it by depriving it of the galvaniser of competition in retail trading. And his "cautious" estimate that abolition of r.p.m. would reduce retail prices of price-maintained goods by about 5 per cent on average and that the saving to consumers might amount to £180 million served to crystallise attention and indicate the size of the stake. His *Hobart Paper* followed his earlier longer work in 1954, *The Economics of Resale Price Maintenance.*

The Institute itself has no view on policy except to provide the opportunity for independent analysis of its economic implications. Professor Yamey's *Paper* fully justified the statement of the aims that has stayed at the head of the prefaces to all the *Hobart Papers:* to provide a stream of authoritative, objective and readable commentary to the formation of public opinion and policy.

A second edition of the *Hobart Paper* was published in 1961 as part of a symposium entitled *Radical Reaction.* The original *Paper* has long been out of print, orders for it have been accumulating, and it was thought helpful to publish a further edition. The text of the original *Paper* has not been changed, except for minor revisions.

The Institute does not necessarily accept the analysis or conclusions of its publications; they are solely those of the author.

Hobart Paper 2 *Norman Macrae*
March 1960

To Let?

Representative government, as Tom Paine hoped, can draw on the wisdom of all sections of the community; but at its worst it impoverishes and enfeebles the community by capitulation to articulate or persistent sections at the expense of the long-term general interest. Much so-called "economic policy" can be understood only in terms of pressure from organised producers—in trade associations, trade unions or other groups. Too often politicians with meagre understanding of the free society have succumbed to the temptation to subordinate the interest of man as consumer to his supposed interest as producer. Politicians would be well-advised to reconsider their customary compromises on policy in which expediency has too much weight and principle too little.

The common assumption underlying the *Hobart Papers* is that rising incomes are creating scope for long-term policies that require and permit wider freedom in personal and business life. These policies become not only economically advantageous but also politically feasible when employers and employees are prepared to abandon the defence of established interests and to welcome the creation of new opportunities in trade and work. The economic is not the only criterion by which the success of policy may be judged; but, even where policy is shaped mainly by political or social purposes, the judgement cannot be made without measuring and counting the cost of diverting resources from their most economic employment.

Rent control in Britain started as a siege expedient in the first world war to minimise hardship and forestall inflationary wage-claims. Forty-five years later it has degenerated into a device for favouring a sizeable group of house occupiers at the expense—apparently—of an insignificant minority of voters. In this *Hobart Paper* Norman Macrae examines the consequences of the Government's pledge at the recent General Election to take no further action in this Parliament on the decontrol of rents. He writes with feeling and authority of the effects on family life, on the building of new houses, and on the shape of our cities. It has been easy for well-meaning sentiment to range itself on the side of rent control, but the sentimental have rarely faced the real issues at stake. Mr. Macrae here unites emotion and intellect in support of returning the provision and repair of homes to the free market in order to serve social justice and to ensure better use of the nation's resources.

It is sometimes argued that the "basic" necessaries of life, such as housing, should be a "first charge" on the communal purse, a "social service" available to all at the public expense. There is something to be said for such a view when, in Seebohm Rowntree's language, there is primary or secondary poverty: when incomes are too low to buy the necessaries, or when people with adequate incomes squander them. Even then there would be no justification for imposing the expense on one group of people—those who happen to own houses. A better result might be to make up incomes from public funds and control the way in which the addition was spent. But with the virtual disappearance of primary poverty, incomes are increasingly sufficient for people to buy living space in the open market without assistance. The effect of subsidising house-room is to divert purchasing power to less essential goods and services and so to distort the scale of values of the recipients. Secondary poverty, too, is happily dwindling: people who are invited to vote on issues of war and peace must be presumed to be capable of deciding between a better home and more clothes or a car, or between a house or flat in a city centre or suburb. Not least, the argument of poverty—of income or judgement—invariably ignores the educational role of personal responsibility. People who can afford market rents but who are supplied with house-room on the cheap are not learning to use their judgement as are those who make the choice on where and how to live—and pay for it themselves. It is precisely because house-room is a basic requirement of life that individual judgement and decision should be given full rein.

These are some of the issues concerning our sense of values, our way of life, and our economic arrangements raised by Mr. Macrae's *Paper.* No political party comes really well out of its handling of the rent problem. Whether it was right to give what Mr. Macrae calls the "expedient pledge," and whether it may be right to break it if it can be shown to be contrary to the general interest, are political matters: Lord Goddard for one has called for an end to rent control because it is unjust. But this *Paper* is concerned primarily with the economic issues. Although the Institute is not committed to Mr. Macrae's diagnosis or conclusions, it commends them for public discussion and decision.

Hobart Paper 8
January 1961

Alan R. Prest

Reform for Purchase Tax

The common assumption underlying the *Hobart Papers* is that rising incomes are creating greater scope for policies that permit wider freedom of choice in personal life. They do not automatically solve all social or economic problems; they require to be accompanied by changes in the legal and institutional framework of society in order that the opportunities they present may be translated into reality.

In this *Hobart Paper* Dr. A. R. Prest was invited to re-examine the origins, principles and effects of purchase tax, and offer recommendations for policy. The purchase tax introduced in the last war yielded a modest supplement to other revenue although its primary purpose was to absorb purchasing power. It has now become a main source of government revenue in peace-time. And, so long as public expenditure remains high, reform of the purchase tax that reduced its yield would need to be accompanied by new taxes or increased revenue from other taxes.

This itself restricts the freedom of consumer choice by guiding it away from taxed to untaxed commodities (and services). Further, the demands of revenue have produced a wide range of tax rates that, in effect if not in intention, have discriminated between commodities, firms, industries and consumers. Not least, the desire to use purchase tax as an instrument in the management of the economy has led to frequent variations, often in conjunction with variations in hire purchase controls, so that they have disturbed or disrupted some of the youngest, scientifically most advanced, and generally most progressive industries.

Although it is not often so regarded, the purchase tax levied at the wholesale stage is a government-devised restriction on competition since it remains invariable whatever reductions in costs and prices can be made possible by efficiency at the retail stage. It is true that resale price maintenance in any event prevents or inhibits price competition over a large part of the market for consumer goods, but a government restriction of competition is not made less objectionable by the existence of a private (or, rather, government tolerated) restriction.

If it is essential to raise revenue by taxing commodities and services, purchase tax is not necessarily the best way to do it. A sales tax at the retail stage on a wider range of commodities and at a generally lower rate has advantages. Is the change practicable? If so, how can it begin? Not least the fundamental reason for raising the large revenue yielded by the purchase tax is that it is required to finance government expenditure. And the reason why discussion of reductions in purchase tax is discouraged is that if its yield is reduced it must be replaced by other taxes that may be difficult to devise and from which the politician may shrink because he thinks them politically unpopular. To envisage a radical reduction in purchase tax may, in the last analysis, require changes in government policy, not least perhaps in recasting the social services in order to avoid abortive expenditure by matching assistance with needs and requiring payment from those who can afford it.

With the exception of the question of government expenditure many of these issues in the development and future of purchase tax are raised and rigorously analysed by Dr. Prest. At a time when the next budget is being pondered by the Chancellor of the Exchequer, by his civil service advisers, by popularity-minded politicians, and by industries that may be affected by changes in purchase tax, the long-run interests of the consumer and of the economy at large are apt to be given secondary attention. Dr. Prest's review and recommendations, which are based on the needs of the general interest, should receive widespread discussion.

Hobart Paper 10 *Colin Clark*
March 1961

Growthmanship

The purpose of the *Hobart Papers* is to contribute a stream of authoritative, informed, independent and readable commentary to the formation of economic opinion and policy. The general theme underlying them is the scope for increased freedom of choice made possible for consumers by rising incomes, and the policies best designed to enable them to take advantage of widening opportunities. The intention is to apply this criterion to particular public policies as they ripen for decision.

For some time the discussion of British economic policy, both at home and in the under-developed countries, has centred on the possibilities and difficulties of growth. There have been two main issues: first, whether growth should take precedence over stability in the value of money; secondly, how best to promote it. The fashionable view appears to be that the British economy has been stagnant, and that its growth should be stimulated by increasing capital investment. It seemed to the Institute that it was time these views were subjected to the test of analysis and evidence before opinion crystallised further.

For the author of this *Paper* we were fortunate in being able to draw on one of the distinguished members of our Advisory Council. Mr. Colin Clark needs no introduction to economists, students, businessmen, politicians, journalists or any interested in economic growth. He has studied growth in many countries and has written about it in pioneering works throughout his career as an academic and professional economist.

He subjects current thinking on growth to rigorous examination and gives impressive reasons for arguing that healthy and continuing growth is not possible with persistently rising prices and that the role of investment in growth is much more complex than many economists have supposed. Of special interest to students of economics is his warning against the writings of those who have applied or misapplied the thinking of Keynes in changed conditions. Here Mr. Clark questions the development of economic doctrine and teaching now common in British universities.

The author assails the policy that has been pursued in Britain and the Commonwealth, not least in India, and finds misdirected investment at home (especially in the nationalised industries and agriculture) and in the under-developed countries. He reminds us that much of the current preoccupation with growth is not new, and that much of what is new is wrong.

This *Paper* amply maintains Mr. Clark's reputation as a lively and stimulating writer. His courageous independence supplies an indispensable ingredient in British economic thinking. And common-sense and humanity inform his recommendations for policy.

Hobart Paper 14
October 1961

D. S. Lees

Health Through Choice

One of the areas of public policy in which it is commonly assumed that wants must be supplied collectively is that of the social services. This assumption has been challenged in general terms by Colin Clark, Alan Peacock and Michael Fogarty, and, in the more specific field of saving for retirement, by an earlier Hobart Paper *Pensions for Prosperity.* Until recently, much of the academic discussion of the principles underlying the National Health Service has been conducted by sociologists who are not only philosophically inclined towards collective provision but also show little interest in the economic implications. An attempt to reconsider the reasons for and the results of the National Health Service was made by Professor John and Mrs. Sylvia Jewkes in *The Genesis of the British National Health Service.*[1] The present study by Dr. Dennis Lees complements the Jewkes study by an analysis of the inescapable economic dilemmas created by a health service financed out of general taxation. It is the first analysis of its kind by an economist in Britain.

Dr. Lees returns to first principles. He refutes the view that health is in principle different from any other service rendered to consumers. He questions many of the arguments used in defence of a state health service by academics and by politicians of all parties. He challenges the claims that the National Health Service should be credited with the improved health of the British people. He emphasises the dangers to the patient and to the medical professions, not least in the prescribing of medicines, of political control based on short-period electoral calculation. And, in total, he is sceptical of the social, the political, and the economic mystiques that have been built around the National Health Service.

When Dr. Lees first published his doubts in an article in the *Lloyds Bank Review*[2] they attracted wide attention. So far, there has been no convincing reply. In this Paper he takes his analysis further by a systematic, step-by-step examination of the arguments for and against the National Health Service

1. Basil Blackwell, 1961.
2. The Economics of Health Services, April 1960.

in particular and a state health service in general. His conclusion is that, provided those in need are helped generously, there is no reason why people should not be free to buy health services from competing suppliers by paying for them directly or with the aid of private insurance. He reinforces the argument at various stages by drawing on experience in the USA, Australia, New Zealand, Sweden, and other countries, in most of which there is lively public debate on alternative methods, state and private, of organising and financing medical services.

Hobart Paper 17
April 1962

J. E. Meade

UK, Commonwealth and Common Market: A Re-appraisal

So far, with the exception of Colin Clark's *Growthmanship*, the *Hobart Papers* have been concerned primarily with markets—for commodities, services, labour—within the British economy. This is the first *Hobart* to be concerned specifically with an international market. Its author is the distinguished economist, Professor James E. Meade, whose academic work in international economics and wartime and post-war service as the Director of the Economic Section of the Cabinet Offices will assure his analysis and judgement a wide hearing.

Professor Meade's *Hobart Paper* is being published at a time when the preliminary negotiations on the UK's entry into the Common Market are well advanced but when there is time for disinterested analysis to be weighed before the decisions to join the Common Market and the terms on which to join or to stay outside it are taken. It restates briefly the classical advantages of free trade but it is concerned chiefly with the conditions which the UK should require in the interest not only of herself but also of the Commonwealth and of the western world at large. It is thus designed to offer proposals that should be in the mind of the statesmen and public servants who are conducting the negotiations.

The question whether or not to enter the Common Market has liquified political and philosophical opinion of all shades and it may be some time before it recrystallises. There appear to be conflicting reasons both for joining the Common Market and for staying out. Some urge that we join because we should participate in an experiment in international economic integration that may raise living standards by making possible division of labour over much of the Continent, others because the Common Market would make it possible to organise state activity over larger areas than single sovereign states. Some argue we should stay out because the Common Market has a high tariff around it against the Commonwealth, the countries of the European Free Trade Area and the USA; others because membership would prevent Britain from being run as a self-contained direct economy. On both sides there is a mixture of idealism and interest. Some business men may be in favour of joining because they would have access to a larger market within the shelter of the common tariff; some trade union leaders oppose entry because the Common Market would weaken their control over the British labour market; and so on.

Professor Meade's analysis sheds light on these diverse approaches. It can be read as arguing either that we should join the Common Market *provided* certain conditions are satisfied, or that we should stay out *unless* they are satisfied. Although he emphasises the advantages that could flow from an outward-looking Common Market that aimed to liberalise economic relations with the outside world so that it could extend to embrace the other countries of the EFTA, the Commonwealth and the USA in a grand North Atlantic market, he is also sensitive to the dangers of an inward-looking Common Market that created a cosy economic corner on the Continent.

Professor Meade's survey of the economic and financial implications is conducted with special reference to the consequences for the Commonwealth. He classifies the relevant aspects into five groups: the implications for the other members of EFTA, UK agriculture, Commonwealth trade, sterling and the balance of payments, and labour migration. The emphasis on the Commonwealth explains why there is no direct discussion of other central aspects such as the legal framework of the Common Market relating to restrictive practices, cartels, trade unions, and the maintenance of competitive institutions generally.

The Institute offers this *Hobart Paper* as a contribution to public discussion of the terms on which Britain should enter the Common Market and possibly to direct attention to the policies she may need to evolve if the conditions cannot be obtained and she must seek economic salvation outside it.

Hobart Paper 18
June 1962

Henry Smith

The Wage-Fixers

The Institute has published several contributions to the analysis of the labour market. In 1959 Professor B. C. Roberts' *Trade Unions in a Free Society*, and his second edition in 1962, argued that if trade unions were "to make a constructive contribution to the future welfare of the nation they must come to terms with the market economy, which is an essential feature of a free society, and not seek to prevent it from working." In 1961 Professor D. J. Robertson's Hobart Paper No. 12, *A Market for Labour*, analysed the labour market "as a market and not as some kind of social institution" and as the instrument for allocating labour to its most economic employments. In 1961 *Agenda for a Free Society* contained an essay by Sir Henry Slesser, Solicitor-General in the 1924 Labour Government, on the legal powers and privileges of trade unions, and by Mr. John Lincoln on the manner in which the rights of labour could be embodied in a legal contract that would avoid the criticisms levelled at trade unions. The present *Hobart Paper* by Henry Smith considers the remuneration of labour as fixed by arbitration in a free labour market.

Mr. Smith is well qualified to write on this subject. He is a distinguished economist with much experience in public service as a member of government committees and as a war-time civil servant. He has been a wage arbitrator for nearly 14 years and has clearly given much thought to his duties, and as Vice-Principal of Ruskin College he has close connections with the world of trade unions and adult education. His special knowledge of and sympathy with the workers' point of view ensures that he is not likely to overlook arguments in their favour. In this *Hobart Paper* he has attempted two tasks: first, a personal statement of the way in which he sees his duty as an arbitrator; second, a more general discussion of the conditions in which wage arbitrators could and should work. In general he defends the principle of wage arbitration from its critics and absolves it from the charge of spreading inflation, which he claims is the responsibility of general monetary and fiscal policy. He is critical of the attempt of the government in the wages pause and the period of the "guiding light" to inhibit the work of arbitration by indicating narrow limits within which wage awards may be made; he claims that if arbitrators are to be degraded to the role of "slightly dirty rubber stamps" there may be a shortage of men ready to serve. And he makes a case for "comparability" of wages paid for labour of a particular kind in all industries and regions.

For those concerned with the underlying economic principles of wage policy, Mr. Smith's *Hobart Paper* is of interest for his analysis of the degree to which arbitration should reproduce the wage rates that would rule in a free labour market, the case for and against decentralised collective bargaining, the extent to which wages determine or are determined by the prices of the product or service, and the significance of the economic principle of the "marginal product" for the distribution and remuneration of the labour force. In place of vague generalisation tinged with political prejudice, Mr. Smith offers a cool, refined analysis of the underlying economic forces that determine the distribution of the fruits of industry and innovation. Opinion may differ on the relevance for these matters of the legal framework of society—not least that relating to employers and trade unions—and the resulting relative strengths of competitive and restrictive practices in the markets for commodities and services. It could be held that settlement of wages through free collective bargaining supplemented by arbitration cannot yield the socially most beneficial result if the legal framework of the market permits employers or employees to hold each other up to ransom or the community by passing on higher costs to the consumer.

Although, as the author of *The Economics of Socialism Reconsidered,* Mr. Smith is in principle a critic of an economic system resting on free markets, he accepts it in practice as the most serviceable arrangement short of extensive changes in the economic and political structure of society. He has written an authoritative, if controversial, contribution to the current discussion of the role of wages policy in a free, expanding economy.

Hobart Paper 20 *A. R. Ilersic*
March 1963

Relief for Ratepayers

A long neglected "consumer" in economic literature is the ratepayer, who not only finances the necessary machinery of local government but also pays for services which it supplies. The revaluation of property and the introduction of new "poundages" in 1963 offer a convenient occasion for a re-examination of the structure of local government, of its sources of finance, both local rates and government grants, and of the range of services that have come to be organised and managed by it.

Accordingly, the Institute invited an economist who has specialised in local government, Mr. A. R. Ilersic of Bedford College, University of London, to explain the effects of the 1963 revaluations on ratepayers of all kinds, the sources of local government finance and the implications for policy of the changing social and economic environment of the second half of the twentieth century.

Mr. Ilersic has written an informative and thought-provoking survey of the financing of local government that should be of interest to ratepayers of all kinds—industrialists, business and professional men, traders, householders and tenants (who pay rates often without knowing it), to teachers and students of economics, to public administrators and local government officials and, not least, to all who form opinion and create policy on local government.

Mr. Ilersic says that the prospect of rising local government expenditure provokes two lines of thought: first, whether existing sources of revenue are adequate or new ones need to be found; secondly, whether local government should go on supplying services originating in the nineteenth century when the bulk of the new urban communities were housed in insanitary towns and homes, when they were too poor to make provision for the vicissitudes of industrial life and too ignorant to be aware of the need for education or public health.

He examines proposals that have been made in recent times for charges for local government services such as education, car parks, health and libraries, and for reducing the burden on the public sector by permitting or encouraging the purchase of services on the open market.

The Institute is not necessarily committed to Mr. Ilersic's analysis and conclusion but offers his *Hobart Paper* as a contribution to the discussion of the reconstruction of local government.

Hobart Paper 24
October 1963

Sir Sydney Caine

Prices for Primary Producers

A common thread that runs through the Hobart Papers is the characteristic approach of economists to the study of economic activity through the analysis of supply and demand in markets. They examine the circumstances in which markets work well or badly and the environment required for them to yield the optimum social advantage. The discussion is therefore in terms of prices and costs, the conditions affecting supply (techniques, etc.) and demand (habit, income, etc.) and the inter-relationships of producers and consumers.

These techniques can be applied with effect to a problem that is looming ahead: the raw material and food products of the under-developed countries. Agricultural nationalism is having to be modified in face of the recognition that larger groupings to facilitate freer exchange between the industrialised and the under-developed countries are essential if living standards are to be raised. The French rebuff to the British application for membership of the Common Market, the limited success of the European Free Trade Association, and the changing relationships between Britain and the Commonwealth countries have provoked increasing interest in proposals for international commodity agreements to stabilise prices or the earnings of primary producers, to avoid disconcerting fluctuations in the export of food to industrialised countries, or similar objectives.

The Institute therefore considered it would be helpful to publish a reconsideration of the economic principles underlying international commodity agreements. We were fortunate in persuading Sir Sydney Caine, the distinguished economist who has extensive practical experience of colonial administration and knowledge of international commodity markets, to undertake this task. He has written a concise but incisive economic analysis of the attempts at stabilisation and has illuminated it from his experience and other examples going back to the 1930s and covering a wide range of commodities including cocoa, coffee, rubber, sugar, tea, tin and wheat. He discusses the role of price fluctuations in equating supply and demand. He reveals the often conflicting aims of stabilisation schemes and shows they may not remove fluctuations but throw the burden of adjustment to changing market conditions on to the volume of production. He argues indeed that, although attempts to modify extreme instability might be possible, variations in price are in principle desirable. His review of the remedies and preventives tried since the 1930s should provoke second and sobering thoughts among those who have uncritically adopted a specific that has returned to fashion despite its weaknesses revealed over many years in many countries, and in many products. Sir Sydney's approval of some forms of stabilisation schemes is highly qualified, not least because even when well-conceived they will be operated not by omniscient altruists but by fallible humans subject to day-to-day political pressures. He recommends that the solution lies less in ambitious comprehensive systems of government regulation than in "helping the ordinary man to help himself" by creating the legal and monetary framework in which he can anticipate the fluctuations unavoidable in a world in which consumers are free to change their minds and technical invention is rapid and unforeseeable. It is ultimately in this way, he thinks, that the West can best assist in strengthening the economies of the primary producing nations.

Sir Sydney's analysis is also relevant to the discussion of the forms in which aid can best be given by the industrialised West to the underdeveloped countries. A previous *Hobart Paper,* by Mr. Colin Clark,[1] questioned the view that the requirement was massive investment in capital. This approach, formerly made fashionable but now being abandoned by writers, such as Professor J. K. Galbraith, who over-simplified the issues, has been replaced by an emphasis on investment in people through education and training. Sir Sydney's analysis suggests that even this assistance, though helpful, is less fruitful than encouraging the entrepreneurial qualities of judgement in recognising, running and responding to risks that lie at the root of western economic progress.

1. *Growthmanship,* Hobart Paper No. 10, IEA, 1961, 2nd edition 1962.

Hobart Paper 25
February 1964

Alan Peacock and Jack Wiseman

Education for Democrats

Education is a service that too many social scientists, educationalists and politicians assume must be provided by government. Recent reports by the Newsom, Trend and Robbins Committees on primary education, research, and higher education respectively, all concluded with recommendations that would enlarge or entrench the role and intensify the control of the state. The Robbins and the Trend Committees showed themselves aware of the dangers of increasing state authority in education, research and scholarship but offered few proposals for strengthening a private sector relatively free from control by politicians.

The publication in 1962 of *Minerva* by the Committee on Science and Freedom, which speaks for eminent academics in many countries, reflects the concern of scholars for the independence of learning and research. Developments in higher education in the communist countries and in the young universities in the newly independent African and Asian states should give educationalists cause for concern. But the conclusion is too rarely drawn that the government piper will ultimately call the tune.

Since the mid-1950s, and earlier, economists in the USA have considered the problems of establishing a private market in education. In Britain the theme is being taken up by the younger economists. This *Hobart Paper* is the work of two of them, Professors Alan Peacock and Jack Wiseman of the University of York, formerly students and colleagues of Lord Robbins at the London School of Economics. The Institute invited them to reconsider the institutional framework and financial arrangements that seemed desirable to permit scope for a variety of private or state educational institutions from primary schools to universities that best met the requirements of a free society. The social survey conducted by Mass-Observation for the Institute revealed a sizeable demand for a choice between state and private education.

Professors Peacock and Wiseman have clearly stated their premises and have reached conclusions by economic analysis that seems inescapable. They have produced a short study that is scholarly in its reticence and meticulous in its phrasing but that strikes at the root of the social and economic thinking that looks to the state for the advancement of attention education and ignores the potentialities of spontaneous private initiative. They question some of the central arguments and proposals of the Robbins Committee: they regret that educational policy may be determined too much by responses to emergencies rather than by reference to the values and principles of a liberal democracy; they do not accept that the independence of universities would be adequately assured if fees supplied 20 per cent of the total income; they are not convinced by Robbins' apprehensions about loans for students; and in general they are not satisfied that any system for channelling state funds direct to educational institutions would ensure freedom from political control. The authors amass an impressive array of argument in making their case for a system of vouchers, bursaries and loans that would give parents the freedom to choose between private and state schools and colleges. They also review the arguments that might be urged against them and reveal their hidden political assumptions.

This *Hobart Paper* is the first examination in Britain of the possibilities opened up by restoring choice in education to parents. Assisted by information, grants and the removal of market imperfections and privileges, families would be able to require schools and colleges to compete among themselves for pupils and students. The supply of education would be reinvigorated by new impulses to innovation and experimentation. Not least, education (and teacher salaries) would increasingly be taken out of politics.

The stereotypes of current debate on education have prevented us from seeing the possibilities of this new approach. Whatever the problems arising out of the detailed proposals made by Professors Peacock and Wiseman, the attitude they typify, that the initiative in education should be taken from the politician and be given to the parent or student consumer, is one that should no longer be ignored.

Hobart Paper 26
July 1964

Colin Clark

Taxmanship

In 1964 the consumer can assert his preferences directly through more or less competitive markets for only some 60 per cent of his income. For the remaining 40 per cent, taken from him in taxes, rates and social insurance contributions, he can assert his preferences only indirectly and at many removes through four- or five-yearly general elections, occasional by-elections, consumer councils for the nationalised industries, representations to members of parliament or local councillors, the formation of pressure groups, complaints to the Press. There is room for differing judgements on the relative effectiveness of the market place and the ballot box as methods of indicating and enforcing the consumer's preferences: both should be subjected to continuous rigorous analysis.

Rising incomes, improved social expectations and enhanced personal responsibility must influence judgement about the scope for the market mechanism. They mean that the use of the welfare state to redistribute income, in cash or kind, from the better-off to the less well-off or from the more responsible to the less responsible is evaporating. For if incomes rise and become more equal, so that more people are paying the state in taxes, rates and social insurance contributions as much as they receive in social benefits, and if they can be trusted to make choices in the markets for consumer goods and to learn from their mistakes, they can also be allowed increased choice in the goods and services for which they pay the state—education, health, housing, pensions and others. And to the extent that they prefer private to state services it would be possible to reduce the proportion of income taken from them from 40 per cent to a lower figure at which it would not discourage effort and output.

After a decade of uncritical euphoria following the Beveridge report, the pioneer of this thinking could not expect an unqualified welcome. And Mr. Colin Clark, whose *Welfare and Taxation* in 1953 questioned the basic assumption of universal state welfare, did not receive rapturous applause. But he has long attracted international repute as the pioneer without honour in his own country. He supported Keynes long before he became fashionable, and questioned Keynes when he became fashionable. He opposed the "protection" of agriculture in Britain and of manufactures in Australia. Long before others he questioned the high rate of economic growth in Soviet Russia. In *Growthmanship* (Hobart Paper 10) he argued, against the fashion, that economic growth could not be accelerated artificially by capital investment but took place mainly in consequence of improvement in human resources. And in this *Hobart Paper* he develops his argument of 1945 (which Keynes accepted in principle) that taxation beyond 25 per cent of the net national income produces inflation and that the way now to reduce it from 40 per cent to 25 per cent is to dismantle many state welfare services and return to the average family a large part of the income taken from it so that it can make better provision for itself.

This theme is not yet popular or fashionable. But, unlike other social scientists anxious to influence and exercise power in one or other of the political parties, Mr. Clark has persevered by encouraging others to develop his theme particularly in welfare services—some of them in *Hobart Papers.*

Mr. Clark now produces evidence from many countries in support of his two central arguments: that the further taxation exceeds 25 per cent of the net national income the stronger the stimulus to inflation, and that the recent analysis of taxation paid and social benefits received by individual households in Britain and information from other countries suggest that the scope for reduced taxation best lies in allowing people to buy welfare services in the market instead of compelling them to buy through the state. He argues that in time it would be possible to reduce taxation to something near 25 per cent of the national income, and he shows how this reduced percentage would comprise expenditure taxes (in place of income taxes), taxes on capital, on company profits, land tax, indirect taxes, and a tax on value added.

The Institute does not necessarily accept the details of Mr. Clark's analysis and conclusions, but he has, as usual, written a stimulating challenge to accepted thinking that should influence thought on social policy in the future when much fashionable doctrine is forgotten.

Hobart Paper 28
July 1964

John Carmichael

Vacant Possession

Since 1915 the capacity of the consumer to assert his preference, as purchaser or tenant, for housing has been limited by statutory controls. Choice in housing has also been influenced by a complex of housing subsidies and income tax rebates on mortgage interest. Policy has been conducted largely by reference to, and at times almost dictated by, the existence of people with incomes considered too low for them to pay market rents. There has been much debate among social scientists on whether housing is a fit object of provision by private suppliers for profit or a social service that should be supplied by public authorities at less than its market price. Housing becomes embroiled with party politics. It has become the object of *causes célèbres*—from the scandal of houses at 2s 10½ d. per week by the Lanarkshire city council to the high rents charged by notorious landlords.

Housing policy has been largely dominated by prejudice, and the economists have had little of the public ear. The sociologists, the moralists, and the politicians are apt to be impatient with the inconvenient scarcity of resources, the need to ration them, and the logic of rationing either by price or by official controls. They therefore often fail to ask what, to the economist, is the key question: *Why* is there a "housing problem" but not a "food problem," a "clothing problem" or a "toffee apple problem"? Mr. John Carmichael suggests solutions.

He reviews the supply of and demand for housing in the last 50 years that have kept rents below market levels and have brought subsidies for tenants of privately-owned houses, council building, the under-occupation of houses by older people and the shortage of homes for younger people. He argues that the continuation of rent controls has exacerbated the very housing problem they have been intended to palliate. He maintains that the policies of both the main political parties have failed to provide housing for people who need it most, and that subsidised housing is often going to people who do not need it at all. And he blames both parties for their failure to recognise that ensuring housing for people "in need" necessarily requires the use of a measure of need. He argues that the subsidy should go in depressed rents. And he maintains that only an effective market, possibly even with higher rents, would attract resources into the building of houses to create the surplus without which the "housing problem" cannot be removed. In 1936–7 some 370,000 houses were built, mostly by private enterprise; since the war targets of 300,000, 325,000, 350,000 . . . have been made offerings by Housing Ministers who take the credit if the target is reached and are eloquent with excuses if it is missed.

Vacant Possession emphasises the author's concern to end the shortage by creating a surplus which will overcome one of the most serious obstacles to mobility of labour.

Housing has become so entangled with party politics that Mr. Carmichael has had to examine party dogmas as well as academic argument. His analysis and conclusions will not be palatable to sociologists who have discussed the subject in terms of nebulous housing "needs" and ignored the institutions best designed to satisfy housing *demands.* They will also probably be unpalatable to politicians of all parties who have used housing as a political instrument, the control of which they would be loath to lose.

Hobart Paper 29
September 1964

F. W. Paish and J. Hennessy

Policy for Incomes?

Since the end of the war the British economy has suffered continual strain from persistent inflation. The politicians have been under pressure to "jack up" demand for goods and services to a level high enough to maintain "full employment." The outcome has been unemployment averaging less than 2 per cent of the labour force compared with the 3 per cent average which Beveridge used (and Gaitskell accepted) as the definition of "full employment."

"Unemployment" is still commonly thought of in its pre-war sense of loss of work for long periods, although most people registered as "unemployed" are out of work for less than eight weeks. Yet in a progressive economy with a high rate of change in techniques, trade, tastes and habits it would be possible to envisage an unemployment rate sometimes rising to 5 per cent or even more as compatible with a high and rising standard of living and as necessary to maintain and raise it.

On the other hand if people were enabled to adapt themselves quickly to changes in supply and demand it would seem possible to maintain a dynamic economy with very little involuntary unemployment except for people leaving declining firms, industries or regions and being retrained for other jobs or moving to where labour is scarce and better paid. The obstacles in the way of movement are numerous: restrictive practices operated by business men or enforced by trade unions, sometimes in collusion; rent restrictions which have discouraged people from leaving subsidised council or private homes; the high cost of buying and selling houses and flats; the practice of "ploughing back" company profits which has encouraged the survival of the fattest; the failure to save out of high earnings for periods of loss of income; the concentration of trade unions on maximising immediate pay and neglecting redundancy benefits; the huge agglomerations of labour and capital in nationalised industries which create vested interests against movement; the subsidies which discourage farmers and others from taking to other employment; high rates of taxation which diminish the incentives to change from older to newer investments and enterprises; not least import duties and other forms of protection which incite capital and labour to remain where they are instead of moving into new or growing industries. All these influences have raised the percentage of unemployed it is necessary to tolerate in a changing economy. In a vigorously competitive economy it would be possible to have high demand, rising standards of living and full employment without persistent inflation.

So far, apart from action on monopoly, restrictive practices, food subsidies and rents, post-war economic opinion and policy had shirked the political measures required to master inflation. There have been demands for "incomes policy," which would limit the rise in earnings to the increase in the output of goods and services. It is the economics of this policy within the existing institutional framework that Professor F. W. Paish and Mr. Jossleyn Hennessy examine.

In Part I Professor Paish considers the two kinds of inflation according to their source—"demand inflation" and "cost inflation," the relationship between inflation and the money supply, and trade unions as monopolists of labour. He discusses the desirability and feasibility of controlling wages, profits and prices, and the difficulties of enforcing controls—the strains on employers, on trade unions and on government. But his main purpose is to analyse the recent movement in earnings, wage rates, demand and unemployment in an attempt to discover the limits of unemployment within which there is room for an effective "incomes policy." He concludes that within the range of 2 and 2¼ per cent unemployment could be supplemented—but not replaced—by a "wages policy" to withstand inflation. If unemployment is below 2 per cent an "incomes policy" would be ineffective because it would not be able to withstand the pressure of the demand for labour, and if unemployment is above 2¼ per cent an "incomes policy" would be unnecessary.

In Part II Mr. Hennessy seeks to ascertain what practical lessons, if any, in incomes policies can be derived from Europe's post-war experience. He shows that only one country—Holland—has attempted a "genuine" incomes policy under the control of a statutory authority, and that it has virtually broken down. Since the "incomes policies" of all other countries have been confined to exhortation and arbitration, Mr. Hennessy's choice of examples falls on Sweden because of her reputation for good labour relations and on Denmark because her system of centralised and synchronised collective bargaining has often been held up as a model. None of these countries has controlled inflation, prevented wages from rising faster than productivity, reorganised wages and salaries in such a way as to satisfy the demand for "social justice." And it indicates evidence of the strains analysed by Professor Paish.

There will be especial interest in Professor Paish's refined analysis in his conclusion that within narrow limits there is room for an effective "incomes policy." These limits—¼ per cent—are so narrow that in practice it would seem precarious to make them the basis of an incomes policy. The practical conclusion for economic policy from both Professor Paish's theoretical analysis and Mr. Hennessy's European review would seem to be that an "incomes policy" is either unnecessary or abortive, and that the way to maintain high employment and rising living standards and yet avoid inflation is to control the supply of purchasing power in relation to output and resources and remove the obstacles to the movement of labour within the economy.

Professor Paish and Mr. Hennessy have produced two stimulating discussions each of which the reader will feel impelled to study in the context of the other.

Hobart Paper 30 *Donald Denman*
December 1964

Land in the Market

The market for land has preoccupied public discussion for several years largely because of the movement of population and industry into areas favoured by the public for their amenities or by industrialists for their cost or other advantages. The predictable results have been an increase in the price of land, especially for house building, exceptional profits by landowners and by individuals who acquired land on which to build property in relatively high demand, and increased activity by politicians in proposing solutions.

In these circumstances the Institute invited Dr. D. R. Denman of the University of Cambridge to analyse the market in land, to appraise the solutions, and to examine alternative suggestions for policy. He has responded with an essay that follows the high standard set by the distinguished contributors to the *Hobart Papers:* a combination of scholarly approach, animated writing and stimulating discussion of policy. He analyses the economics of the land market within the legal and institutional framework of common law and statutory rights of property; and he reconsiders the fundamental quasi-legal concepts of rights and justice on which the discussion rests. Throughout his *Paper* he emphasises: first, that buyers and sellers in the market for land are concerned not with exchanging physical areas of grass or woodland but rights established by law and made valuable by the interplay between supply and demand; second, that in consequence, "landowners" are not a small number of wealthy country gentlemen but millions of people with varying rights to dispose of homes, shops, farms or other property occupying land; third, that disregarding the unambiguous rights of individuals may not (in normal times) be the best way to serve the more indeterminable rights of "the community."

In his examination of the reasons for movements of prices in land and the buildings erected on it, and of the numerous proposals for taxing the increases in prices and values, or for transferring them from individuals to the community, Dr. Denman returns to the first principles of economics in his emphasis on price as the means of bringing supply into harmony with demand. He reviews the conditions in which the compulsory purchase of land by individuals, municipal corporations or the state can be justified, but argues that the buyer should pay a price which compensates the owner for current and expected satisfactions. He questions the proposals for transferring the increments in land values from the owners to the community by arguing that if they are passed on to individual house buyers they cannot be enjoyed by the community, and that if land prices are not allowed to rise the increment can be enjoyed neither by the community nor by individuals. He argues that if there are to be levies for betterment there should be compensations for detriment. In particular he is sceptical of the proposal for a Crown Lands Commission, which he argues might accelerate the increase in land prices and/or reduce the supply of land available for house building. His main conclusion, again following first principles, is that if it is desired to keep down price in land the only way is to increase supply by removing restrictions on densities in urban areas and on building in green belts and elsewhere.

Instead of the devices for preventing would-be sellers of land from coming together with would-be buyers, Dr. Denman suggests that the market in property and land should be overhauled so that it serves buyers and sellers better, and that urban renewal might be facilitated by compulsory reallocation of land that would remain in private ownership rather than be transferred to public control.

Dr. Denman has concentrated discussion of the many aspects of a very large subject into compact space. The Institute thinks it will be found educational and invigorating to teachers and students of the economics and the law of property in land, to people who own, buy and sell rights in land, to economists, journalists and others who contribute to the formation of opinion, and to people in public life who make policy.

Hobart Paper 31
February 1965

Gottfried Haberler

Money in the International Economy

The purpose of the *Hobart Papers* is to contribute authoritative, independent and readable commentary to discussion of the economic analysis of policy. Their general focus is the system of inter-related markets within which buyers and sellers exchange goods or services and the legal and institutional framework within which markets best serve man as consumer.

Such a framework requires laws to provide security for contracts and to govern the conduct of industry, and institutions to provide a monetary system that enables contracts and industrial activity to take place with confidence in their outcome. The structure of a monetary system for the British economy was brilliantly analysed by Professor E. Victor Morgan in Hobart Paper 27, *Monetary Policy for Stable Growth.* To discuss the requirements of a monetary system in the world economy we invited the internationally distinguished economist, Professor Gottfried Haberler of Harvard University.

His analysis of the fundamentals of the international monetary mechanism since the nineteenth century closely examines the methods of correcting disequilibrium in the balances of payments between countries with nationally controlled currencies. He analyses first, the market methods of fixed exchanges under gold or similar standards and of variable exchange rates which float freely or are adjusted periodically; secondly, the non-market methods which comprise *ad hoc* controls of imports or capital flows, such as the recent British 15 per cent surcharge. He categorises market methods as general or non-discriminatory and non-market methods as particular or discriminatory. His conclusion that the discontinuous but fairly frequent adjustment of exchange rates ("adjustable peg system") is inferior to either fixed exchange rates or freely floating exchange rates will be closely studied and analysed by readers who have watched recent British economic policy. He considers whether continuing depreciation in exchange rates under flexible exchanges or a dwindling gold reserve under fixed exchanges is the more effective deterrent to inflation, and concludes that since there is too little experience so far with floating exchanges the choice remains one of technical judgement. He suggests that there might be experiments with limited flexibility of exchange rates by widening the gold points, occasional but not too frequent adjustment of exchange rates and allowing some non-reserve currency countries to adopt flexible exchanges.

Professor Haberler's discussion is conducted with reference to the argument that there is a growing need for an increase in international monetary reserves and liquidity. He questions the theoretical basis and the empirical evidence for the argument and indeed points to possible dangers of making liquidity too easily available to national currency systems because governments might then become indifferent to the need to maintain equilibrium in the balances of payments by making necessary but unpopular changes in internal economic policy on prices, wages and other costs.

Professor Haberler's conclusions and judgements are based on a study of international monetary affairs over 30 to 40 years and on analysis of recent events in many countries: the USA, Canada, Germany, France, Italy and South America as well as Britain. He questions views that have been held or made fashionable by economists or central bankers in the last few years and is concerned to envisage a structure of interconnected monetary systems that are as far as possible beyond the influence of national politics.

By going back to first principles in his analysis of international monetary policies Professor Haberler has raised many fundamental issues that will enlighten the scene for teachers and students of economics and stimulate reappraisal by economists, bankers, politicians, and others concerned with national and international economic policy.

Hobart Paper 32
March 1965

C. T. Sandford

Taxing Inheritance and Capital Gains

It is common property of economists of a wide range of thought that the consumer is more likely to be able to exert his preferences in a competitive than in a monopolistic order. A high degree of concentration of property strengthens monopolistic tendencies and weakens the equalising force of competition. The bulk of private property remains in surprisingly few hands: some 3 per cent of the population own much more than half, 97 per cent own the rest. The distribution of property ownership is therefore an urgent subject for analysis as part of the institutional framework of society. The use of death duties to encourage the dispersal of property is usually associated with the Italian economist, Eugenio Rignano. Lord Robbins also advocated reform of the death duties in the 1930s and again after the war. In 1938 the Liberal Party published a report on the distribution of property, *Ownership for All,* which urged the replacement of duties levied on estates by taxes on legacies received by heirs. Surprisingly, the Conservative Party, in spite of verbal adherence to "a property-owning democracy" in the 1950s, did not alter the structure of the death duties in its 13 years of office: less surprisingly in view of its preference for public ownership of property, the Labour Party repealed the legacy and succession duties in 1949 and raised the estate duties.

Mr. C. T. Sandford, an economist who has made a special study of the death duties, has two purposes. First, he has reviewed discussion of the reform of death duties as a means of dispersing property ownership. Secondly, he offers original proposals for what he calls a "capital receipts tax" to be levied on all receipts not subject to income tax whether inherited property, gifts or gambling winnings, and including capital gains on owner-occupied homes or investments, but allowing for losses; he argues it would be a better method of taxing capital gains than that proposed by Mr. James Callaghan.

Mr. Sandford's skilful presentation of the arguments in favour of replacing the estate duty by an inheritance (or legacy) tax should direct attention to a long-neglected reform in the British tax structure if the desire is to reduce the inequalities in the ownership of property. Since the Labour Party is not opposed to private ownership in the form of homes, National Savings, unit trust investments, and even equities in industry, there may now perhaps be agreement in all parties that if property is to remain privately owned it is desirable to reduce the wide gap between the ownership of much by the few and of little by the many. So long as the power of the political parties and the state is massive, it is desirable to permit centres of independence based on property. Yet the concentration of property ownership remains a main reason for the persistence of privilege, monopoly, and political pressures on Parliament. Gross inequality in property ownership makes for inequality of opportunity which in turn may intensify inequalities of property ownership. To break this vicious circle a change in the death duties would seem to be an essential reform.

Mr. Sandford's interesting proposals for taxing all forms of capital receipts may be more controversial. The usual case for taxing capital gains is that they add to purchasing power and should therefore be taxed no less than income. Mr. Sandford discusses the extent to which taxes on capital might discourage effort and enterprise less than taxes on income. So far the British tax system ignores capital except in the form of estates passing on death. The rates of duty on estates have been raised so high that they are tolerable only because of the large number of loopholes. The solution lies not in devising methods of closing the loopholes or of multiplying penalties for tax avoidance, since other devices would be evolved, but in new forms of taxation of capital receipts which mitigate the harmful effects of very high taxation on income.

In view of the apparent failure of Mr. Selwyn Lloyd's tax on short-term capital gains, it is timely to re-appraise the whole subject of taxes on capital. Lawyers, accountants, and other specialists in taxation are usually too immersed in detail to see the wood for the trees, and politicians are too prone to take short-run views because of the effects of electoral opinion. Coming from an independent economist, Mr. Sandford's discussion and proposals are therefore particularly valuable. He argues that current estate duty rates are too high and his proposals for an inheritance tax would yield less revenue but, he claims, do more good by spreading ownership of property, be more equitable as between forms of ownership, and be less discouraging to effort. If the inheritance tax were developed into a "capital receipts tax" the yield would be higher, so that there might be some room for a reduction in taxes on income.

Hobart Paper 36 *Michael Canes*
June 1966

Telephones — Public or Private?

Micro-economic analysis of the prices and costs of individual goods or services and their adjustment at the margin by individual suppliers and demanders can be no less enlightening in the public than in the private sector of the economy. Macro-economic analysis, with its precarious assumptions and projections, has not been conspicuously illuminating when it has been applied to publicly-provided or publicly-organised services such as nuclear energy, steel, social insurance, schools or doctors. And it would seem to be no more enlightening if it were applied to a public service that has received too little economic scrutiny, the national telephone system provided by the General Post Office. Projections of the number of telephones that would be "needed" by industry or private households in 1975 or 1985 would not only have to be based on assumptions about the demand for and the supply of telephones and competing methods of communication but would also shed no light on the required organisation of supply or the inducements of penalties required to ensure that demand was satisfied. These problems can be illuminated only by the application of micro-economic analysis to individual demand, to the motives ("social service" or commercial profit) which lead individuals to supply telephones and to the prices and costs that emerge in consequence. Macro-economic calculations of the total number of households or of businesses that might want telephones at some point in the future or of the productive capacity of firms making telephones may be of interest as indicating possible broad orders of magnitude, but they are subject to such wide margins of error that they degenerate into little more than exercises in sophisticated arithmetic that yield *simpliste* inferences for public policy.

In view of the scarcity of such market analyses of public services, the Institute invited a talented young American economist, Mr. Michael Canes from the University of Chicago, who has studied business administration and who has some knowledge of the American telephone industry, to embark upon a comparative study of the British and American telephone systems, their relative degree of success in furnishing the telephone services demanded in their countries, and to offer conclusions for public policy in Britain.

Mr. Canes has researched and written an informative, closely-argued and uninhibited study of the telephone systems in Great Britain and the United States that will be new to most British readers. In general he finds that the American system is much more effective in providing the variety of services required by industry and private users. And he ascribes the superiority primarily to the difference in the method of organisation. He finds that the American method of decentralisation and of private and, to some degree, competitive supply is more accountable and responsive to the American consumer than is the British government-provided service to the British consumer. He traces the origins of the telephone service in both countries, the divergent ways in which they have developed, and the contrasting methods of supply and of government regulation or supervision. His central proposal is that Britain should experiment with decentralisation, competition and private provision. He supplies a convincing array of economic arguments for supposing that a change in the method of organisation would yield results beyond those that could be expected from re-arranging the existing system.

Mr. Canes's *Hobart Paper* should help to stimulate fundamental reappraisal of public policy on the telephone service in Britain. We are grateful to Professor George Stigler of the University of Chicago, Professor Jack Wiseman of the University of York and Professor B. S. Yamey of the University of London for commenting on early drafts of the *Paper.*

The Institute offers Mr. Canes's analysis and conclusions as a refreshing re-interpretation of the economics and public policy of telephone services that should help formulate a more satisfying system for the British consumer.

Hobart Paper 37
August 1966

F. R. Jervis

The Company, the Shareholder and Growth

One of the main parts of the legal framework of the private sector of the economy is that governing the founding and conduct of companies with limited liability. Criticism of the organisation of industry in Britain in the form of companies does not usually distinguish between the role of the company as an economic unit and as a legal creation. It is not difficult to show, as has been done in the USA in two classic works,[1] that the growth of the company is very much a function of the framework created by the law in giving it specific rights and obligations. The creation of the holding company, for example, has made possible the development of very large diversified businesses which exhibit economies of large-scale financing, and possibly risk-spreading, but also often dis-economies in management, technique and marketing. Limited liability also made possible the aggregation of small savings into a large capital fund but thereby widened the gap between the shareholders as the ultimate owners and the directors and managers as the immediate controllers. Since the war company law in Britain has been recodified in the 1948 Companies Act and re-examined by the Jenkins Committee which reported in 1962. The Institute has contributed to this discussion in this and other series. The government is preparing a Bill thought to be based largely on the recommendations of the Jenkins Committee, which economists have considered not sufficient to meet the conditions of the changing British economy.

In this *Hobart Paper,* Dr. F. R. Jervis, a specialist in business administration, reconsiders the organisation of companies within the existing legal framework and suggests desirable changes. First, he argues that by over-expansion companies become larger to satisfy the internal aspiration of directors and managers rather than the desirable requirements of increased economic efficiency and growth. Second, he maintains that company expansion sometimes takes place without consulting the shareholders and even in opposition to their interests. Here he offers a short modern re-statement of

1. A. A. Berle and G. C. Means, *The Modern Corporation and Private Property,* Macmillan, New York, 1933 and Walter Lippman, *The Good Society,* Allen and Unwin, 1938.

the argument of Horace B. Samuels in his celebrated *Shareholder's Money.* Dr. Jervis raises two fundamental issues that cannot be ignored in the next Companies Act. British industry has in some sectors been expanding physically without growing commercially either in terms of real output or in response to the preferences and judgments of the owners.

If either or both of these charges is substantiated, British industry is less efficient than it could be, not because of the principle of limited liability company organisation, but because the laws covering the conduct of companies have permitted them to develop in ways that do not satisfy the purpose of maximising the efficiency of resources, and have thus caused the private interests of those who run companies to diverge from the general interest of consumers.

It may be argued that large firms controlling companies with physically dissimilar products may be efficiently run and be able to reap economies of large-scale management, financing, marketing and risk-spreading. Unilever would seem to be an example, and in international markets such companies can grow not because of monopolistic power but because of their ability to reduce costs below those of smaller competitors. Dr. Jervis's view is that in organisations with dissimilar products there are increasing managerial costs of administration and co-ordination. It is true that arguments for "rationalisation" used in the 1930s were not well-founded and that the strength of some mergers rested more on market dominance and the power to exclude competitors than on the capacity to satisfy consumers.

Dr. Jervis's argument is timely. It has long been evident that individual shareholders are not able (or not interested enough) to exercise a direct influence over the boards of their companies; what influence they exert is indirect by selling the shares of companies with which they are dissatisfied.

The views of the institutional shareholder are heard too infrequently rather than too often. The effect is to leave the boards of many British companies with a vacuum which they find themselves having to fill by exercising control without reference to their sizeable blocks of shareholders. This is a central problem of the divorce of ownership from control that remains to be solved. Certainly the life office doctrine, that ownership can be exercised without responsibility, cannot be upheld. They are virtually trustees for their policy holders' money and, even less than individual shareholders, they cannot influence companies indirectly by selling their shares because they often hold blocks too large to dispose of without alerting other shareholders and adversely affecting the market.

Hobart Paper 39 *N. J. Gibson*
February 1967

Financial Intermediaries and Monetary Policy

One of the most essential parts of the legal framework is the provision of a system of money and banking to lubricate production and distribution. In 1959 the report of the Radcliffe Committee on the Working of the Monetary System doubted the efficacy of monetary policy in part on the ground that the development of financial intermediaries—banks, building societies, hire purchase finance companies, insurance companies, superannuation funds, investment and unit trusts—was frustrating governmental policy in controlling the supply of liquid resources available for use as money.

In 1960 the Institute published a symposium of essays under the title *Not Unanimous,* in which Professors R. F. Henderson (now at the University of Melbourne, Australia), E. Victor Morgan, F. W. Paish and the late Wilfred King doubted the economic theory and application of the Radcliffe Committee; Sir Roy Harrod ventured the view that "more can be learnt in this slim volume about the 'working' . . . of our monetary system than from the Report itself." It may, nevertheless, be as a consequence of the Radcliffe Report that both Conservative and Labour Governments since 1960 have tended to make less use of monetary policy and more use of selective controls over financial intermediaries on the ground that they were frustrating monetary policy. After seven years it may now be time to consider whether this position is theoretically tenable and whether the practical policies that have emerged from it have been effective or had desirable results.

In this *Hobart Paper,* Dr. N. J. Gibson, a young economist specialising in financial institutions at the University of Manchester, re-examines the development of financial intermediaries in recent times and considers their capacity to influence government monetary policy. His general conclusion is that their growth has contributed to the efficiency with which scarce resources are put to the most desirable use, that they have not materially negatived monetary policy, that where they have an effect it can be offset by the monetary authority, and that if government provides a stable economic environment there would be less occasion for direct disturbance of the activities of financial intermediaries. Dr. Gibson deploys his description and argument with careful economic analysis and copious statistical illustration.

His argument and conclusions are very different from those we have been accustomed to expect from economic writers and commentators in the last few years. They have been conspicuously absent from government policy and from the thinking of economists who have advised recent ministries. In view of the failure of efforts by governments of both parties to run the economy by techniques which have ignored the underlying reasoning elaborated by Dr. Gibson, his *Hobart Paper* provides a timely reminder of economic principles ignored and of economic consequences that seem unavoidable if they continue to remain unheeded.

Apart from its interest for economists, politicians and civil servants closely concerned with economic policy, Dr. Gibson's *Paper* will be valuable for teachers and students of economics as a concise but authoritative account of financial institutions and their impact on monetary policy.

The Institute is grateful to Professor E. Victor Morgan of the University of Manchester and to Professor Harold Rose of the London Graduate School of Business Studies for commenting on drafts of the manuscript. The Institute offers Dr. Gibson's analysis and conclusions as a scholarly contribution to a department of economic policy in which there is evident need for fundamental rethinking.

Second Edition, 1970

Professor Norman Gibson's *Hobart Paper* has since 1967 found a wide welcome amongst students and teachers of economics.

For the Second Edition Professor Gibson has revised the text. He reviews the development of financial intermediaries since 1967, emphasises the increasing recognition of the changes in the supply of money, and identifies the chief culprit in the failure of government to master inflation, since the authorities manipulate the supply of money to maintain the market price of gilt-edged securities to facilitate servicing the national debt and raising loans for government expenditure. He writes that it provides "a fundamental clue to British monetary policy since the Second World War." He questions whether this objective of governmental financial policy is well conceived, doubts whether the understandable anxiety of government to maintain the demand of investors for government securities should be the over-riding *desideratum* and whether it need conflict with the objective of mastering inflation.

Hobart Paper 40
August 1967

F. G. Pennance

Housing, Town Planning and the Land Commission

One of the most difficult parts of the legal framework to erect is the structure of rights of the ownership and disposal of property and land. In Great Britain three voluminous reports during the war by Barlow, Uthwatt and Scott were followed by legislation that has been defective. Another effort is being made in the Land Commission Act, 1967, which could have far-reaching consequences on the use of land in housing, town planning, agricultural and other purposes.

The Institute therefore invited Mr. F. G. Pennance, Head of the Economics Department at the College of Estate Management, to amplify into a *Hobart Paper* a lecture he delivered to an audience of chartered auctioneers at Oxford in March 1967. He combines the qualities of authority, independence and clear thinking required for *Hobart Papers* and has tried to describe recent legislation and its economic implications in language suitable for lay readers as well as for specialists. With the minimum of technical terms apparently inevitable in a technical-legal-economic subject he has written in short compass a review that will be of exceptional value to teachers and students of economics as well as to professional specialists in the selling and buying of land and property, and to observers, writers and politicians concerned with public policy.

What has emerged is a penetrating analysis of the economic effects of the Land Commission and of the betterment levy established by the 1967 Act. He doubts whether it is desirable to tax the development value in land by special machinery rather than as one source among others of general taxable capacity. He questions whether the Land Commission should combine its powers to acquire and manage land with its power to collect the betterment levy. He sees no argument for a land commission to hold and supply land for house builders and looks rather to more flexible town planning, building densities, housing standards, subsidies and rent control to provide a better solution. He maintains that the middleman function proposed for the Land Commission would have little advantage for suppliers of housing and industrial building and normally none for sellers of land. He sees little room for the much-publicised "Crownhold" form of tenure. He doubts whether the effects of the levy on housing development will be significant or beneficial and therefore judges that the long-term effect in increasing the influence of public authorities over the use of land would be undesirable.

The main useful role Mr. Pennance sees for an independent land authority is in stimulating the market to work more efficiently by removing the restrictions on it. He ends with an ingenious proposal; to replace much of the paraphernalia of town planning legislation, to treat development rights in land as a saleable commodity and to invite tenders from the general public in the expectation that efficiency in the use of land would be increased.

The *Paper* serves to illustrate the analytical approach Mr. Pennance is adopting with Mr. Hamish Gray of the Institute in their researches into the housing market on which a report will be published in 1968. Their approach differs fundamentally from much other work on housing in its micro-economic emphasis on the supply of and the demand for housing, in contrast to studies embracing projections of housing "needs" based on assumptions about the size of families and other technical categories.

In his present study Mr. Pennance has written a thoughtful, thorough and stimulating analysis that will clarify the economic issues often concealed in the legal and technical phraseology of the legislation and most consequent discussion. His questioning of accepted thinking should provoke discussion among economists and land specialists, and his apparently simple but radical proposal provides an alternative to the tortuous tangle of administrative regulation and discretion.

The Institute is grateful to Mr. Ralph Turvey and Mr. W. A. West for commenting on early drafts.

Hobart Paper 41 *M. H. Cooper and A. J. Culyer*
March 1968

The Price of Blood

The analysis of pricing systems and market relationships in this *Paper* can be applied to commodities and services in the private and public sectors of Western economies, to capitalist and communist economies, and as an analytical tool to all substances that can change hands whatever the ethical, aesthetic or philosophical attitudes of the analyst. Its possible application to, or extension in, water, fire services, refuse collection, and other services supplied wholly or partly free was discussed by young economists in a recent IEA book.[1]

The origin of this *Hobart Paper* lies in the experience in November 1965 of a member of the Institute who, after waiting for a major operation, went into a nursing home because a private bed in the hospital at which his surgeon operated had not been free for two months and seemed unlikely to become available for some time. Bleeding after an operation created an emergency demand for blood from outside sources. Two hospitals, a blood bank and a new donor had to be tapped before the required amount was assembled in time for a life-saving transfusion. The patient asked the pathologist who had assembled the supplies whether voluntary donation was adequate to save life; he replied that emergencies were not unknown but he hoped it would never be necessary to pay for blood as in other countries.

This experience later led the Institute to commission Messrs. Michael H. Cooper and Anthony J. Culyer, Lecturers in Economics at the University of Exeter, to analyse the methods of generating blood supplies in Britain and other countries, to assess their effectiveness and to make proposals for improving and extending channels of collection to remove the possibility of loss of life through shortages. Mr. Cooper is well known for his books on the economics of pharmaceutical supplies and Mr. Culyer has been teaching the economics of the social services and writing a book on the subject with his colleague.

The analysis of blood as a commodity in terms of supply and demand, of

1. *Essays in the Theory and Practice of Pricing,* Readings in Political Economy, No. 3, IEA, 1967.

"shortage" and "adequacy," and of a price may strike the non-economist as distasteful, particularly if he has in mind recent developments in transplantation and in what has been called "spare parts" surgery. This attitude is understandable although it is also part of the common antipathy to buying and selling and "commercialism" in general. It is not surprising that emotionalism and sentimentality, not least from social administrators and sociologists, has clouded the nature of the problem: to ensure that supplies are as large as they can be made to meet demands. A professor of social administration recently said that in the USA "'professional' donors from 'Skid Row denizens,' drug addicts and others . . . live by selling their blood." In contrast he said that in Britain there was "no shortage. . . ." "It is freely donated by the community for the community. It is a free gift from the healthy to the sick irrespective of income, class, ethnic group, religion, private patient or public patient." That this romanticised idyll may conceal shortage is suggested by the inquiry among doctors discussed in this *Paper*. A blood donor writing to the *Daily Telegraph* on 1 March, 1967, referred to his experience in Wormwood Scrubs. He described "the occasional visit of the transfusion unit [which] would arrive to find a brilliantly organised stream of volunteers—murderers, rapists, con-men, fraudulent company promoters and a great variety of other long-term prisoners." It would seem that blood in our voluntary system is drawn from as wide a social and occupational range of donors as in the "professional" system of the USA.[2]

The authors begin by clarifying attitudes and issues in their extreme form by "caricatures": opponents of the notion of a market in blood, and economists who would analyse it as a possible solution of, or a contribution to, the problem of generating the required supplies. The extremes are an ingenious expository device. The first extreme accurately describes the attitudes of many doctors, patients, social critics and others who believe pricing not merely superfluous or inefficient but also wicked. Economists who see some value in analysing the possible effects of pricing do not fit as readily into the other extreme; they would anticipate that fruitful results might emerge from experimenting with a pricing system in countries where blood was supplied exclusively by voluntary donors, but they would find no fault with a voluntary system, unless possibly it were found more costly than pricing.

The authors apply market analysis to the interactions between supply, demand, and price and examine the case for and against payment for blood.

2. The subject is discussed in Professor R. M. Titmuss's forthcoming book, *Commitment to Welfare*, Allen & Unwin, 1968.

They examine the conditions in which pricing might produce supplies that would not be offered in a wholly voluntary system. They conclude with carefully-worded, tentative propositions that as a scarce commodity blood can be submitted to economic analysis, that pricing has been shown feasible by inference from shortages in Britain and from the experience of other countries, that the introduction of pricing (or non-monetary inducement) in a dual system of voluntary and paid donors might reduce waste and increase supplies, that information is lacking about the reasons why people donate (or do not donate) blood and that there is a lack of information on the costs of assembling blood both in a voluntary and in a pricing system.

The authors have found it difficult to validate their economic analysis by empirical studies because of the lack of official statistics on the cost of generating, collecting, transporting, storing and transfusing blood (and the wastes of local over-supply). They have, however, been able to draw plausible inferences from the available data. The regrettable obscurantism of the Ministry of Health and the National Blood Transfusion Service on information that should be public property has, nevertheless, made it difficult for independent observers to assess the possible efficacy of the two systems or the effect of introducing pricing in an effort to supplement the supply of blood generated by the voluntary system. The "free" blood in a voluntary system requires the use of considerable resources, including television and press advertising. It is therefore misleading and short of deceptive to compare the "free" blood of a voluntary system with the paid blood of a "commercial" system. It has been found impossible to confirm or reject the estimate of £7 per pint expenditure in collecting blood in the voluntary system indicated independently by two medical sources. The authors suggest that more expenditure on advertising and methods of encouraging voluntary donors might be less costly than a pricing system; but there is little information about costs in both systems, and they conclude that in the long run the cost advantage will probably lie with pricing.

They have made an unanswerable case for a trial period in which the voluntary donor is supplemented by the fee-paid donor so that the results can be judged in practice, and not prejudged by doctrinaire obfuscation. The ultimate test is whether both systems in harness would yield larger supplies than the voluntary system alone. Pricing may repel some voluntary donors or shift them from volunteers to professionals, but the authors argue it would tap new sources.

The Institute wishes to thank Professor J. M. Buchanan of Virginia University and the three medical doctors who commented on an early draft:

Mr. R. S. Murley, a surgeon, Dr. Ivor M. Jones and Dr. John Seale, physicians. They are not committed to the author's analysis and conclusions. The *Paper* is published for economists, doctors and the public at large who may be patients one day, as an application of economic analysis that yields thought-provoking conclusions on a problem in which rational thinking must overcome emotional feeling in arriving at a solution that may reduce suffering and save life.

Hobart Paper 42 *E. G. West*
June 1968

Economics, Education and the Politician

It is a superstition of social science that the citizen is competent to make valid choices as a voter or as a consumer of everyday or household purchases but not in decisions concerning what may be grouped as welfare services—education, medical care, housing and pensions, to name the four most important. This, indeed, is one of the main intellectual buttresses of the view that the citizen can be left as a consumer to decide the disposition of his income in the market for consumption but not in the market for welfare.

Since its foundation ten years ago Institute authors have questioned this dichotomy: research by its staff and a widening range of economists in the universities has repeatedly confirmed that it is not well-founded. From its first work, *Pension in a Free Society,* in 1957, followed by *Hobart Papers* on rent restriction, medical care, education, taxation and expenditure, housing and the land, the Institute has broken new ground in economic analysis of the supply of and the demand for welfare services and the possibilities of, and the desire for, markets in welfare. In 1963 it supplemented its economic analyses by empirical field researches into the state of public knowledge and preferences in taxation and in the education services, in medical care, and in pensions. In 1965 it followed with a longer study of the institutional framework of education and with a second and fuller empirical field research embodied in *Choice in Welfare, 1965.* The conclusions of most of these works have challenged the conventional view held alike by academics, by politicians and by opinion-forming journalists on public preferences in welfare and on the possibilities of reform. Despite the consequent shift in the balance of intellectual judgement, academics concerned with education (mostly sociologists or social administrators) persist in favouring a system of monopolistic, state-controlled, standardised, universal, comprehensive education. This is in itself a perplexing facet of the relationship between intellectuals and government, and of the view of academics on the appropriate province of government in academic life. The anxiety of academics for freedom of scholarship might have been expected to incline them towards scepticism, even cynicism, certainly opposition to government control over education. Yet in 1968 the prevailing attitude is almost exactly the opposite.

What *New Society* has recently described as "the intellectual directors of education . . . who have not yet got their knighthoods," as distinct from the educational establishment comprising chief education officers, union officials and school headmasters, share this largely uncritical view of the role of government as the source of finance for education and as the controller of its organisation, staffing and curricula. Among the names listed were Professor Brian Simon, Mr. Brian Jackson, Mr. Howard Glennerster, Professor Peter Townsend, Dr. Michael Young, Professor D. V. Donnison, Dr. Ian Byatt, Professor Peter Hall, Professor John Vaizey and Mr. Tyrrell Burgess.

The second batch of policy-makers or opinion-formers are the politicians. It has long been a complaint of observers that the main spokesmen for the Labour and Conservative parties are barely distinguishable in their views on education policy. The two leading figures commonly named have been Mr. C. A. R. Crosland, when he was Minister of Education, and Sir Edward Boyle, a former Minister of Education. It does not follow that all the influential members of their parties share their views on the future relationships between government and education; nevertheless, with few exceptions Labour has stood for increasing governmental control of education and the Conservatives, with a few more exceptions, have stood for much the same policy. But liberal politicians in all three parties have shown interest in the work of IEA authors on the evolution of methods of introducing choice and independence into education, not least through the mechanism of the voucher system.

The third group of influential opinion-makers are the journalists, not least the education correspondents of the national newspapers. Except for a handful, particularly in the *Times Educational Supplement,* they seem too committed to existing administrative institutions and short-term political consideration to contemplate radical development of a freer market in education. They showed interest in the efforts of Enfield parents to maintain choice in the structure of state education. But in education "credits" as a means of strengthening choice they have evinced little interest or voiced opposition based in ignorance of what was being proposed and on the pretext of "administrative impracticability."

Economists must persist in discovering whether the same principles that have brought plenty and rising standards in consumption—competition, choice, consumer authority and responsiveness of suppliers in markets—can be applied to education. It is part of the purpose of Dr. E. G. West's *Hobart Paper* to extend the argument from analysis and principle to that of administrative and political application. He has endeavoured to apply the reasoning of his earlier pioneering studies[1] to the circumstances of education policy in 1968 and to the difficulties that can no longer be denied of finding enough finance from taxation to provide education not merely at rising standards but even at standards long taken for granted. The main administrative device Dr. West deploys is that of the education "credit" (voucher) and he shows how it could be used to avoid situations such as that at Luton where the local authority found itself unable to provide schooling for many children at the primary stage, and more generally in the "deprived" areas as described by the Plowden Report, in order to attract additional finance for education and to raise standards in all forms of education and in all its stages.

Dr. West seeks to refute the objections advanced by academics and others to the notion of expanding choice and encouraging suppliers of education to increase the total supply. In the last resort it may be that the practicability of the education "credit" cannot be judged except by introducing an experiment on a scale and for a period sufficient to yield conclusions for more general application. In the meantime administrative difficulty is no decisive objection to the idea of the "credit," which is essentially a device for distributing purchasing power rather than "free" education in order to enlist the closer interest of parents, to galvanise additional resources for education, and to make education a subject for family and household budgeting so that it receives at least as much consideration as decisions about clothing, or furnishings, or motoring, or holidaying.

The academics, the politicians, the journalists, have been so preoccupied with immediate problems of education financing and with the blind alley of "social cohesion" and the supposed need for "integration" of state and private education that they have failed to give much attention to a much more fundamental requirement: a new device to excite interest in education, to enlist the active day-to-day attention of parents, to make the suppliers of education more responsive to the preferences of consumers, and not least to direct a larger proportion of the national income to education than can be raised in taxation. For many years most academics, politicians and journalists have not had a new thought with much relevance for the fundamental requirements except the recurrent plaint that there is not enough money for education and that government must find more from taxation. It is time they abandoned their false scents and embarked on a more radical approach to the organisation and financing of education.

1. *Education and the State,* IEA, 1965, and his contribution to *Education: A Framework for Choice,* Readings in Political Economy 1, IEA, 1967.

Dr. West also throws new light on the reasons why such market inequalities as he documents in the state sector are tolerated by well-meaning politicians pledged to equality in education. His revealing application of economic analysis to the behaviour of party politicians and administrators disposes of the benign image of men free from motives of power, ambition or personal gain and inspired only by the highest ideals. For economists perhaps the most significant distinction between the calculations of politicians and those of business men is that the former are less exposed to question or challenge by competitors than the latter in the market place. Thus, in education Dr. West shows how the aim of policy has shifted imperceptibly from promoting the best interests of the child to perpetuating the power of those in charge of the existing apparatus—a goal business men might cherish but competing business men render unattainable in the market place.

Dr. West's *Hobart Paper* is designed for readers who are concerned about education as parents, as citizens, as taxpayers, as well as for readers who are concerned with the economics of education as teachers and students. The *Paper* challenges much accepted doctrine, much conventional unwisdom, and much of the accepted attitudes of almost all the parties and pressure groups—sociological, administrative, trade union and political. No reader can conscientiously doubt the need for far-reaching departures in educational policy after reading Dr. West's indictment of shortcomings in the dominating state sector which would not be tolerated in the least important industry or service conducted by private business men.

The Institute offers this *Hobart Paper* as the effort of a conscientious academic of high integrity and a developed social conscience to import into the discussion of education a new element that has long been lacking but that must be considered as a means of removing the demonstrable deficiencies of our educational system.

Hobart Paper 43
July 1968

Sir Sydney Caine

Paying for TV

One of the services in which the possibility of a market with competition between suppliers and choice for consumers has been doubted, opposed or operated imperfectly is broadcasting. Several government inquiries have reported on the structure of the broadcasting industry; several have pointed to the possibilities of competition and choice, but the last one, the Pilkington Committee of 1960, recommended governmental controls with a maximum of monopoly and a minimum of competition.

Now that new contracts have been awarded by the Independent Television Authority under substantially the same system as before (the Pilkington recommendations for more centralised operation were not accepted), the Institute is publishing a *Hobart Paper* by Sir Sydney Caine, an economist who has been a distinguished civil servant, university administrator and Deputy Chairman of the ITA. He reviews the structure of British television and its two central economic characteristics—the separation of income from expenditure and the divorce of the viewer's payment by licence duty from his receipt of the television programmes. He analyses the financial results of the system for the viewer, the suppliers of programmes, and the Exchequer; and the methods by which the BBC and ITA programmes are paid for. He examines the fundamental issues of policy arising from the tenuous relationship between the resources available to television and the demand for programmes and from the technical conditions in which the services are supplied to the degree that they create a monopoly.

He explores five of the possible financial changes in the existing limited local monopolies of the independent television companies financed by advertising revenue: that they be provided by a public corporation or corporations; that, as recommended by the Pilkington Committee, the ITA control the sale of advertising time and buy programmes from contractors appointed as the programme producers; that their contracts be awarded provided profits above a stated figure are put to reduction of charges; that contract rentals be based on income or profit; and be put to competitive tender. After analysing the first three proposals, and dismissing them as unsatisfactory or impracticable, Sir Sydney concludes that the balance of advantage has shifted towards competitive tender.

But he goes further. He does not accept that the existing structure is unchangeable. He argues that monopoly is not inevitable and emphasises the possible advantages of extending advertising to channels now financed by licence duty. He concludes that the structure could with advantage be changed by extending the principle of Pay-TV to all channels as the means of establishing for the first time a market in television in which the income and expenditure of the suppliers of programmes will be more closely related and the payment by viewers and the receipt of programmes more closely and graphically linked. Although this transformation may appear "revolutionary," Sir Sydney argues that, combined with the continued acceptance of advertisements, it would establish for television the system of financing which is accepted for the Press and which has ensured for it a much higher degree of independence than it could have exercised if it had been financed by governments from taxation. And, while he sees the practical difficulties, not least those of costs, in changing to Pay-TV, Sir Sydney maintains it is the most hopeful solution in the long run and that its practical possibilities should be fully investigated before decisions on the structure of the television industry are made.

Sir Sydney's *Hobart Paper* is made all the more timely by the prospect of an extension in the licence of the company experimenting with Pay-TV in London and Sheffield. Lord Pilkington, an enterprising business man, has protested proprietorially in *The Times* (20 June, 1968) that his Committee concluded unanimously that Pay-TV supplied a service for which viewers were prepared to pay fees sufficient to cover its cost, "it would significantly reduce the value to viewers of the BBC and ITA services": programmes broadcast on Pay-TV services in return for fees would not be available to BBC viewers who paid by licence duty or to ITA viewers who paid nothing. Pay-TV, he claimed, restricts rather than widens the range of programmes available "to ordinary viewers" and "it is essentially a minority service for urban viewers who have cash to spare." It is possibly, though not certainly, true that the existing system of Pay-TV in small and limited areas restricts the programmes available to the "free" viewers of BBC and ITV; but the argument of limitation of choice would be far weaker if Pay-TV were universally available and would have no application at all to a system in which all channels were operated by Pay-TV.

A significant advantage of Pay-TV would be to attract extra revenue for expansion and improvement of the television system. Yet Professor R. H.

Coase, a member of the IEA's Advisory Council, has recently argued that at costs of only a penny to fivepence per viewer per hour (depending on programme costs and audience size) it need not prove expensive.

The notion that television is a public service that only government should control is not supported by experience in the USA, Canada, Australia, New Zealand and other countries. There it yields a wider range of programmes than the narrow range provided by "a public service" that might not descend to the depths, but would not rise to the heights, of the programmes supplied by independent services. Experimentation in television broadcasting ought not to be prohibited. A public system of broadcasting must be defective if it cannot tolerate experimentation.

Sir Sydney's *Hobart Paper* aptly illustrates the purpose of the series in discussing fundamental principles underlying economic policy that tend to be submerged below administrative convenience and political expediency. Not least it demonstrates that it is feasible for the direct influence of the consumer to be brought to bear even on a service in which technical considerations have appeared to limit the possibilities of competition and choice in a market.

Hobart Paper 44 *A. A. Walters*
January 1969

Money in Boom and Slump

The most essential element in the legal institutional framework is the provision of a monetary system which permits the economy to work with the minimum of friction and the maximum of scope for adaptation to change in the conditions of supply and demand. Since its foundation in 1957, Institute publications have emphasised the importance of the quantity of money as a fundamental function of government. When in August 1959 the Report of the Radcliffe Committee on the Working of the Monetary System concluded unanimously[1] that the important element in government control of the economy was not the quantity of money but the general state of "liquidity" in the economy, the Institute invited six distinguished monetary authorities, Professors F. W. Paish, E. Victor Morgan and R. F. Henderson, Mr. Peter (now Lord) Thorneycroft (who had resigned as Chancellor of the Exchequer in 1957 because he considered the Government had not effectively controlled public expenditure and the quantity of money), and the late Sir Oscar Hobson and Mr. Wilfred King, to examine the Committee's analysis and conclusions. Their findings were published in January 1960 under the title *Not Unanimous* in which they found that the quantity of money was a central element in government management of the economy. Their conclusion had been anticipated in a broadcast in October 1959 by Mr. John B. Wood, then an economist with Lazard Bros., and a trustee of the Institute from 1962 to 1968, in which he voiced his doubts about the economic analysis in the Radcliffe Report which consigned monetary policy to a "subordinate" role in management of the economy. He argued that Radcliffe was wrong in urging that the quantity of money should be controlled in order to manage interest rates rather than the general level of prices, and that the Bank of England could not determine both the level of interest rates and the amount of National Debt it held: the choice of one decides the other. In November Lord Robbins noted in a House of Lords debate the faint praise with

1. The nine signatories were: Lord Radcliffe (chairman), Professor A. K. (now Sir Alec) Cairncross, Sir Oliver Franks, Viscount Harcourt, Mr. W. E. Jones, Professor R. S. Sayers, Sir Reginald Verdon Smith, Mr. George Woodcock, and Sir John Woods.

which Radcliffe had damned monetary policy. In July 1964, Professor E. Victor Morgan outlined in *Hobart Paper 27* a sophisticated structure of rules to govern the conduct of monetary management as a superior alternative to the "physical" control of hire-purchase and other funds by rationing. He argued that Radcliffe and other critics of monetary policy had exaggerated its limitations and that its risks arose in large part from defects in government policy.

Until the early 1950s it was thought that Keynes' analysis of "liquidity preference" in the effect of monetary policy on the economy had disposed of the quantity theory of money, which for decades had indicated that the quantity of money was a decisive influence on the level of money incomes. Since the early 1950s the Keynesian view has been increasingly challenged in the USA by the Chicago school of economics headed by Professor Milton Friedman, who has formulated the quantity theory of money in a more sophisticated form and who has found historical support for it. In this *Hobart Paper*, Professor A. A. Walters, one of Britain's outstanding younger economists, examines the evidence of British monetary history since 1881 and concludes that, until at least the Great Depression of 1929, there was a clear relationship between the quantity of money and the state of activity in the economy, and less conclusively but still significantly for the period since 1945. For most of this period the effect of the supply of money on prices and incomes was significant, and it was in the direction predicted by the quantity theory. He concludes that the stock of money cannot be ignored in government monetary policy on managing the long-run stability of the economy.

Many in British academic economics, practical banking, financial journalism and politics will have to modify or abandon long-held, uncritically harboured, cavalier predilections and illusions about the unimportance of money in economic policy. Although much analytical refinement and empirical research remains to be done, it would seem that money is likely to move nearer the centre of the stage in governmental management of the economy in the 1970s than it has been for half-a-century since the 1920s. Management of the quantity of money holds out a better hope than physical controls and financial rationing of mastering inflation and constructing a monetary environment within which the economy can respond to changing techniques and demands. For this we have to thank mainly a small body of economists who refused to be stampeded by the over-simplifications drawn by over-zealous acolytes from Keynes' supposed destruction of the classical system of economic thought; patient analysis and research have demonstrated that Keynes' emphasis on liquidity preference (the preference for cash and the influence on it of the rate of interest on less liquid assets) does not mean that government can let the quantity of money vary uncontrolledly so long as "liquidity" is managed to maintain the value of gilt-edged or "full employment." Money has been a perennial pre-occupation of economists for 200 years. It can be both a lubricator of exchange which John Stuart Mill explained in 1848 and a monkey wrench, as Professor Friedman has described it, when it is not controlled. Perhaps economists need to return to the efforts made by Professor F. A. Hayek to devise a "neutral" money that would lubricate without fouling the works.

The Hobart Papers are normally directed to lay readers as well as specialists and are therefore written in non-technical English. Professor Walters' study has employed econometric methods and mathematical devices which some readers will find difficult to follow. We have made an exception in this case in order to dramatise the importance of the recent researches by American and British economists for British monetary policy in the 1970s.

The Institute has to thank Professor F. W. Paish for offering comments on the text in early draft. Like him and the Advisory Council, it is not committed to Professor Walters' analysis and conclusions, but offers the Paper as an impressive demonstration of the results of economic research and its significance for monetary policy.

Hobart Paper 46
May 1969

Harry G. Johnson and John E. Nash

UK and Floating Exchanges

For Britain as an international trading community that exports a fifth of its annual product to pay for imports of food, raw materials and, increasingly, consumer goods, the creation of an international monetary system in which traders can receive and make payments for goods and services is a prime essential. Whatever difficulties Britain has had in creating an efficient home economy have been exacerbated by an inefficient system of international payments. Whether or not the devaluations of 1949 and 1967 have enabled Britain to compete effectively in world markets, discussion has turned increasingly to the advantages and disadvantages of moving from fixed to floating exchange rates.

This is an issue that divides economists not only of different schools of thought but also economists who broadly agree on the merits of a free economy within a liberal world order. Some see advantages in a system that would link national currencies in much the same way as those of counties, provinces or states within a single political unit; and they tend to favour fixed exchanges not least because the loss of currency reserves with accompanying weakening in the exchange rate acts as a discipline on politicians tempted to expand the money supply in order to raise prices continuously and maintain a high level of employment. Others see fixed exchanges as a denial of the working of markets in international currencies where continuous adjustments in rates would bring supply and demand into balance without the disturbances associated in post-war years with fixed exchanges.

To present the argument on both sides for students and teachers of economics as well as businessmen, bankers and people concerned with public policy in international monetary affairs, the Institute invited Professor Harry G. Johnson and Mr. John Nash to state the opposing views. Professor Johnson has written a characteristically cogent theoretical analysis of the arguments for floating sterling and Mr. Nash an impressive account of trends and influences in the international monetary system which lead him to doubt the wisdom of floating. The two essays thus constitute a contrast of method and approach as well as in argument. Professor Johnson writes essentially as an academic economist with nevertheless an insight into the working of international monetary institutions; Mr. Nash writes primarily as a practising banker with nevertheless an insight into the theoretical implications of alternative exchange systems and an academic competence in the subject.

It may be that when the theoretical arguments have been exhaustively deployed the view of readers on whether sterling should be linked with other currencies free to float will depend not so much on economic subtleties as on individual judgement about which system is likely to give politicians the less scope for mismanaging their domestic economies in ways that most suit their often short-sighted political interests.

Hobart Paper 47 *F. W. Paish*
June 1969

The Rise and Fall of Incomes Policy

In September 1964, when the incomes policy was in its infancy, the Institute invited Professor F. W. Paish, whose incisive economic analysis of British monetary policy has shed much light on the working of the British economy, to analyse the economics of "incomes policy" and Mr. Jossleyn Hennessy to indicate what lessons could be learned from attempts to operate "incomes policy" on the Continent. Their two texts were published as *Policy for Incomes?* In the last five years "incomes policy" has had a chequered career that has finally ended in all but generally recognised failure: only politicians and others whose intellectual reputations are at stake refuse to confess defeat. Although it may have dammed an increase in incomes in an industry or a group of industries for a time, it has patently failed to prevent inflation; it has diverted attention from the fundamental changes in the British economy that should have been undertaken and that would have had to be undertaken if it had not had such a long trial; and it has created new stresses and strains that would have been avoided if it had not been introduced or if it had been abandoned as soon as its failure had become apparent. In this period Professor Paish and Mr. Hennessy revised their texts for second, third and fourth editions in October 1966, February 1967 and October 1968.

The economic destruction of "incomes policy" has now changed from its merits, which are seen to be few, and its demerits, which are more obvious, to the reasons for its failure and the extent to which statistics record its unhappy history. In considering a further publication on the subject, the Institute decided that the time had come to complement *Hobart Paper 29* with a second *Hobart Paper* that would examine the newer issues as they had evolved in the five years since 1964. Professor Paish has written an almost entirely new text. In it he closely examines the statistical evidence on wage rates, earnings, the wage trend, output per man-hour, productivity and productive potential, income from employment, unemployment and unused productive potential, personal incomes and consumption, the balance of payments and stock accumulation, labour costs and export prices, and the terms of trade.

Professor Paish's close analysis of the recent economic history also provides an incisive commentary on government policy and the power of trade unions in conditions of high employment, and also material for judging the likely trend of economic events in the home economy and in the balance of payments with other countries. He concludes that the required surplus on overseas account to finance current trade and repay debts is unlikely to be reached by 1969 and that the desired target of a £500 million surplus is unlikely to be reached until the second half of 1971 at the earliest. He judges that, even if increasing confidence in sterling lessens the desire of external creditors for repayment of debt, it would be necessary to maintain a surplus of £300 million a year or more. This aim, he argues, implies that incomes must "never again" be allowed to rise as fast relatively to output as in the last few years; and this, in turn, that the margin of unused productive resources and the average level of unemployment must be higher than it has been since the end of the war.

These will be regarded as unwelcome conclusions from a rigorous analysis. They arise not from the dismal science of economics but from the application of its logic to the political failures of government since the early 1960s. The unpalatable truth will have to be faced sooner rather than later that incomes policy is no more likely to be effective if government cannot prevent inflation than sitting on the safety valve of a well-stocked steam engine is likely to prevent the escape of steam. If the economy had been made more mobile and flexible by removing the elements of monopoly in industry and the trade unions, it might have been possible to avoid serious inflation with unemployed as low as 2 per cent, although even that would be difficult in an economy that requires to be responsive to changes in international supply and demand. But recent British governments have done very little to make the economy sufficiently adaptable; instead of removing obstacles to movement—restrictive practices, rent restrictions, ploughing back profits, the dis-incentives to saving, the agglomerations of labour and capital in nationalised industry, subsidies to the inefficient and out-dated, high taxation, and import restrictions—they have had to resort to the doubtful expedient of resisting increases in incomes by persuasion and law. Their failure could have been, and was, foreseen before it was introduced, but the "fair minded" pragmatic British might not have been convinced until it was tried. Five years may be long enough, and the present Government has at long last had to turn to reform the powers of the trade unions. But even that will not be sufficient if the other impediments to the free movement of labour and capital are allowed to remain undisturbed.

Hobart Paper 48
August 1969

F. G. Pennance and W. A. West

Housing Market Analysis and Policy

In Great Britain the structure of rights in the ownership and disposal of houses and land has been the subject of an almost continuous stream of legislation spanning a century or more. During the last half-century the stream has become a spate. The Institute's researches into housing since 1967 have been conducted by Mr. F. G. Pennance, head of the economics department at the College of Estate Management, with the collaboration of Mr. Hamish Gray. Mr. Pennance sums up and goes more deeply into the economic theory of the housing market and the implications for housing policy; and to put the economic discussion into its institutional setting the Institute asked Professor W. A. West to contribute an essay on the legal framework.

Mr. Pennance concentrates on rigorous economic analysis. Making no concession to sociological sentimentality or political predilection, he goes to the economic roots of the housing market and his intellectual reticence does not inhibit him from unequivocal judgement on policy.

Analytical rigour is especially essential in an area of public policy too long confused by false sentiment and emotion, not only from politicians of all parties but also from academics in the sociological faculties of the universities.

Mr. Pennance distinguishes between the market as a mechanism for allocating the supply of housing and the distribution of income to which it has to accommodate itself. As in medical care, education and saving for retirement, supply and demand have been almost inextricably confused in much social commentary. The common fault has been to attribute to "imperfections" in the market the mal-distribution, the bad condition, and the deprivation of housing, dramatised in the television pseudo-documentary Cathy Come Home—faults properly ascribed to the mal-distribution of income. Not the least damaging conclusion has been that since the housing market has been inoperative, housing must be "provided" by government for people with low incomes.

From his analysis of the economics of the housing market Mr. Pennance concludes that fundamentally the formidable obstacles to humane reform lie not in its "imperfections" but in the obstacles put in its way by government—in building and town and country planning controls, in rent restrictions, in the differential taxation of owners and tenants public and private.

The government does damage not only by its acts of policy, however well-intended, but also by fear of its continuance or return. The most potent damage is perhaps done by the continuance, and uncertainty about the expansion, of rent controls. The inability of politicians to revise rent controls with the social and economic changes of the last half-century has stuck British society in a quagmire of out-dated legislation in which humane reform is baulked by political elephantiasis; and the fear of rent restriction, sensibly modified by Mr. Henry Brooke in 1957 and by Mr. Richard Crossman in 1965, still paralyses the supply of housing to let. Even in Australia, where rent restriction has been almost entirely abolished, its relic in some 40,000 houses in New South Wales out of a total of 1.5 million in the Continent still inhibits the inflow of funds to houses for letting.

It is hopeful that discussion has changed from the notion of housing as "a social service" to the prospects of re-creating a market. Mr. Pennance rejects the doubts, voiced by Professor D. V. Donnison, that the prospects are remote because the market has been virtually inoperative for 50 years. Scepticism about the possibility of re-creating a market in housing may originate in part from distaste of "the market" as a social instrument and this in turn from the understanding of "market forces." Economists are themselves partly to blame for failing to explain that "market forces" are acting as buyers and sellers. Far from the market being difficult to re-create, it tends to re-create itself spontaneously wherever they are allowed to come together in voluntary exchange of goods and services, and it is government that prevents the emergence of markets by suppressing them. But the scepticism of subconscious resistance to re-creating markets has provided a tendency to placate the critics by supposing that the market can be re-created step by step in stages. Mr. Pennance offers cogent reasons for gradual restoration but he also argues that a more rapid approach to a market may, paradoxically, be more practicable than a slower, piecemeal approach.

Economists and politicians who have lately come to see the merits, or inevitability of the market are disposed to concede that while it might be the best solution "in the long run," in "the real world" other solutions, less satisfactory but more "practicable," must be taken. The truth, as Mr. Pennance emphasises, is that half a century of "short-run" responses to "urgent practical problems" have built up a massive social problem that no gradual process may suffice to resolve. Short-run practical expedients have successively destroyed the market, and it may be that nothing short of a drastic reform will re-create it.

Professor West's essay on the legal framework with which the housing market has had to contend is a concise compendium of the main legislation and its effects. He writes primarily as a lawyer but to his account of the law and its administration (or mal-administration) he adds legal philosophising and uninhibited judgements, many highly critical, some leading to a general impression that much of housing law is an ass. And he throws out provocative proposals for legal reform, some of which would uproot the law as it stands. Professor West's clear and authoritative account leaves the reader wondering that any elements of housing market can have survived in the face of legal impediment and encumbrance.

Hobart Paper 50 *Brian Hindley*
July 1970

Industrial Mergers and Public Policy

One of the essential parts of the legal and institutional framework is the environment within which industry can most effectively serve society by responding to consumer preferences. Since 1890 the USA has developed a structure of anti-trust ("trust-busting") laws. Although imperfect and sometimes lagging behind technical development, it has helped to maintain a generally although not always competitive economy. In Britain, the development of anti-trust laws is more recent, but since 1948 a series of measures directed against monopoly and restrictive practices has created the substance of British "trust-busting."

The structure of industry is thus the result of two sets of elements: the economic and the legal. Economies of scale in technique, management, marketing, financing and risk-taking tend to increase the size and reduce the number of units of control, known as "firms": diseconomies tend to reduce the size and increase the number. But at a given point in time, or in a given period, the structure of industry is also the outcome of the legal and institutional framework that permits or even encourages the development of firms that are larger (or, less frequently, smaller) than their optimum economic size.

In recent years the British economy has seen the emergence of mergers not only between firms that seem natural complements in horizontal or vertical integration but also "conglomerates" that seem to have no evident common identity.

Dr. Brian Hindley of the London School of Economics turns to an analysis of possible structural imperfections in British industry and what seems to be government policy desirable to ensure that it serves the general interest of the consumer. His *Paper* comes at the point when IRC has spent several years and large sums of public money encouraging mergers it considered desirable and preventing others it considered undesirable. Dr. Hindley examines the rationale for its activities by discussing the reasons why firms merge with one another and asks why their judgement should be thought inferior to the judgement of an outside body such as the IRC. As a major reason for doubting whether mergers between firms serve the consumer, he discusses possible divergences between the interests of owners and managers. He contends that researches do not provide sufficient support for government-sponsored activities such as those of the IRC, but concludes that the possibility of conflict between managerial decisions and the interests of owners and the general public remains.

It does not follow from this, he argues, that a panoply of official bodies should be established. The problem could better be dealt with by removing the market imperfections that give rise to it. This solution would require an environment in which the threat of take-over to a slack management was substantially increased. Such an approach could mean an increase in merger activity. Dr. Hindley examines the criteria by which mergers should be judged. He concludes, first, that the government should ban concentration-increasing mergers between firms in the same activity, second, that it should allow other types of merger to proceed unchecked.

He believes that much of government policy towards industry is based on the supposition that managers can act at variance with the interests of owners. But he does not think that this is a sufficient justification for that policy. He concludes that better reasons are required if government policy towards industry is to continue in its present forms.

Hobart Paper 51
December 1970

Brian Griffiths

Competition in Banking

The money and credit that lubricate exchange are intimately linked with the service of banking, commonly regarded as part of the institutional framework of the market economy that falls within the realm of government regulation. Yet banking, like other financial institutions, is not organised as competitively as it might be. In its examination of the conditions required for the effective functioning of a market the Institute has studied industries and services in which competition is conventionally conceived as impracticable or undesirable. So the first 50 Hobarts contained studies of medical care, television, libraries, transport, education, housing, pensions, parking, telephones, blood. For the first of the second 50 we have invited Mr. Brian Griffiths of the London School of Economics to write an analysis of the means by which banking could be made more competitive.

He has examined banking as a service to individuals and industry. Two characteristics distinguish it from other services. First, for diverse reasons, it works within a self-created network of agreements to restrict competition in the price (rate of interest) it charges borrowers and pays lenders, the so-called "cartel." Second, it is subjected to more complex and inhibiting regulation by government through the Treasury of the Bank of England, than other services to individuals and industry. He is critical of both restrictions.

He argues that the restriction of competition in the main element in which banks could compete, the rates of interest on loans and deposits, is not only disadvantageous to the individuals and industries that lend to or borrow from them, but also banking itself. He elaborates a nine-point programme for the restoration or creation of competition and rebuts the main objections: that the Bank of England would lose control of interest rates, instability of the gilt-edged market would make control of the cash base impossible, the cost of credit would rise, there would be excessively risky investment and bank failures, the conditions of competition could not be obtained unless monetary policy is changed, and the "syndicate" ensures that the supply of Treasury bills is sold and their interest rates are stable. He considers the alternatives to competition: lending-deposit ratio, fixed maximum interest rates on deposits and liquidity controls over financial institutions.

This is a timely contribution to academic and public discussion when a new government is for the first time for decades sounding a new vote of economic philosophy in emphasising the importance of competition. It seems to be prepared to withstand predictable objections to competition since a former government of the same political complexion 40 years ago weakened or destroyed competition in agriculture, coal mining, transport and other industries and services.

The Government's early intentions foreshadow the construction of a more liberal market economy, and Mr. Nicholas Ridley, the Minister responsible for policy on competition, has indicated that an official enquiry into restrictive practices in banking is not unlikely. If the disposal of immediate problems as they emerge is not allowed to conflict or frustrate it, banking will be expected to make itself more competitive. In these circumstances it would be wise for banking to anticipate the structural changes indicated by economic analysis, as in Mr. Griffiths's *Paper,* and that would otherwise be expected by public opinion and parliament. The development of secondary financial intuitions[1] would seem to make inevitable a thawing out of the rigidities in banking.

The Institute is grateful to Professor E. Victor Morgan and Mr. Michael Green, Editor of *The Banker,* for making comments and suggestions that Mr. Griffiths has taken into account in preparing the final text.

1. Professor Norman Gibson, *Financial Intermediaries and Monetary Policy,* Hobart Paper 39, IEA, second edition, 1970.

Hobart Paper 52 *Robert McKie*
March 1971

Housing and the Whitehall Bulldozer

Several early Hobarts discussed the functioning of markets in goods and services in which they are commonly thought to have limited application. Housing is one in which there are two sharply contrasting views: that the market should have minor use since housing is "a social service," and that the failure of the market has been due more to government than to the inherent nature of the service. Mr. Norman Macrae analysed the devastating effects of rent restriction; Professor D. R. Denman demonstrated the consequences of obstructions in the market for land; Mr. F. G. Pennance, one of the most penetrating and incisive economists in housing, analysed the economic consequences of the Land Commission and in the working of the housing market; and Professor W. A. West discussed its institutional setting.

In *Hobart Paper 52* Dr. Robert McKie presents a further study of housing with two significant differences. First, he writes as a political scientist as well as an economist who approaches housing with the sympathies but not the sentimentality of the sociologist. His *Paper* is especially valuable for non-economists: social administrators, town planners, architects, surveyors, transport engineers, public officials, politicians and others who study, influence or determine policy often with too little regard for the economic implications. Second, he does not discuss reform of the institutional framework but accepts it with its existing imperfections and discusses what improvements can be made in the crippled housing market. He concedes he is "taking a view" about what is "politically possible," an approach that Institute authors are normally asked to shun like the plague since they are asked to write as economists and not as politicians, and to "take a view" unnecessarily and avoidably inhibits them from examining causes and consequences that may be excluded by assumptions about what politicians, themselves often wrong, will regard as practicable or expedient.

Dr. McKie analyses the conditions of supply and the demand for housing. On the demand side he begins with a review of the history of public policy on housing in Britain and tries to identify the reasons why government aid was given in the form of subsidised housing rather than direct monetary grants to consumers. Opinion in recent years has moved away from grants to suppliers and in favour of grants to customers, the central advantage of which would be to reconstitute markets which have been allowed to seize up in education and medical care as well as in housing. On the supply side he critically reviews government policy on slum clearance and concludes that it has tragically reduced the supply of housing capable of rehabilitation in the search for high standards, crystallised in Parker Morris, which have prevented people with low incomes from buying the house they preferred and could pay for without endangering health or safety. The Parker Morris episode has been a sad blunder of an approach that permitted technical criteria to take precedence over economic, enthroning "the expert" at the expense of the customer. It is to the credit of the new Government that it learned much in opposition but one's welcome for the statement by Mr. Julian Amery, Minister for Housing and Construction, that the Government is prepared to accept a lowering of standards in private house-building in the hope of reducing building costs, would have been more enthusiastic had he encouraged some relaxation in the public sector; Parker Morris remains however sacrosanct and inviolate. Yet, as Dr. McKie emphasises, Parker Morris standards are higher than the minimum required for health and safety and generate rents higher than some potential consumers would wish to pay. There seems no good reason why consumer demand and preferences should be denied in council but blessed in private housing.

This flaw in official thinking—that housing policy has been determined by technical rather than economic criteria—explains the title of the *Paper*, adapted from the seminal work, *The Federal Bulldozer* by Professor Martin Anderson, now an adviser in the White House. Professor Anderson, whose book profoundly affected thinking in America, sub-titled his book "A Critical Analysis of Urban Renewal, 1949–1962." Dr. McKie's study also discusses the maintenance of income, but the "urban renewal" or slum clearance that bureaucratically cleared large areas containing houses of originally low standards that could be rehabilitated, without regard for the new homes for their occupants, is the aspect that may be most relevant to housing policy in the 1970s. Dr. McKie describes "cellular renewal" in the twilight zones as the most helpful way of rebuilding towns given the existing out-dated and defective legal framework. He discusses a method of revitalising areas of old housing without the massive and wasteful investment of resources and the upheaval of comprehensive redevelopment. This approach would encourage local councils to co-operate with local builders and developers who are ideally equipped for small-scale renovation and renewal.

The central difficulty here is the low or precarious return on the investment sufficient to attract local builders and investors. The tragedy is that 55 years of rent control has almost choked off all private capital. And even the advent of a Government that intends to enable rents to approach their market level may not be sufficient to heal the capital market. (Even in New South Wales, where rent control applies to only 50,000 out of 1,500,000 houses, private capital is still slow to be risked.) The evil that rent restriction does lives after it. And the threat that it may be restored even before it is abandoned may make essential and extra-ordinary effort of co-operation between builders, developers, building societies, insurance companies and local authorities, perhaps backed by government guarantees, if the capital market is to be revived.

The empirical content of Dr. McKie's *Paper* comprises a summary of researches in Peterborough and other towns. Much of this work was conducted without specific reference to the price of alternative housing, although the sample investigated were informed of prices in the local housing market and owner-occupiers were asked to estimate the market value of their homes. Since the Institute has pioneered research into preferences based on prices in education and medical care, it would regard price-tagged research as necessary to complement Dr. McKie's findings. It is desirable for housing research generally to emphasise expectations both in the distribution of existing income between housing and other expenditure and in increases in real income.

Hobart Paper 55 *Douglas Rimmer*
April 1973

Macromancy

Hobart Paper 55, like No. 10 by Dr. Colin Clark, *Growthmanship,* discusses a collection of macro-economic concepts used by economists to measure economic advance in general and the growth in the "gross domestic product" in particular. Dr. Clark analysed the "mythology" of investment as the then widely accepted sure path to economic growth and warned against the overuse or misuse of Keynesian economics. He put the implication for policy tersely:

> An excessive preoccupation with economic growth, advocacy of unduly simple proposals for obtaining it, and the careful choice of statistics to prove that countries with a political and economic system you favour have made exceptionally good economic growth and that countries administered by your political opponents have made exceptionally poor economic growth. (p. 12)

Mr. Douglas Rimmer, Senior Lecturer in Economics in the Centre of West African Studies at the University of Birmingham, now examines more closely the use of GNP as the criterion of economic progress and the rate of investment as the determinant of the increase in gross domestic product. And, like Dr. Clark, he ends with astringent judgement on the mischievous implications for policy that have followed the use of these macro-economic concepts. He insists that supplementing or replacing these preconceptions (or, perhaps more explicitly, misconceptions) by income distribution or employment opportunities are "changes in brand names, not in the recipe." These attitudes have been common at the United Nations and were reflected in the 1969 Pearson Report on international development.

The austere analysis leads to three conclusions: that indefinable and almost inconceivable concepts of "social welfare" be abandoned, that the developing countries make more use of markets without protective tariffs, licensing, subsidies and controls on employment, and that economists concerned for social progress in developing countries would be more justified to advocate voluntary initiatives rather than government compulsion:

> The policies defensible by economic canons . . . invoke Adam Smith rather than Dr Raoul Prebisch or Professor Jan Tinbergen.

Mr. Rimmer's work is based mainly on his studies of West Africa, but his analysis and inferences also apply to other developing countries and more generally to the industrialised countries of the West.

Hobart authors are usually asked to indicate the implications of their analysis for policy. Mr. Rimmer robustly responds that economists may properly confine themselves to demonstrating that economic criteria in common use ("the preconceptions") are baseless without having to put better ones in their place. And his reason goes to the roots of the subject: it is that economists do not know what constitutes the well-being of populations or the means of promoting it. To suppose otherwise is pretentious: "The premises of alchemists and raisers of the dead are modest by comparison with such 'macromancy.'"

Mr. Rimmer is highly critical, though more in sorrow than in anger, of his fellow-economists who work on the developing countries.

> So far as the prescriptive literature of development economics rests on these fundamental concepts, the whole corpus is reducible to ideology. The declared purpose and the prescribed basic strategy of development are essentially rhetorical.

Economists of all schools would recognise the value of macro-economics, properly used. It is its misuse, and/or over-use, which is at issue.

In all, Mr. Rimmer has compiled an acutely analytical examination of the main concepts used in development economics. And his conclusions are none the less important for contemporary thinking and policy because they offer warnings on what economists are not justified in recommending rather than grandiose proposals for large-scale action by government. This Hobart Paper is in the best tradition of a series of which No. 1 by Professor Basil S. Yamey was described by a reviewer as "an academic polemic."

The Institute is grateful to Professors Yamey and Alan Peacock and to Miss Sudha R. Shenoy of the University of Newcastle, Australia, for reading and offering comments on an early draft which the author took into account in his revisions.

Hobart Paper 56
August 1973

L. M. Lachmann

Macro-thinking and the Market Economy

The *Hobart Papers* are intended to contribute a stream of authoritative, independent and lucid commentary to the understanding and application of economics. Their characteristic concern is the optimum use of scarce resources and the extent to which it can be achieved by markets within an appropriate legal framework. The first 50 were published from 1960 to 1970. The second 50 in the 1970s will continue the central study of markets and of the environment created by government.

The interest in the working of markets explains the essentially micro-economic approach, the study of individuals, families, firms or other homogeneous groups as buyers and sellers. Several *Hobart Papers* have been the work of distinguished economists who have used the technique of macro-economics, i.e., the study of the behaviour of aggregates such as national income, expenditure and production. Economics comprises micro and macro elements but their relationship is rarely clarified. Since the 1930s economists who have followed the same 40-year-old approach of J. M. Keynes have often appeared to say, or to think, that macro has 1) replaced 2) or is superior to 3) or is distinct from, micro-economics. And this confusion has for many years been translated into text books and "popular" writing from laymen. Professors Armen Alchian and William R. Allen's *University Economics*, which should be better known in Britain, puts macro-economic analysis of fluctuations in employment, national income and output in its place as "relying on the basic theorems of micro theory."

In this Hobart Paper the methods of analysis of macro-economics and leading macro-economists are further examined by Professor L. M. Lachmann to see how far they yield valid hypotheses about human activity and prescriptions for policy. He divides macro-economics into two main schools: 1) the first, the neo-Ricardians, led in Cambridge (England) by Professors Joan Robinson, Piero Sraffa, and Nicholas Kaldor, 2) and the second, the neo-classical school, represented mainly by Professors Paul Samuelson, Robert Solow and Sir John Hicks. In a recent article[1] Professor James Tobin

1. "Cambridge (UK) v Cambridge (Mass.)," *The Public Interest*, Spring 1973.

is highly critical of the Cambridge School in England and defensive of Cambridge in the USA; in this *Paper* Professor Lachmann is severely critical of both. He finds the analyses of both schools defective on the ground that they have lost sight of the micro-economic foundations of economic behaviour. Although those economists who seem to be critics of the Cambridge School claim to have inherited the micro-economic approach of the neo-classical economists such as Leon Walras and Vilfredo Pareto, Professor Lachmann argues that they have not fully incorporated the essentials of neo-classical economics and that their thinking is no less defective than that of the Cambridge School.

To go to the roots of these fundamental differences in the thinking of economists, Professor Lachmann has had to conduct a highly theoretical discussion that will be easier for economists than for beginners or non-economists. The more fundamental the differences, and the arguable errors, in economic thinking, the more abstract the reasoning must be. If macro-economists have been using poor reasoning and emerging with bad recommendations, it is essential to re-examine the fundamentals of their methods. There is no easy way to grasp their conclusions without an effort to understand how and why they think as they do. This *Hobart Paper* is therefore more theoretical than most have been, but newcomers to economics and laymen will find it rewarding if they persevere in their effort to understand it, perhaps in a second or third reading, because the implications for policy could be radical.

If Professor Lachmann is right, much of the thinking of economists for the last 40 years has misled a generation or two of students, teachers, popularisers of economics in the press and broadcasting, businessmen and politicians. For the inference would be that macro-economics has a useful role to play in economic thinking and policy only if its underlying micro-economics are understood. It is safely used by economists who are constantly aware of the substructure of individual decisions in buying and selling; it is unsafe in the hands of economists who think it *replaces* the substructure, or that it is sufficient to assume that individuals, or individual entities like families and firms, will act in the way that conforms to macro-economic laws, rules, tendencies or generalisations typically made about the behaviour of large groups such as a country, an economy, or a society as a whole.

The reader who masters Professor Lachmann's analysis will find that the implications for policy are far-reaching. He briefly indicates the erroneous conclusions that have been drawn from macro-economics for current policies in the Western countries; the control of incomes and wages as a means of mastering inflation, the management of economic growth, ensuring technical progress, and the monetary policy required for a progressive, open society.

Professor Lachmann's analysis is scholarly but the implications of his approach are revolutionary: for the teaching of economics, for the authority with which economists offer advice, for the respect in which they are held by industry, government and society in general.

The Institute would like to thank Professor Armen Alchian and other economists for reading an early draft and offering suggestions which the author has taken into account in his final revisions.

Hobart Paper 57
February 1974

Keith Hartley

A Market for Aircraft

The *Hobart Papers* are intended to contribute a stream of authoritative, independent and lucid commentary to the understanding and application of economic analysis. Their characteristic concern is the optimum use of scarce resources and the extent to which it can be achieved by markets within an appropriate legal and institutional framework. The first 50 were published from 1960 to 1970. The second 50 in the 1970s will continue the central study of markets of their legal and institutional environment created by government.

The theme can be approached by asking, for each commodity or service examined, whether the market is working as competitively as it could be made to do; if not, whether its defects or "imperfections" are remediable, or derived from technical conditions that are ineradicable, or from economies of scale (or other circumstances) that can be nullified but only at a disproportionate cost; and, if the market cannot be enabled to work tolerably in the interest of the consumer, whether a better method of registering his preferences and apportioning resources to satisfy them is practicable and preferable.

It might be thought that aircraft are a product in which a competitive market is impracticable. So it would seem from the practice of successive British governments. Mr. Hartley contends the contrary. After a close analysis of the conditions of demand for military and civil aircraft and of the conditions of their supply, he concludes that aircraft for the RAF and for British "public"[1] airways are not produced as economically as they could be

1. The word "public" in the sense of governmental (nationalised, socialised, municipalized) is avoided in IEA publications because it is misleading or is commonly used ambiguously—for three reasons roughly corresponding with Abraham Lincoln's celebrated trilogy: "of," "by," "for" the people. It implies control *by* the people, which is usually tenuous or nonexistent. It implies that the commodity is produced or the service conducted *for* the public, which is usually debatable and difficult to prove. And it implies disinterestedness of purpose by "public servants" or "public officials" in contrast to the self-seeking of private ("commercial") services which is question-begging, and fastens attention on *motives* that may be secondary to *consequences.*

and that they would be produced more economically if the market were made more competitive. For, he argues, "the imperfection of this market is a direct result of government intervention rather than any underlying technical characteristics."

The failings he diagnoses are government errors of commission and omission: he argues that government policies or practices of inciting mergers of aircraft manufacturers, subsidising established firms, and on the planning, handling and costing of contracts are themselves obstacles to competition between suppliers from overseas, chiefly the USA and Europe (90 per cent of expenditure on military aircraft is allocated non-competitively).

Mr. Hartley's case may seem to rest on his judgement of past and possible policies, but he also pursues his argument on a ground that is more difficult to resist. He insists that the ultimate cost of the subsidies and wastes in procuring aircraft in imperfect markets is the sacrifice of resources for use in other ways: for the private aircraft industry or more widely in the hospitals, schools, housing, etc. that could otherwise have been built. This conception of cost is fundamental in economics since it was formulated by the Austrian economist Friedrich von Wieser (1851 to 1926). Yet it is central to a rational judgement between policies requiring resources in alternative uses—in government buying of aircraft as well as in the economy at large. Advocates of additional expenditure of resources on plausibly "good" purposes like education or medical care—or even defence—rarely recall that it implies denying resources to other purposes. Still less do they demonstrate that the resources would add more to the total national product in the use they prefer than in other uses.

It would seem that in the artificially imperfect market for aircraft created by government, the consumer—tax-payer or fare-payer—is largely ignored in the effort to serve the options or purposes of politicians in power, technocrats obsessed with technical progress no matter the cost, and subsidised manufacturers. Mr. Hartley has no difficulty in disposing of some of the arguments for special support resorted to when the British aircraft politico-military industrial "complex" is under attack. The balance-of-payments argument for state support is dissected and shown to be at best slender: civil aircraft make a smaller contribution than other comparable industries except shipbuilding since it also became a state-supported preserve. The defence argument is "a costly illusion": the US industry is more competitive and has a substantial cost advantage (as is implicitly recognised by the British Government in its buying policies, e.g. Phantoms, Boeings, etc.). The net benefits of technological advance are difficult to discover and measure. On the apparently weightier argument that a removal of subsidies from British industry would play into the hands of US monopolists, Mr. Hartley counters: "the use of a large-scale US firm is hardly likely to result in a higher price than a small-scale British monopolist." In any event, buying from the least-cost source of supply would not always favour the US: there are more than 20 airframe firms in the West.

Nor does Mr. Hartley accept the common *canard* that the state has had to supply capital for aircraft because private investors could not or would not. He observes that if the private capital market has not supplied funds for civil aircraft it is because there are more profitable uses elsewhere, but that the magnitude, risk or time-scale of the investment is no necessary obstacle.

The production, marketing and purchase of aircraft is rarely discussed in books on economics for students or for laymen who want to know what economists can say that will shed light on the subject. Mr. Hartley provides a concise but crystal clear account of the mechanism by which government negotiates with aircraft suppliers and provides aircraft for the RAF and British Airways (BEA and BOAC). He discusses the economic theory and political economy of the Rolls-Royce RB-211 engine, Concorde, and other aircraft and engines that have provoked sometimes feverish controversy in recent years. And he concludes with clear-cut, unconventional proposals for reform: ranging from the winding-up of the Review Board for Government Contracts introduced in 1968 to the proposal that the British aviation companies should become more specialised sub-contractors to international consortia. Nor does he shrink from the logic of his analysis. He concludes that the state should withdraw from the ownership (but not necessarily from the financing) of civil airlines and that the aircraft manufacturing industry should shed 50,000 to 100,000 employees whose skill could make a larger contribution in other industries.

The Institute has to thank Dr. Brian Hindley and two economists in the universities and Whitehall who prefer to remain anonymous for reading an early draft and for comments that Mr. Hartley has taken into account in his final revisions, although he has not always agreed with their interpretation of events or accepted their advice. It has also to thank Sir Peter Masefield for reading the penultimate text.

Hobart Paper 58 *G. C. Allen and Chiaki Nishiyama*
March 1974

The Price of Prosperity: Lessons from Japan

Differences in economic, social and cultural conditions make international comparisons in the use of markets difficult or precarious, but it may be fruitful to study some outstanding examples of other economies in North America, Europe or Asia that have a record of exceptional achievement to see whether lessons may be learned in Britain or what other methods than the development of market systems might account for more rapid growth.

Certainly by the conventional objective assessments of economic growth, such as measurements of Gross National (or Domestic) Product, it would appear that Japan has, for a lengthy post-war period, far outstripped any Western economy. To discuss the extent to which the Japanese economy has characteristics which differ from those in Britain, the Institute invited two distinguished economists from both countries to outline their interpretation of the Japanese achievement.

Professor Chiaki Nishiyama, although still a comparatively young man, has made a considerable reputation in his country and is well known among Western economists. Professor G. C. Allen is widely acclaimed in Britain for his acquaintance with the Japanese economy that has yielded several authoritative books over 35 years, as well as for his studies of the British economy familiar to students of industrial structure in world universities.

The *Paper* opens with a well informed essay by Professor Nishiyama which concentrates on the two main causes to which he attributes the strength and rapid expansion of the Japanese economy. The first is the system of collective responsibility, *Ringisho,* in which the participants in an enterprise discuss and reach decisions under the chairmanship of the president and are therefore ultimately committed to its successful execution; Professor Nishiyama describes the system as "group dynamics à la Japonaise." The second is the strict monetary policy pursued by Japanese governments despite the uncomfortable adjustments and redeployment of resources it necessarily entailed.

Professor Nishiyama rejects the opposition to economic growth of the "environmental" and "social welfare" lobbies on the ground that it probably raised the real incomes of the Japanese people faster than any alternative policy could have done, including that of heavy government expenditure on the social "infra-structure." Expenditure on the environmental "infrastructure" (roads, sewage, etc.) did not keep pace with economic growth, and an increase in the coming ten years is expected to reduce private investment from 15 to 10 per cent, but Professor Nishiyama maintains there was no argument for developing a "welfare state" which he thinks is "now apparently bankrupted after more than 30 years' experiments" in various parts of the world." He estimates that the exceptionally rapid growth in the 1960s raised income per head from being lower than that of any Western country to approaching that in France and Germany, and that by 1980 average industrial wages are expected to be twice those of Britain and 80 per cent of those in America.

These figures may be compared with two recent prognostications. Lord Rothschild has authoritatively warned that slow growth in Britain would in 12 years reduce its living standards to only half those of France and Germany and about equal to that of Italy. Britain's world influence would suffer an equivalent decline. And Sir Geoffrey Howe, Minister for Trade and Consumer Affairs, said that in 20 years Britain would be overtaken by Spain and Portugal "in prosperity." It seems that Lord Rothschild's apprehensions are supported by a survey of the Hudson Institute which found that France would be the most powerful nation in Europe by 1985 because of its rapid economic growth and that Britain would have fallen behind Austria and would be jostling Spain at the bottom of the European table.

Professor Allen assesses the Japanese economy as seen by an economist in Britain. After reviewing Japanese *Ringisho* and monetary policy he discusses other explanations of the Japanese achievement: her fresh start after the war with new leaders and new policies; US aid; an ample supply of rural labour available for high-productivity industrial work; industrial relations distinguished by employers' strong sense of responsibility for the well-being of employees and a trade union organisation that offered no impediments to technical progress; the high quality as well as the large quantity of industrial investment; high standards of management in industry and government and a creative relationship between the two; a keenly competitive economy; a monetary policy which while maintaining a strongly expansionist trend has, until recently, kept inflation in check; and, above all, adaptability to change. After rapid growth has now come the demand for more leisure and more investment in the social "infra-structure" by private as well as government effort to deal with congestion and pollution. Like Professor Nishiyama, Professor Allen concludes that heavy investment in industries that have yielded returns quickly in market values has been a major cause of the rapid improvement in living standards. Professor Allen argues that the strength developed by economic growth will enable Japan to adapt herself quickly to the changes in the world's energy market.

How far there are lessons for Britain in the Japanese record of growth must remain for individual judgement. Professor Nishiyama was invited to analyse the main reasons for Japanese growth. Professor Allen points to the striking differences between Britain and Japan in their social organisations and their attitudes towards economic progress and contends that Japan's institutional arrangements have been far more favourable than Britain's to economic development during the last 20 years. Hence the more rapid improvement in Japan's living standards. There can be little doubt that faster growth is possible in Britain. The main question is whether her people want it strongly enough to overcome their resistance to change and their predilection for structures and methods that may have been appropriate or up-to-date 70 years ago.

The Institute offers Professor Nishiyama's and Professor Allen's complementary essay as comprising an exceptionally well-informed study in the market and non-market requirements for economic growth and rising living standards that should give economists, industry, the trade unions, politicians and publicists more than the customary food for thought.

Hobart Paper 59
July 1974

Colin Robinson

The Energy "Crisis" and British Coal

Hobart Paper No. 59, by Professor Colin Robinson of the University of Surrey, is especially timely. It examines the nature of the "crisis" in world energy and the supposed exhaustion of supplies in the future that has been widely publicised in recent years by natural scientists, fuel technologists and people anxious about the environment. The "crisis" has been supposed to have become more acute or more imminent since the last months of 1973 and the constricted supplies and higher prices of oil from the Middle East. The centre of interest of Professor Robinson's Paper, and its main merit in throwing light on the subject, is its analysis of the effect of pricing on the demand for and the supplies of fuels—coal, gas, oil, and the newer forms of nuclear and solar energy—in the 1970s and beyond. The main analytical argument is that the role of price has been ignored or understated or misunderstood by non-economists and that, if its effects on demand and supply are taken into account, the conclusions drawn by them are unfounded. And here he draws on the nineteenth-century classical economist W. S. Jevons who, roughly a hundred years ago in the 1860s when there were similar apprehensions that the reserves of coal would be exhausted, argued that the rise in the price of coal as deeper seams were worked would discipline the demand for coal (and, Jevons might have added, stimulate the search for other fuels).

Professor Robinson prefaces his analysis of the current supposed "crisis" by a discussion of the world energy resources, which concludes that there is no more of a "crisis" now than there has ever been or is ever likely to be in the sense of an exhaustion of supplies of fuel. Here he observes that the associated concern about the exploitation and pollution of the environment derives essentially from its treatment by man as though it were "a free good," and that if and where it is exploited by over-use the reason is precisely that no price is, or perhaps can be, attached to it. The implication for policy is that prices should be attached where pricing is possible and other means evolved for rationing its use where pricing is impracticable. It may be difficult for non-economists to see that the environment can, like the former common land enclosed for farming, be a scarce commodity that is despoiled if no one has an interest in conserving and protecting it.

In forecasts of the demand for energy Professor Robinson argues that naïve "models" have been used in which the growth rate in the past has simply been projected into the future with no logical supporting argument. They are defective also because they take little or no account of the effects of changing price. Professor Robinson concludes that some current "models" fall short of the economic sophistication in Jevons a century ago, not least because they do not embrace the effects of price *expectations.*

In two respects he argues the market will not deal with the problems of pollution: the effect on climate and the safety of nuclear power plants. Here he thinks there may be a case for government controls, possibly by international agreement.

Professor Robinson differs from Professor M. A. Adelman who has argued that the OPEC countries are operating a conventional cartel, because there is little prospect that a member country will defect and no prospect of anti-trust action.

In considering the effect of the energy "crisis" on Britain, Professor Robinson focuses attention on the coal industry. He denies that successive British Governments have run down the industry since the end of the war and argues that government policy should now be not to give the industry more protection against competition but less. His estimate that, in addition to the 260,000 employed, at least 140,000 wage-paid miners, and perhaps as many as 200,000, would have been required in 1973 to replace imported fuels indicates the high cost of subsidising coal in terms of the number of workers that would have to be withdrawn from other industries. He examines the four arguments for subsidising the coal industry—the effect on the balance of payments, the security of supplies of fuel, the avoidance of rising oil prices, and the "social" effects—and finds them all wanting. On the contrary, he argues that the fuel oil tax should be removed, the electricity supply industry should be allowed to decide commercially which fuels to burn, coal imports should be freed, and the National Coal Board be allowed to compete more freely with other fuels. In brief, he argues that a much more radical revision of fuel policy is desirable than has been contemplated by recent governments.

The Institute wishes to thank Professor Duncan Burn and technical specialists in three oil companies for reading an early version of Part I of this *Paper* and for offering comments that have been taken into account in the final revisions. The Institute commends Professor Robinson's Paper to students and teachers of economics, and to people in government, industry and the communications media, as a concise and clearly-argued analysis of the energy "crisis" and of the application of pricing theory to its clarification.

Hobart Paper 60
October 1974

R. L. Carter

Theft in the Market

Scarcity is a characteristic of resources used not only in buying and selling, including lending and borrowing, saving and investing, but also in other forms of human action outside formal markets and without the advantage of money pricing. In 1936 Professor R. H. Coase analysed the firm as an entity in which resources were allocated by substitutes for pricing—committees, standing orders, etc.; and it is of interest that firms have developed "internal" or "transfer" pricing as surrogates for "real" market pricing in the effort to approach economic rationality in the sense of the real sacrifices or opportunity costs of using resources in one way rather than another. More recently the application of economic analysis—micro rather than macro—has been extended more adventurously and more confidently to a widening range of non-market situations: antagonism/adversity, crime, charity, education, fertility, labour "participation," leisure and its uses, marriage, politics, racial discrimination, revolution, statistical decision-making.

Some years ago, the Institute considered whether economics could shed light on the increase in theft and the relevance of insurance. At about the same time Professor S. Herbert Frankel suggested the Institute might study the development of private police—private security services—and how far it reflected the under-financing of the government/county police forces. It seemed possible to link these two related subjects in a single study, and the Institute invited Dr. R. L. Carter, then Lecturer in Economics at Brighton College of Technology, later Professor of Industrial Economics at the University of Nottingham, who had written a highly commended essay on the pricing of fire-prevention services[1] and had specialised in the economics of insurance for a doctoral thesis,[2] to apply economic analysis to a combined study of theft, its prevention or detection by police or private security services, and the impact of insurance.

1. "Pricing and the Risk of Fire," in *Essays in the Theory and Practice of Pricing,* IEA Readings No. 3, IEA, 1967.

2. "Competition in the British fire and accident insurance market," University of Sussex, 1968 (unpublished).

Hobart Paper 60 is the result. Dr. Carter begins with what may seem a surprising statistic: that the theft "sector" is equivalent to 2 per cent of national income. A consideration of private and governmental control of theft losses leads him to two central questions. First, what is the optimum quantity of police protection? It may be technically possible to prevent all theft but at such high cost in alternative uses that it is more rational—more "economic"—to tolerate some theft, disagreeable though that course may be on social or moral grounds. Second, do nil-price police services reduce the incentive for individuals or firms to arrange private protection?

An ancillary question is what is the effect of nil-pricing on the total protection—is it more or less than it would otherwise be? Here the economic interest is similar to that of the effect of providing state education or medical care free or at nil prices.

Dr. Carter finds that in the two decades from 1950 to 1970 expenditure on private security grew twice as fast as on the police (and even more if *internal* expenditure on guards, night watchmen, etc. by private firms and government establishments were included). The economic question is how far the county police forces are under-financed because individuals cannot pay for more police protection; and, further, how far individual payment is precluded because police protection is a "public good" from which individuals cannot be excluded and therefore have a "free ride" (for which they cannot be made to pay), and how far it is a private or personal service for which they could or should be made to pay directly rather than by taxation. Here the analysis touches on the American theory of the economics of politics recently developed by The Virginia School headed by Professors J. M. Buchanan and Gordon Tullock.

Dr. Carter describes the rapid growth of the British security industry and provokes the question how far it is complementary to or competitive with the county police forces. He argues that over a wide range of their services private security firms are different from and therefore not in competition with the police. On the other hand, insofar as they reflect a demand for police protection not satisfied by the "official" police, and draw on staffs that have served, or could serve, with the police, they are competitive. Dr. Carter indicates that the attitude of police chiefs varies from approval (Sir Robert Mark, Commissioner of the Metropolitan Police) to disapproval (Mr. William Palfrey, former Chief Constable of Lancashire). How far opposition arises from understandable apprehension about competition and how far from anxiety that private "police" will be inefficient is not clear. Dr. Carter shares the anxiety on general political grounds about a "private police force" and its possible dangers, but concentrates on analysing the economics of the demand for and the supply of police protection and of the interrelationship between the county police forces and private security services.

In his discussion of the insurance industry Dr. Carter presents an interesting analysis of the division of risk between insurer and insured (by deductibles, co-insurance or first-loss insurance), the effects of "moral hazard," and the degree of refinement in pricing (premium-setting). He refers to the 1964 agreement not to compete in accepting high risks, and thereby raises the question whether it is for insurers to exclude undesirable risks or for the consumer to exclude himself by self-insurance if he considers the price (premium) too high. More competitive pricing might have helped to check the increase in theft by encouraging the individual or firm to take more care in protection by burglar-alarm systems, etc., and by penalising those who were careless.

A further valuable discussion is of information on theft prevention and on how it should be provided at nil price by government and at a market price by private agencies. This is an aspect of the economics of information, again largely developed in the USA by Professor George Stigler (University of Chicago) and others.

Dr. Carter's conclusions emerge from his analysis and will strike many in Britain, in the police force and outside it, as unconventional or even provocative. His proposal that the police should extend the range of advisory, cash-carrying and other services for which they charge market prices will strike many as conflicting with the over-simplified orthodox notion of the police as "a public service" that has arisen from inadequate distinction between police services that are "public goods" and those that are private goods. His suggestion that standards of theft prevention in private and government buildings be raised confronts the familiar difficulties about uniform standards for varying risks (as judged by the individuals or companies or politicians in power). The proposal that manned security firms be licensed would make government judge and jury insofar as (local) government police compete with "private police." And his commendation, at least in principle, of the suggestion by Professor Gary Becker (also from the University of Chicago) that thieves be fined in proportion to the harm they do raises profoundly interesting practical and moral issues in the treatment of crime.

Apart from the merits of Dr. Carter's careful and documented analysis, his Paper also draws attention to developments in the application of economics to human activity conventionally thought to be beyond the confines of economics. The Institute has to thank Mr. George Schwartz, formerly of the London School of Economics and a specialist in the economics of insurance, and Mr. Henry Smith, formerly Vice-Principal of Ruskin College, Oxford, for reading and offering comments on an early draft that Dr. Carter has borne in mind in his final revisions.

Hobart Paper 62
April 1975

Samuel Brittan

Participation Without Politics

The characteristic approach of the Hobart Papers has been to study the nature of markets and the reasons for their effectiveness or deficiencies. In particular they have investigated whether a "market failure" was due to the inherent nature of the market or to avoidable defects in the institutional environment within which it is expected to work, and to consider which other arrangements might be superior. The nature of "the market" is still widely and persistently misunderstood by laymen—from politicians to lawyers. It is here clarified by Mr. Brittan. He argues that the market as a technical device for registering consumer preferences and apportioning scarce resources to satisfy them can be employed in a wide range of social and political circumstances and systems with private or socialised ownership of property. The extent to which it is effective or defective depends largely on the legal and institutional framework created by government and on public attitudes to the morality of its rewards and penalties. It can be frustrated in practice even where, as in Britain, it is intended to operate in principle. It has rules of the game that may be disagreeable, but without which it cannot yield its benefits. Mr. Brittan indicates the "corrections," largely to redistribute income and deal with "externalities," required to make it serve the public interest. He argues that the market can be used to serve whichever purpose is desired, material goods or leisure, and that it is not in conflict with the urge to give "free" without payment.

The market has often been confused in public debate and associated with some schools of social philosophy rather than with others. Mr. Brittan shows there is no such necessary association with politico-economic systems, capitalist, socialist or communist. Unreasoning fears of the market have prevented countries in varying stages of economic development from benefiting from it as an economic-technical instrument to record wants and allocate resources and as a source of information. Markets have been misused or abused (in a technical sense) in Western industrial societies, abused (in a pejorative sense) or not used (officially) in collectivist societies in Eastern Europe, and suppressed even where they have shown advantageous spontaneous growth in developing countries in Africa and Asia. The market is normally associated specifically with the English classical liberal school of economists from Adam Smith to Lionel Robbins, but it has been argued that the writings of classical economists who broke away from the liberal tradition such as Karl Marx, and of writers like Engels and Lenin who followed them in devising collectivist economic systems, did not envisage or require the abolition of the market as an instrument for allocating scarce resources.

The post-war practices of countries in Eastern Europe that have increasingly used markets in varying forms have conflicted with the teaching of the older collectivist economists who condemned the market. The difficulties of allocating resources without markets have led East European economists—such as Liberman in Russia, Ota Sik of Czechoslovakia and Béla Csikós-Nagy of Hungary—to devise market systems.[1] And there has been increasing acknowledgement of the writings of Ludwig von Mises, F. A. Hayek, Lionel Robbins and others who for decades argued that markets could not effectively be replaced by centralised direction.

The theoretical distinction (and confusion) between the market as a technical device and its institutional environment is clear enough. The important question remains whether to work effectively the market requires decentralised ownership and disposal of the means of production or whether it can be incorporated into an economy where the means of production are owned in common, although controlled by central planners. The late Professor Ludwig von Mises was the leading proponent of the view, expounded in a celebrated article in 1920,[2] that rational economic calculus required market pricing which in a socialist economy was possible for consumer goods but not for the factors of production because they were not traded. This view was contested for several decades by economists since F. M. Taylor, H. D. Dickinson and others in the 1930s, who claimed that rational calculation could be incorporated into a socialist economy by a market mechanism. In more recent times it has been argued, most notably by the late Professor Oskar Lange, the distinguished Polish economist, that the computer could make the task easy.

1. Some of them are discussed in four IEA studies: Margaret Miller, Teresa M. Piotrowicz, Ljubo Sirc, Henry Smith, *Communist Economy under Change*, IEA, 1963; Margaret Miller, *Rise of the Russian Consumer*, IEA, 1965; Béla Ciskós-Nagy, *Pricing in Hungary*, Occasional Paper 19, IEA, 1968; Ljubo Sirc, *Economic Devolution in Eastern Europe*, Longmans for the IEA, 1969. An early IEA text that discussed trade with East European countries was Alec Nove and Desmond Donnelly, *Trade with Communist Countries*, 1960.

2. "Economic Calculation in the Socialist Commonwealth," *Archiv für Sozialwissenschaften*, 1920.

Mr. Brittan argues that the computer may help in static but not in dynamic conditions.[3]

In recent years Mises' early criticism has received more attention from economists in socialist economies.[4] Economists favourable to the view that the means of production should be owned in common differ among themselves on how far markets can be introduced into such a system. The view of a close student of collectivist economies, Professor Alec Nove, is that "Change towards greater reliance on market elements will come," although "Resistance to change is very strong in the political organs of the USSR . . ."[5] The interesting question for economic policy on the use of the market in practice is whether change can come more readily in an economy where the means of production are owned in common but controlled at the centre or where both ownership and control are decentralised.

It may be that a reason for resistance to the use of the market is that the price it produces as its fulcrum has the same effect on income as that of a regressive tax: a given price takes a larger proportion of a lower than of a higher income. This view may explain the reluctance to use the market, especially for "essential" goods or services such as education, medical care or housing. In turn it may also lead to a general dislike of the market as an insensitive instrument that bears disproportionately on people with relatively low incomes (or with disabilities that make them "disadvantaged" or "underprivileged"). Mr. Brittan meets this objection with a proposal for a minimum income guarantee as the better solution than disrupting the price system and thereby losing its rationing and other functions. Here he goes beyond the IEA study group that in 1970 argued for a reverse income tax as a form of income guarantee.

If there is interest in the market as a mechanism in communist as well as capitalist countries, it is not surprising that it also crosses party boundaries

3. Professors F. A. Hayek and Lionel Robbins had maintained in the 1930s that the solution of the numerous simultaneous equations required for rational calculation was impossible without a market. In 1967 Lange replied: "Let us put the simultaneous equations on an electronic computer and we shall obtain a solution in less than a second . . . the electronic computer does not replace the market. It fulfils a function which the market was never able to perform." ("The Computer and the Market," in C. Feinstein (ed.), *Capitalism, Socialism and Economic Growth,* Cambridge, 1967).

4. Professor Fritz Machlup in *Tribute to Mises,* Mont Pelerin Society, 1975.

5. "Economic Reforms in the USSR and Hungary, a Study in Contrasts," in J. Chapman and Shun Msi-chou (eds.), *The Economics of the Communist World,* reprinted in Alec Nove and D. M. Nuti (eds.), *Socialist Economics,* Penguin Modern Economics Readings, 1972.

in Britain. The Economics Editor of *The Times*, Mr. Peter Jay, recently argued that the market had both supporters and opponents in two main political parties. Exponents of "pro-market" monetary and fiscal management (as in Mr. Denis Healey's control of the money supply), of private or government investment judged on returns, and of freeing international trade were found in both parties. And, equally, "anti-market" industrial policies (such as those of Mr. Anthony Wedgwood Benn and Mr. Peter Walker), "white elephants" such as Concorde, Maplin and the Channel Tunnel, were also supported by politicians in both parties. The attitude to the use of the market has no necessary identification with allegiance to British political parties. There is on many fundamental issues more identity of outlook between wings of both parties than within them, and it may be that more economically coherent political groupings will be formed round an understanding of the market as a convenient device for rationing scarce resources.

Mr. Brittan also examines the possible scope for markets in a society in which the urge to material consumption is replaced by degrees of altruism. He argues that markets, which are commonly associated with the acquisitive society, can be used whatever the basic motives that move men.

The *Paper* thus based on Mr. Brittan's recent and new writing comprises a concise explanation of the market that will educate the newcomer to economics and edify the practical man (or woman) in industry, government and communications who uses or judges markets, as well as students and teachers of economics who have been brought up to regard the market as unnecessary or undesirable.

Hobart Paper 64
October 1975

Alan Maynard

Experiment with Choice in Education

The IEA approach considers whether resources are better deployed in markets than organised by government, and how far market principles and pricing can be introduced into the production of goods and services organised by government. Since the Forster Act of 1870 education has increasingly been organised by government with diminishing use of market techniques and pricing. Economists with an analytical approach are disinclined to accept that the form of organisation developed for education in the past century is necessarily the optimum.

Since the Institute was established it has questioned conventional economic thinking and practice, and has sought to discover where neglected market analysis and market organisation could be applied with advantage to the consumer. In 1962 it began to prepare field studies to test the assumption, from people in all schools of thought, that reforms in the welfare services were "politically impossible" even where they might be desirable. The results were analysed in three reports: *Choice in Welfare,* 1963, 1965, 1970. In 1964 the Institute invited Professors A. T. Peacock and Jack Wiseman to write *Education for Democrats,* an analysis of the organisation and financing of education in general, which discussed vouchers and loans as means of moving initiative from suppliers to consumers. In 1965 Professor E. G. West wrote *Education and the State,* which found that private education had developed extensively in the nineteenth century without state control. In 1966 Professor A. R. Prest analysed fees and loans in *Financing University Education.* In 1967, *Education: A Framework for Choice,* Professor Mark Blaug debated the economic pros and cons of vouchers with Professor West. Also in 1967 two Research Monographs, *Universal or Selective Social Benefits?* and *Taxation and Welfare* reviewed the private and governmental financing of welfare services, including education, and public attitudes to them. In 1968 Professor West in *Economics, Education and the Politician,* applied economic theory to the behaviour of politicians and administrators in education. Hobart Paper No. 64 by Alan Maynard of the University of York, now continues this IEA "tradition" of re-examining the origins, organisation and financing of education.

His *Paper* takes further the possible use of vouchers for pupils (nursery, primary and secondary) and loans for students (undergraduates and others) examined in the earlier IEA studies.

The genesis of the voucher is traced by Professor E. G. West[1] to Tom Paine in *The Rights of Man.* It was advocated by Archbishop Bourne, in 1926. But it has been left to economists to refine the concept: here, as elsewhere, the pioneer was Professor Milton Friedman.[2] The Institute in its early days saw the relevance of the voucher not only as a solvent for the frustration of parents but also as a generator of new revenue to remedy the deficiencies of tax finance. It seemed that the voucher could raise revenue for education beyond the reach of taxation. This hypothesis was tested by the *Choice of Welfare* researches and confirmed to a degree that impressed the sceptics, but went unheeded by policy-makers and educationists. More recently it has been vindicated by Professor West who concludes that total expenditure on education in Britain would have been larger if the state, in 1870, had not jumped on "the galloping horse" of education in the nineteenth century because the effect was not to urge it on, but to slow it down.

The truth would seem to be that more funds might be raised for education if payments were voluntary rather than compulsory. For to the historical support there is added the commonsense reasoning that people will pay more for a service if linked with payment than if it is not. In essence the proposition was put by two Labour Cabinet Ministers: in almost the same language Lord Houghton and the late R. H. S. Crossman[3] said that people would pay directly for better services for themselves than they would pay taxes that bore no relation to the services they received.

How far this is true of state services may be debatable, but it has the ring of truth in education, especially in rising incomes when people who have enjoyed paying for choice in food and clothing, in motoring and holidaying, are confronted with state services such as education and health in which they have little choice or influence.

In 1974 the increasing stringency of central and local government finance led the Government to appoint the Layfield Committee of Inquiry into Local Government Finance. In November it invited the Institute to submit evidence on "the scope for placing local services on a more commercial footing." "The Committee were interested in the idea of a voucher scheme . . ."

1. *Education and the Industrial Revolution,* Batsford, 1975.

2. *Capitalism and Freedom,* University of Chicago Press, 1962.

3. Douglas Houghton, *Paying for the Social Services,* Occasional Paper 16, IEA, 1967; R. H. S. Crossman, *National Superannuation and Social Insurance,* Cmnd. 3883, January 1969.

The Institute submitted Papers by some 20 authors published since 1960 discussing the financing of local services from housing and libraries to fire-fighting and refuse collection. In addition it commissioned Mr. Maynard, who had written Hobart Paper No. 54, *Rates or Prices?* (with Mr. D. N. King), to compile evidence on vouchers and loans, and Mr. Alan Jenkins, an economist who has studied local government recreational amenities, to submit evidence on sports facilities.

Mr. Maynard's *Paper* makes an informed contribution to the discussion of local government finance and illuminates the issues for a wide range of observers: from those who think that the deficiency of local government finance can be remedied by new local taxes, or shifting the burden to central government, to those who believe that the deficiency of finance cannot be remedied by higher or new taxes and that new methods of financing are long overdue. It should thus be welcomed by critics as well as by supporters of education vouchers and student loans.

In response to the Layfield Committee's emphasis on the effects on local authority finances of new methods of raising revenue, Mr. Maynard has gone far in discussing eight kinds of voucher schemes in outline and three in detail. Here the Institute obtained the co-operation of the Kent County Council Education Department and the assistance of Mr. John Barnes, Vice-Chairman of its Education Committee, in arranging discussions with the County Education Officer and other officials. The general problem was how far an academic study could go in indicating the feasibility of a new technique before the political authority and the administrative machine have decided on the variant (of voucher) most likely to be practicable. Mr. Maynard has gone some way to indicate how a voucher scheme might be introduced by adding an "Agenda" on the administrative steps that seem desirable, modelled on the procedures used by the State of New Hampshire in its experiment in vouchers in March 1975.

On the financial implications Mr. Maynard has referred to *Choice in Welfare*. These findings were unexpected by the politicians who are presumed to be in touch with public opinion, by education administrators who advise on what is feasible, and by teachers who might be thought in closest touch with parents. The reports showed that families in all income-groups would add substantially to a voucher to obtain the school of their choice. Mr. Maynard suggests that the Government bring these findings up to date. He also discusses vouchers that are taxed. A third kind could be "sold" for a nominal price. Clearly, the voucher is a flexible device that could create choice in many ways and attract revenue.

In the Chicago University tradition that hypotheses should be tested, and speculation on conjecture supported by evidence before they influence policy, Mr. Maynard urges experimentation. Experiments should, in principle, be welcomed by the unconvinced as much as by hopeful supporters, for only experiments can resolve the argument. In the USA, in recent years, social policy has been made with an effort by pilot studies to test the likely consequences. The education voucher experiment in California (Alum Rock) is being followed by the experiment in a more widely tenable voucher in New Hampshire and possibly in a third kind in Connecticut. In Great Britain the Kent County Council governing party has shown an interest in investigating the voucher to the extent of making its officials available for discussions and supplying information about education in Kent, as a possible kind of area in which a voucher might be tried for a period. The material assembled so far may encourage Kent CC to pioneer its own feasibility studies of the administrative procedures. And perhaps other education authorities will be encouraged to follow where Kent has led the way.

In his discussion of the effects of the voucher on the balance of power between local and central government, Mr. Maynard reaches views that must be subject to the form of the voucher employed. But it seems clear that local authorities would remain the owners of schools, the employers of their staffs, and retain the powers to lay down standards. Moreover, the finances for education would reach local authorities and their schools, not from central government, as it has done increasingly, but from local parents. The voucher could thus strengthen local government in order to fortify local democracy and decentralise decision-making.

It would be natural for some to be sceptical of the untried voucher which can have far-reaching medium- and long-run effects on the structure of education as well as on pupils, teachers, administrators, parents and the balance of power between local and central government. In the USA the voucher has been examined and experiments supported by academics and others of a wide range of philosophic sympathy from so-called "left" to so-called "right."

The voucher is a radical innovation that conservatives of all parties and occupational groups will predictably resist. Their most cogent reason is that it would disturb the existing system of state education. That is an objection which social scientists cannot accept. If they did, it would justify the suspension of innovation and confirm the continuance of existing thinking and practice whether they served the public interest or not. The voucher would "disturb" the system; but the sacrifice of potential improvement is too high a price to pay for avoidance of "disturbance" to any system of education. Politicians will not discourage the scholar from trying to think of new ways of improving existing practice. In their new book on welfare economics[4] Professors C. K. Rowley of the University of Newcastle and A. T. Peacock of the University of York, writing as philosophic liberals, say, after a penetrating discussion of the economic theory of welfare, policy and of alternative means and conflicting aims: ". . . the voucher solution, in an appropriate form, presently dominates the field as the most attractive means of education support."

The further method of financing education examined by Mr. Maynard is that of student loans. Not least in his review of objections to loans is the "working-class" argument that they would diminish the access to higher education of people with lower incomes. His pointed comment is that there is no evidence to suppose that the ordinary people are less capable of valuing choice in higher education than they are in everyday purchases.

The Institute is grateful to Professor West who generously agreed to read the text and make suggestions that Mr. Maynard has borne in mind in his final revisions.

His Hobart Paper is a timely contribution to a debate on the future of education in particular and local government services in general that will continue as long as state education fails to satisfy the citizens who pay for it.

4. *Welfare Economics: A Liberal Restatement,* Martin Robertson, London, 1975, p. 128.

Hobart Paper 66 *Wilfred Beckerman*
December 1975

Pricing for Pollution

The "consumption" of the environment can be analysed by economists in the same way as commodities and services in general. The environment—pure air, clean water and so on—is a scarce resource that is used in the production of goods and services by industry, public utilities, nationalised industries, local and central government. It must therefore be "economised" so that it is used only to the point at which its social costs are covered by the social benefits. And this is equally true of scarce labour, equipment and capital used in production. The question is whether industry or government can be induced to economise its use more effectively by charges than by direct regulation.

The economic functions of a charge (a price) as a means both of reducing the use of a resource and also of imposing a penalty on the amount used is not easy for non-economists to grasp. This may be perhaps why Dr. Beckerman was unable to persuade more than one other member of the Royal Commission, Lord Zuckerman, to share the economic thinking embodied in the minority report. The majority of 7 members include 5 scientists (one in industry), a civil servant, and a cleric. Some were not opposed in principle to the use of charging as a means of controlling pollution but they thought it should not be introduced without further inquiries. Dr. Beckerman deals with the doubts and objections. What is surprising is that industry, which is presumably knowledgeable in the working of prices, does not seem to have understood his economic analysis.

The central value of the Paper is indeed the clear and cogent analysis of the economics of charges and direct regulation as alternative methods of controlling pollution. And of especial interest is Dr. Beckerman's incisive dissection of seven objections to charging which indicates that they are, at least in part, founded in intellectual difficulty and error. The unanswerable argument used by Dr. Beckerman to reply to the objections from industry is that people opposed to charges would not argue that their investment projects, or any other use of scarce resources, should be determined by direct state regulation.

Dr. Beckerman's analysis is of especial interest in 1975 when the Layfield Committee appointed in 1974 to investigate local government financing has been gathering evidence from a wide range of sources and is expected to report by the end of the year. Although most of the evidence to it seems to have favoured revised or new forms of taxes, the Institute was asked to submit material on charging for local services. Dr. Beckerman explains that local government would be very much involved in a system of charging for the use of the environment. There are now charges for the treatment of industrial effluent channelled to municipal sewers as a financial disincentive to pollute. Dr. Beckerman's argument is that the principle should be applied more generally to discourage avoidable or uneconomic use of the environment.

A general objection to charging and the use of the price mechanism is that it bears more heavily on people with lower than higher incomes. Here Dr. Beckerman observes that the attempt to redistribute incomes lies at the root of most policies that deliberately misallocate resources. He cites examples from agriculture, tariffs, rents and then nationalised industries, in which controls are designed to even up incomes in favour of consumers or employees. And he concludes that the misallocation of resources might be avoided by scrapping such policies and redistributing income directly.

Moreover, on the use of charging in the control of pollution Dr. Beckerman argues that the "poverty" argument against charging is not even true, since the pollution is caused by industry and the charges would be borne by people with the higher incomes.

A fundamental general implication of Dr. Beckerman's analysis is that it is wrong to regard the environment as an absolute that must be preserved at all costs. This again is where many non-economists have misunderstood the implications of economic analysis and drawn wrong conclusions. Dr. Beckerman cogently demonstrates that it is appropriate to use the environment in the course of production of goods and services.

Dr. Beckerman provides a convenient "refute-it-yourself-master-key" for people confronted by objections to charging in principle (they apply to all scarce resources), and a secondary kit to refute objections on the ground of the impracticability of charging (the same objections apply to direct regulation).

This Paper is an outstanding demonstration of economic analysis and its applications to a department of policy in which decisions must be made by government without much more delay. It will be found enlightening and stimulating by students and teachers of economics, by people in government who resist pricing, by conservationists, environmentalists and ecologists, and not least in industry where too often the functions of price are still misunderstood.

Hobart Paper 67
May 1976

G. C. Allen

The British Disease

Professor G. C. Allen's *Hobart Paper* is a wide-ranging discussion of the origins of Britain's lagging economic progress. He argues it is necessary to go beyond the discussion of monetary management, the magnitude of government spending, or the amount of investment to the deep-seated attitudes to industry and the institutions of education and training to find the causes. He thus begins further back than the debate between the Keynesians and the Friedmanites over the role of money, or between the monetarists and the Hayekians over the "cause" of inflation, to the discussions of the economists in the half century before the First World War such as W. J. Ashley, W. S. Jevons and Alfred Marshall on the development of industry in Britain and its performance compared to industry in North America and Europe. And he thus reinstates the grand tradition of political economy and asks searching and disturbing questions about the nature of society most conducive to economic advance and the weakness he discerns in nineteenth century British society to which can be traced the origins of what has been called the "British Disease."

Professor Allen argues that the fundamental questions are whether the British people have been ready to accept the exertions required in a changing economy, whether the economically progressive countries have not been those that have concentrated on growth, whether Britain's social attitudes and economic institutions chime with modern industrialism, whether the low quality of investment, governmental and private (as distinct from its *quantity*), indicates weakness in the selection and training of civil servants and business managers, and why British industrial relations have become anachronistic to the point of attracting scorn from those who once regarded Britain as their exemplar. It is in the answers to these questions that he suggests the causes lie.

To supply the answers he goes back half a century and traces the deficiencies to their sources in the tardy development of education in science and technology and the reluctance of industry to use engineers and scientists. He goes further back to the industrial revolution and to the influence of the public schools and universities, especially Oxford and Cambridge, which in their preoccupation with classical studies neglected education in the industrial arts; they excelled in providing administrators for government and the Empire but not for manufacturing and commerce. He argues that the civil servants and politicians produced by these institutions were not much interested in industry and did not understand the necessity for systematic training of professional scientists and engineers. Hence the relatively slow pace of adaptation to change compared to the USA, Germany, France and, in recent years, Japan, where there has been more respect for the entrepreneur and where industry values the scientist and has capitalised on technology.

Professor Allen's contention is thus that the main cause of the relative decline in British industry lies in the failure of attitudes and institutions to adapt themselves to a technological-industrial society. The British "cult of the amateur" was inherited from an aristocratic society by its bourgeois successors. The increasing reluctance to accept an hierarchical society means that attitudes and institutions must be changed—gradually to avoid disorder but not too slowly if the British economy is to regain its initiatives. Old methods and leaders of the old type continued in Britain long after their counterparts had been replaced in other countries. In Britain the effort has been concentrated not on change but on conserving the industrial structure, and here the trade unions have strengthened the resistance to adaptation and innovation.

This *Paper* raises many fundamental issues on which economists and others will differ. Perhaps the most basic is whether the main fault lies with people and institutions that put continuity before innovation; or with government that by omission or commission failed to make the economy competitive so that people and institutions would have been impelled to adapt themselves to change; or even more fundamentally with the ideas and teachings of the critics of industrialism among historians and social observers who for a century or more have denigrated the role of risk-taking and investment in industry on the ground that the problems of production have been solved, to egalitarians who have fastened on redistribution as the means of raising the living standards of the "under-privileged," and to those who have taught that work in profit-making industry is necessarily less worthy than in salaried government, the professions, or teaching itself. Some blame may also be attached to representative machinery in government, industry and the trade unions that may not accurately represent the opinions and preferences of the rank and file, so that the voice of those who welcome change was muffled by that of others who preferred to settle for a quiet life.

And the role of the state in controlling a large part of economic activity from transport to education, and from fuel to medical care and housing, is not sacrosanct: in practice political power is not necessarily all-wise and far-sighted but prone to put short-term electoral expediency before long-term objectives.

The Institute wishes to thank Professors Margaret Gowing, Harold Rose and B. S. Yamey for reading an early draft and offering comments that the author has borne in mind in his final revisions. Since the *Paper* touches the structure of industry and the attitude of industrialists, Sir Emmanuel Kay, Chairman of Lansing Bagnall, Mr. Kenneth Corfield, Managing Director of Standard Telephones and Cables, and Dr. John Murray, Chairman of Bedworth Holdings, were also asked to offer observations on the general theme based on their knowledge and experience.

Second Edition

Perhaps the most important observation by Professor Allen in his Postscript to the Second Edition is that, although his argument has been widely accepted, nothing has been done about it. He is one among many economists who feel that, although the nation's leaders have had to accept the analysis of liberal economists on the causes of Britain's ills—not only the slow rate of growth but also inflation, unemployment, the deteriorating "public" services, not least, education and medicine, the growing social tensions and industrial conflicts—they have shown themselves unable to apply the only solutions that seem likely to remove causes. Professor Allen says, that in the nearly three years since the First Edition, complacency has changed to a mood of humility, but there is still little sense of urgency that time is running out. There is still too little recognition that living standards derive from individual effort, exertion and enterprise, and that the vast mass of government expenditure requires taxation that is inimical to all three. There is too little acceptance that government expenditure will have to be reduced by measures more radical than have been considered so far.

Professor Allen contests the view of the American Professor Mancur Olson that "the British disease" is common to other countries at a given stage in industrial development. He insists that it is a *British disease.* To adapt Shakespeare (*via Cassius*):

> The fault, dear Britons, is not in our stars,
> But in ourselves, that we are underlings.

Professor Allen argues that "a nation's future is settled by its choices." Government has used its powers to strengthen the collective activities and collective demands that go against the grain of the market economy; Britain would by now not be lagging behind other countries if government had gone with the grain of the market.

There are here lessons for Britain in 1979 and the 1980s. Indirectly, of course, industry is financing education by channelling its financial treasure through government. It thereby subjects the process to the pressures of party politics and of electoral calculations. It has thus acquiesced in the process by which short-term party politics has replaced the long-term industrial considerations that would have been given primacy in the judgements, decisions and policies on the role of science in industry. The notion that government would take a longer and wider view than would industry has never been persuasive, and never less than in our day when we have seen how government has used its influence in the investment decisions of the nationalised industries and public corporations. There is no reason to suppose it will ever be different.

The one argument that seems to have some weight is that the family influence in British industry has been a weakness because the sons of entrepreneurial fathers have not always inherited their talents but have been content to rest on their oars and have thus neglected the contribution of science and technology. But it has little relevance for public policy. First, relative complacency would have been short-lived if the economy had been more competitive. Secondly, the alternative of political influence in industry would have been, and has been shown to have been, even more weakening, because it is more difficult to discipline complacent politicians than the complacent sons of innovating industrialists.

This is the reply to the critics of British management including the heir to the throne, which would have had to be more cost-conscious, more efficient, better at "communicating" with its workforce if it had been so impelled by the pressures of a more competitive system. That the British economy has not been more competitive is the responsibility of government, not of management.

Professor Allen has written his Postscript in English, uncluttered by jargon or sociologese, that is a lesson to younger economists. The Second Edition of his *Hobart Paper* is a timely addition to the literature on the economics (and social and political history) of Britain's present discontents that will require early and perhaps unprecedentedly drastic solutions.

Hobart Paper 68
June 1976

Gordon Pepper and Geoffrey Wood

Too Much Money . . . ?

It has long been a common belief among economists of all schools, especially those interested in the working of markets, that one of the most important functions of government and elements of the legal/institutional framework is a mechanism for facilitating buying and selling, lending and borrowing by the use of money. A significant change in attitude is not merely that economists have in recent years come increasingly to the view that government has not provided an efficient monetary mechanism since the end of the Second World War. There is now the more fundamental critique that government down the centuries has been prone to mismanage money and that there is no other ultimate solution than to take it out of political control. In a recent IEA *Paper* Professor F. A. Hayek maintained that a gold standard, with balanced budgets, fixed exchanges and limits on international liquidity, has proved the best means of removing the supply and the value of money from the control of government, and Mr. Peter Jay has suggested a Currency Commission as a move to much the same kind of automatic mechanism "insulated from political manipulation," though less radical than Professor Hayek's proposal that government be deprived of the power to oblige its citizens to use only its money as legal tender. The significance of these proposals is their anxiety to take money out of "politics."

The failure of government is seen most vividly in its propensity to increase the supply in response to pressures from vested interests that suffer from underlying economic change, in particular to maintain employment in parts of the economy and full employment in general.

This *Paper* is the work of an interesting combination of expertise in the day-to-day reactions to the monetary environment and academic economic analysis of the immediate and underlying causes. Mr. Gordon Pepper, a Cambridge graduate in economics and an actuary, is a Partner of W. Greenwell & Co. His speciality is the gilt-edged market which in many ways is central to the British monetary system. Gilt-edged transactions often reflect the ebb and flow of funds within the financial institutions. Observation of the gilt-edged market can detect the balance between the demand for long-term finance and the supply of savings in the economy as a whole. Mr. Geoffrey

Wood is a Lecturer at the City University. They analyse the reasons why government has been misled into expanding the supply of money. They recognise that a major factor in monetary expansion is the growing divergence between government spending and the taxation available to finance it, but their concern is to analyse other pressures—technical and economic—that contribute to inflationary tendencies.

Their *Paper* has grown out of research begun at Greenwell's into trends in financial elements in the money and capital markets. These inquiries have been refined and widened to the more general underlying economic causes and consequences. The Bank of England's monthly statistical release on banking statistics, including money supply data, started in March 1972. Since up-to-date analysis of the supply and demand for short-term finance has become possible over the years, it has been demonstrated that exposure to market disciplines can improve economic analysis itself, as well as the working of the economy.

Pepper and Wood analyse the mistakes in government control of the monetary mechanism since the war and the technical errors and fundamental factors at work behind the scenes.

As technical and economic specialists the authors confine themselves to their specialism. Readers interested in the even wider institutional setting of the social and political pressures within which government works may reflect on the scope for avoiding inflation when governments must be concerned with General Elections, or even by-elections, in order to maintain office. This is not a critique of the integrity of politicians but a realistic approach to the task of maintaining a stable value of the currency and of keeping inflation at bay in the real world of modern representative democracies in which governments that should take long views must take short views if they are to remain in office. It is part of the relatively new advance of economics into the working of political institutions known variously as the economics of democracy, the theory of public choice, and other descriptions, and is discussed by Professor Gordon Tullock of Virginia State University and Dr. Morris Perlman of the London School of Economics in a forthcoming IEA Paper.

The Institute thanks Professor Victor Morgan of the University of Reading and Mr. Brian Griffiths of the LSE for reading early drafts and for offering comments and suggestions that the authors have taken into account in their final revisions.

Hobart Paper 69 *E. Victor and Ann D. Morgan*
September 1976

Gold or Paper?

In the nineteenth century and in the first quarter of the twentieth until the Great Depression, currencies in Western industrialised countries were linked directly or indirectly to gold. It is arguable that this link, which prevented governments from expanding the supply of money to suit themselves, was the fundamental condition and reason for the relatively stable value of money that helped the industrial advance and the rise in living standards of the Western world. About 40 or 50 years ago, and increasingly before and after the last war, industrialists argued that the gold link would prevent government from expanding the supply of money to encourage industrial expansion, and that it should be freed from its link with metal in order to control money in the public interest.

Experience in the last 40 or 50 years does not appear to have supported this faith in the capacity of government to control money better than when linked to an outside control. In this *Paper* Professor E. Victor Morgan, joined by a second economist, his wife, reviews the working of the gold "standard" before it fell into disrepute in the 1930s. They conclude that most of the criticisms of "the gold standard" by economists (repeated by politicians) were unfounded and that it was not necessarily deflationary. And they maintain that what went wrong was the failure to understand the conditions in which a gold standard could work most effectively. They review the post-war attempts, notably at Bretton Woods, to create a new world monetary system, but contend that it had the same inflationary and destabilising effects as other systems controlled by government. They also contend that the new proposals of the International Monetary Fund have similar built-in inflationary weaknesses as Bretton Woods, and that its suggestion that metallic gold be replaced by "paper gold" would not avoid excessive expansion in world money or restrict domestic money when restriction was desirable. They therefore argue that the proposal to "demonetise" gold would not be much of an improvement, and that, if metallic gold is to be restored as a control of the supply of money outside the power of government, it can only be by re-establishing a direct link with domestic money that no government has so far been ready to accept. In other words, metallic gold could not be used to control international money unless government accepts it as a control of domestic money and monetary and economic policy. Professor and Mrs. Morgan say the reason why government will not accept gold as a control of domestic money is that it is under persistent pressure to favour groups and win votes by expanding the supply of money. Therefore, to prevent them from responding to these pressures, money must be subjected to an external discipline.

Hence the Morgans argue the time may not be far distant when the Western world will have to return to an outside discipline over the monetary power of government. Since they are sceptical of linking money to parcels of commodities, they conclude that the West will sooner or later have to return to gold. They say that it will not be by international agreement but by one country, or a small group, linking its currencies to gold and others following them. That is how the classical gold standard developed by spontaneous evolution when its advantages were seen, not by formal or solemnly binding international agreement.

Such a country (or group) would require a strong international balance of payments (and gold stock); buy and sell gold at a price near the current market price; control the supply of their currencies so that they were convertible into gold; discipline government expenditure; and maintain rates of exchange determined by the gold parities (but floating exchange rates with non-gold countries).

This is a remarkably clear exposition of the economic case for and against gold. It will be found an ideal text for teachers of economics and a thought-provoking analysis for politicians, bankers, civil servants and others concerned with making policy. It touches on the political obstacles that make it unlikely that government will accept an outside discipline, and will cause the reader to wonder what constitutional changes are required before government can be made to act in the public interest.

The Institute has to thank Professor F. W. Paish and Miss Sudha Shenoy for reading the text and offering suggestions and comments that the authors have taken into account in making their final revisions.

Hobart Paper 80
June 1978

S. C. Littlechild

The Fallacy of the Mixed Economy

British economic thinking and policy has been dominated by what Professor S. C. Littlechild calls the neo-classical "mainstream" and its associated welfare economics. He argues we have largely overlooked the importance of the contribution to thinking on policy in Britain that we could have drawn from the Austrian economists. In his *Paper* Professor Littlechild covers a wide range of topics from the origins of the Austrians in the mid-nineteenth century to the recent revival in their thinking, especially in the USA and more recently in Britain, and to its very direct relevance to government policy in Britain in the last quarter of the twentieth century. Austrian thinking is described as based on the individual, who provides both the method of the reasoning ("methodological individualism") and the source of the valuations ("subjectivism") on which policy must rest.

Professor Littlechild is led to the roots of the reasons for the "market failure" that is said to be a major fault of a system of decentralised private ownership, especially in its neglect of private contracts on the "external" effects and the resulting despoliation of the environment. He turns this criticism into a counter-criticism of welfare economics, which he says has ignored the central importance of imperfect knowledge, the pervasive uncertainty which overshadows all decisions, whether taken in the market or by government. He describes as a "myth" the view that government will necessarily have access to more or surer information than is available to men in the market. And he rejects the conclusion that "market failure" is a sufficient justification for the replacement of the market by government.

This approach leads Professor Littlechild to his critique of the mixed economy, the case for which has been most persuasively argued by Professor J. E. Meade in devising economic policy for "the intelligent radical." The *Hobart Paper* argues that "market failure" has derived not from the defects of the market as a method of organisation but from the imperfection of the framework of laws and institutions within which it has had to work. The intellectually more convincing solution for market failure is therefore not replacement of the market by government but refinement of the legal framework to make property rights easier to identify as the best incentive to the efficient use of resources.

The closely reasoned and scholarly analysis leads to strong implications not only for policy on competition but for the treatment of "externalities," national planning (the National Enterprise Board), and nationalised industry. The main indications for policy are assembled at the end of the final section.

To direct the reader to the central idea and insights of Austrian economics, Professor Littlechild has had to compress a large amount of material into a relatively short space, and a judicious use of italics has been employed to indicate the main propositions. The new feature of *Hobart Papers,* the "Consequences," also indicates the importance of the reasoning by crystallising its effects for 10 classes of readers.

The Institute wishes to thank Professor Israel Kirzner of New York University, Miss Sudha Shenoy of Newcastle University, New South Wales, and Professor Jack Wiseman of the University of York for reading drafts and offering comments and suggestions that the author has borne in mind in his final revisions. His *Paper* should mark a renewed interest by British academies, government and industry in a school of thought that might provide solutions to the problems of British industry that have hitherto proved elusive.

Hobart Paper 81
July 1978

G. C. Allen

How Japan Competes: A Verdict on "Dumping"

One of the markets of which competitors have most anxiously complained has been the international trade between countries with supposedly different backgrounds and costs. Here the most celebrated example is that of Japan, which has been competing more strongly with Britain and Europe in recent years and which is accused of aggressive marketing, not least by selling exports at less than their "cost" while, at the same time, restricting the access of foreign producers to its home market. This argument has recently led to increasing calls and pressures for a tariff and other "protection" against Japanese imports of a wide range of consumer goods against which, it is argued, British industry cannot compete on equal ("fair") terms.

This proposition is examined in Hobart Paper 81 by Professor G. C. Allen, a distinguished and respected economic authority on the industry and trade of Japan. He examines the economics of the Japanese economy without bias, with restraint, and with a cool-headed determination to arrive at the truth. In brief, he concludes that, although some practices would not be used in Britain or Europe and others might be justifiably described as misleading, the success of Japanese industry in competing with British and European industry, despite long distances and high transport costs, is due essentially not to her trading practices but to her superior industrial efficiency.

The corollary that Professor Allen discusses, the inability of British industry to compete in Japanese markets, reflects the failure of British industrialists, management and trade unions to display the enterprise, initiative and efficiency of the Japanese.

The Institute's usual practice is to have early drafts of its *Papers* read by two or more economists. In this case they were Mr. Gilbert J. Ponsonby, who offered observations on the general argument that have been taken into account in the final revisions, and Professor Yikihide Okano, of the University of Tokyo, who fortuitously was on a spell of study at the University of Oxford. Professor Okano's lengthy series of comments were considered so interesting and valuable that, at Professor Allen's suggestion, they have been added to form a Commentary. We thank Mr. Ponsonby and Professor Okano for their comments and suggestions.

Professor Allen's *Hobart Paper* should help to encourage a cooler analysis of the reasons for the success of competition from Japanese imports. It should therefore direct attention away from supposed solutions like protection, which would leave the comparative weakness of British industry untouched. It should instead direct attention to the more fundamental causes of these weaknesses and, by stimulating thought on methods of removing them, indirectly help to strengthen British industry.

The Institute presents this *Hobart Paper* by one of its eminent Trustees as a scholarly, urbane, and clearly-written analysis of a subject that has caused not only heated and unenlightened public discussion but also misguided thinking from economists, mostly at Cambridge, who have not similarly analysed the reasons for the differences in the relative efficiency of British and Japanese industry.

Hobart Paper 82
October 1978

Steven N. S. Cheung

The Myth of Social Cost

The most damaging criticism of the market for some decades but especially in recent years has been that buyers and sellers who exchange goods and services by contract often create costs and benefits ("externalities") for third parties not directly involved in the exchange, so that the market suffers from a serious "failure" in these bargains. It generates excessive production of goods/services that impose costs on others who cannot be compensated, and insufficient of those that yield benefits to others for which they cannot be made to pay. From this diagnosis has followed a series of conclusions for policy varying from a structure of taxes (to discourage output with social/external costs) and subsidies (to stimulate output with social/external benefits) to suppression of the market entirely and its replacement by government.

For some years economists, especially in the USA, have contested the original diagnosis of externalities. They have offered alternative explanations of the supposed divergences between private and social costs/benefits. They have argued that the parties to private contracts will *not* fail to take the externalities into account in their dealing provided there are no barriers to "trading" in external effects. The newer conclusion for policy is the possibility of re-drawing the boundaries of property rights so that such "trades" over external effects can take place. This new perspective on externalities has been slow to filter through to thinking on policy in the UK.

Hobart Paper 82 presents this counter-critique by American, and more recently British, economists on two planes. The central portion is the work of Professor Steven N. S. Cheung of the University of Washington, who has developed the counter-critique in a series of studies known best in the USA. His argument is addressed chiefly to economic specialists in the subject who will find it a microcosm of his writings for some years brought up-to-date in the light of the latest developments in the debate between economists. He has explained his analysis by arithmetical tables designed to show alternative methods of measuring private and social costs. He follows the evolution of the theory of social cost/benefit from its originator of 50 years ago, the Cambridge economist A. C. Pigou, into its most recent forms, and claims that they are all defective. His essay is mainly intended for students and teachers of economics with special interest in the theory of social cost and externalities. His main conclusion is that the originators of "externality" theory relied on invalid assumptions and did not test their results. He holds that the evidence, when examined, reveals flaws in their reasoning. He joins issue both with Professor Pigou, on the basis of counter evidence derived from land-tenure contracts and farming behaviour in China, and with Professor J. E. Meade by contesting his analysis of the pollination and nectar extraction services of bees.

In view of the difficulty that newcomers to economics may have in following this closely reasoned analysis, we invited Professors Charles K. Rowley of the University of Newcastle upon Tyne, a British authority on this development in economics, to outline briefly the importance of Professor Cheung's analysis. Professor Rowley is, with Professor A. T. Peacock, the author of the deepest British economic study of the subject, *Welfare Economics: A Liberal Restatement.*[1] The opening sentence of his Prologue graphically states his verdict: "Society might be far better off if the 'problem' of social cost had never been discovered." The importance of the economics of social cost is that it has considerably influenced British economists and other academics and the governments they have advised. Professor Rowley's exposition will be found easy to follow by beginners in economics and by non-economists.

For readers interested in discussion of public policy, such as of various forms of environmental controls, we also invited Mr. John Burton to write a longer Epilogue designed to apply Professor Cheung's central analysis more fully in language again suitable for the non-specialist and to illustrate it by topical examples from Britain and overseas. Like Professor Rowley he indicates the alternative approach from the study of property rights and of public choice[2] as a more fundamental insight to the reasons for external effects and the naiveté of the proposals for policy drawn from the Pigovian analysis. Both British authors indicate the conclusions that follow for government policy from this superior perspective of property rights and public choice.

If our three authors are right, the continued teaching in Britain of the simplistic conventional approach to social cost/benefit is seriously flawed

1. Martin Robertson, London, 1975.
2. J. M. Buchanan and others, *The Economics of Politics*, IEA Readings No. 18, 1978.

and dangerously misleading. A wide range of British policies from technological and industrial policies and the third London airport to town and country planning, subsidies for the arts, and measures for the protection of the environment are based on this flawed analysis. There is urgent need of re-examining it in the light of the more realistic analysis presented in this *Paper.*

Hobart Paper 84
December 1979

David Greenaway and
Christopher Milner

Protectionism Again . . . ?

International markets provide the means by which nations of the world can trade with one another to their common advantage. But because nations are ruled by governments, and governments are run by politicians with short-term self-interests that may conflict with the long-term public welfare, international trade has been restricted and the international division of labour has been thwarted.

International exchange arises essentially from differences in national endowments of human and material resources, which give rise to differences in costs of production. If these resources were perfectly mobile they would tend to move so that the differences in costs would be reduced or removed, and the advantages of international exchange of products would diminish or vanish. But human resources may not wish or be able to move; and national resources, not least climate, cannot move. The exchange of goods and services is thus both a substitute for the immobility of resources and also compensation for it. To the extent that international trade is liberalised, the disadvantages of immobility are thereby reduced, and the nations and peoples of the world can benefit from the differences in human and national endowments of the diverse countries of the globe.

After the last war the nations of the world seemed to have learned the lesson that, whatever the disadvantages of governments or to the vested interests that pressurised them, the trading nations would have to find ways of exchanging goods and services or take the consequences, which would be not only lower living standards but also increasing international tension and, in the ultimate analysis, war. It was one of the lessons learned from the economic nationalism of the inter-war years 1919 to 1939 that "If goods do not cross national frontiers, armies will."

Since the war the trading nations have therefore made sustained efforts to reduce tariff barriers, exchange controls, currency regulations and other restraints that constrict the natural inclination of people in different countries to trade with one another. In the inter-war years there were refined technical/economic arguments, from Cambridge economists and elsewhere, for tariffs and other restrictions that were taken seriously by economists for a time, but that can now be seen to be at best secondary, and at the worst insignificant or damaging, in comparison with the arguments for international economic integration by trade. Such an argument for restrictions to counter "dumping" was examined in *Hobart Paper* 81 by Professor G. C. Allen.[1]

Hobart Paper 84 is a review of the first principles in the economics of international trade by two young economists, David Greenaway of the University College at Buckingham and Christopher Milner of Loughborough University. It serves as a sobering reminder of the advantages of international exchange and of the dangers of restricting it. They examine the latest technical/economic arguments for limiting international exchange advanced by the Economic Policy Group at Cambridge University. They conclude that the arguments are faulty, that the claims made for what would be a new version of a siege economy are unconvincing, and that dangers for international amity are overlooked.

Messrs. Greenaway and Milner provide the economics student and teacher of international trade with a clear outline of the economic principles and their applications to the real world. Their analysis should make the *Hobart Paper* of value also to all concerned with international trade in the markets for imports and exports of goods and services, as well as to citizens with the future of international accord. By this test the removal of exchange control, argued strongly nine months ago in an IEA paper,[2] must be seen as a move in the right direction. The more individual governments reach international agreement that limits their powers to restrict imports the less they will be under pressure to do so by employers or employees that stand to gain at the expense of the consumer and the public interest in general.

The Institute has to thank Professor E. Victor Morgan of the University of Reading, and Professor Jan Tumlir, Research Director of GATT, for reading an early draft and offering comments and criticisms.

1. *How Japan Competes: A Verdict on "Dumping,"* with a Commentary by Professor Yukihide Okano, IEA, 1978.

2. Robert Miller, J. B. Wood, *Exchange Control for Ever?*, Research Monograph 33, February 1979.

Hobart Paper 85
April 1980

Peter Sloane

Sport in the Market

Throughout its life the Institute has sought to apply market analysis to subjects that are not normally thought to be the province of the economist. *Hobart Paper* 85 by Professor Peter J. Sloane represents an effort to examine recent trends in sport in Britain (and other countries) to see how far economics can shed light on its development when it is analysed as selling a service for which spectators will pay, and therefore with components of supply and demand that determine the price at which it can be produced.

Professor Sloane opens with a discussion of the nature of the service that sport supplies in order to attract its market of spectator "fans." He argues that sports teams have to provide an uncertain outcome so that the spectators are not witnessing a pre-determined contest. The importance of this view is that it seems to provide a reason for restricting competition in league clubs. At one point he divides spectators into two parts, the partisans who want their team to win and the connoisseurs of the sport who come to watch good play. The connoisseurs want the excitement of seeing which side wins; but the partisans want the satisfaction of seeing their side win whatever its merits. The product therefore differs for the two kinds of consumer. In some events partisans may outnumber connoisseurs; the case for restricting competition thus seems to turn on whether the connoisseurs outnumber the partisans. It remains true that teams provide a joint product, and that, although teams compete for players, they do not compete with one another as do firms making distinct products.

After discussing sport in macro-economic terms—its total national size and the extent to which the demand for it as a whole varies with income and other conditions—Professor Sloane moves to the central part of his analysis, the micro-economic supply of sport and the demand for it. Here he analyses the economics of the individual team and the leagues into which teams are grouped to provide the spectacle of individual skill and team co-operation. He reviews developments in baseball and other American sports and then arrives at the subject that will be most in the minds of British readers: the broad comparison between soccer and cricket, the former more competitive until recent years than the latter, and the increase in competition in organising cricket accompanying the Packer development.

Feelings in Britain ran high when the Packer "invasion" was first announced. Whatever the cultural or other elements in cricket, or in sport generally, the economic aspects of supply, demand and price cannot be excluded or ignored. The people who enjoy watching cricket as a game, or who regard it as embodying the national spirit in some sense, must take into account the costs involved in alternative policies: methods of organising sport, the rules governing competition for players or the working of leagues, the sources of income from gate revenue, advertising, sponsors, and other policies. Even if we preferred that cricket or other sport should not be subject to commercial pressures it is relevant to know what the economic pros and cons are before attitudes can be formed rationally. The interesting question here is why the conduct of cricket produced a Packer, and whether a Kerry Packer or anyone else would have appeared sooner or later. The issues are basically economic rather than personal.

Professor Sloane's analysis is thus of interest not only to students and teachers of economics but also to people who enjoy cricket and other sports.

The Institute has to thank Professors S. C. Littlechild and Basil S. Yamey for reading all or part of an early draft and offering comments that Professor Sloane has borne in mind in his final revisions. It offers this *Hobart Paper* as a rare economic analysis of a subject that is of wide interest to the British public and an industry with economic aspects that require to be understood if it is to develop with satisfaction to players as well as to spectators.

Hobart Paper 86 *Ivy Papps*
July 1980

For Love or Money?

The alternative to the market is all forms of production and distributing the product by command, rules, agreements, committees or other methods of organising resources and distributing their product other than price. Government is the most important alternative. The market system establishes co-ordination *between* units of production and distribution by pricing mechanisms. *Within* these units—firms, voluntary associations, clubs, the family—production and distribution are also organised by agreements, rules or other alternatives to pricing.

Dr. Ivy Papps examines the economics of production and distribution in the family. This is one more form of organisation or activity that is not normally thought of as within the province of the economist. That view misconceives the nature of economics. The world is not divided into *activities* that are economic and others that are not; the distinction is between activities that have economic *aspects* and those that have not. For half a century or more economics has been regarded as refining the principles that decide the optimum use of resources. If resources are superabundant, so that there are more than enough for all desired purposes, there is no occasion to "economise" because using more resources in one use does not require resources to be taken from others. Inside firms, voluntary associations, clubs, families, etc., where resources are not superabundant, there remains the task of making the optimum use of their available "scarce" resources. They can therefore be analysed to discover the principles that make for optimum production and distribution.

It does not follow that pricing cannot be used within these units. Large firms sometimes try to use "shadow" or "transfer" pricing for the goods that pass from one department to another, or for services that some departments, such as transport, provide for others, so that they know the cost of resources used in production or possibly use outside services if these are better or cheaper. Clubs use prices for personal services, such as meals, or risk unrestrained demand. Centralised planned societies such as Poland and Hungary have been trying to introduce pricing systems to inform them of production costs and consumer preferences. Dr. Papps shows how the formation of marriage has used bride-price (or dowry) and groom-price (or dower). And families could use pricing (for otherwise "free" telephone calls, etc.) to restrain its members from running-up avoidably high costs. And all these centrally-directed, "unpriced," units can run as well as they do because they can use outside pricing as bench-marks, guides and sign-posts.

Dr. Papps's analysis will be new to many teachers and students as well as to non-economists. She has therefore addressed her exposition to economists as well as other academics and laymen.

Some of her analysis and conclusions will seem common sense, except that she provides an economic explanation for them. Other parts of the analysis and the conclusions for policy will seem surprising, contrary to everyday supposition, and controversial. Dr. Papps explains that the economic theory of the family is still being refined—that some forms of family organisation cannot easily be explained by economic theory—and is therefore reluctant to draw more than tentative conclusions. But her observations on sex discrimination laws, the "Women's Movement," wages for housework, free day-care centres, family taxation, and loans for women students should cause reconsideration of established attitudes and reflection whether recent or current policies are invariably well-thought-out and advantageous for individuals and society.

The Institute has to thank Professor Gary Becker of the University of Chicago, Mrs. June Lait of the University College of Swansea (University of Wales), and Dr. Robert Sugden of the University of Newcastle upon Tyne for scrutinising an early draft and making criticism and suggestions that Dr. Papps has borne in mind in her final revisions.

The Institute presents Dr. Papps's *Hobart Paper* as a thoughtful, well-argued and scholarly effort to show the light that economics can throw on a central institution of British life and to indicate the implications for public policy to strengthen its contribution to British economy and society.

Hobart Paper 87 *F. A. Hayek*
July 1980

1980s Unemployment and the Unions

Hobart Paper 87 is an analysis by F. A. Hayek of the most stubborn obstacle to the efficient working of markets in the British economy: the main cause of the decline of the economic system.

The *Paper* includes three considerably re-written Parts, II, III, and IV, based on material used in BBC broadcasts in 1978. The text has been expanded to explain the argument more fully than was possible in the "air-time" then available, and examples have been added to illustrate the argument.

Part I revises the essence of the argument elaborated in the succeeding essays.

Part II is an analysis of the elementary but fundamental principles governing the distribution of scarce resources to meet consumer demands. It demonstrates the rôle of the market as a device for signalling changes in supply and demand and the required redistribution of resources. Here Professor Hayek emphasises that people use their resources to produce commodities or services for people unknown to them; that there is no adequate substitute for the signalling rôle of prices in guiding producers to the wants, preferences or demands of their unknown consumers. The reasoning here is simple and clear enough for the non-economists but contains penetrating insights into the working of economic systems that are designed to serve the consumer, whether under capitalism or under socialism or communism. He points, for example, to the statistical nonsense of measuring production by the cost of its input of labour and capital rather than by the value of its output, to the political nonsense of job creation that instead creates unemployment, and to the economic nonsense, taught by Keynes and his followers, of supposing that employment can be maintained at full stretch by bolstering total demand. He points to the implication that the real cause of the "de-industrialisation" now loudly lamented by British politicians is essentially the inflation of costs that has made the products of British industry unsaleable.

Part III examines three alternative policies on the attitudes to, and the use of, markets. The first is to refine the framework of law, especially to corral social costs known by the economists' jargon of "externalities." The second is to attempt to direct economic activity from the centre. This method is ineffective unless there is agreement on the objectives of policy, which is possible only by coercion in a socialised society, but not in a free society with maximum individual liberty. The third alternative is to remove the domination of the market by monopoly—whether in the corporativism of employers and employees in collusion with government or in the syndicalism of trade unions.

In this discussion Professor Hayek covers the futility of "incomes policies": the power of the market to minimise coercion; the difficulty of reconciling the most effective reward for effort with a "just" reward; the superiority of a system guided by abstract rules in serving the consumer over a system in which there is deliberate pursuit of the interests of known people; the contrast between primitive society with more scope for altruism and industrial society with more scope for removing poverty; the conflict between high-mindedness and the maximisation of wealth to raise living standards; the error of Keynes, dramatised by the poet who wrote that aiming for heaven makes life hell. And Professor Hayek shows the relevance of these insights for Britain.

Part IV then applies the economic analysis of the necessity for market signalling to the labour market in Britain. Examination of the powers given to the trade unions by the privileges conferred by trade union law, and their effects on wage differentials, unemployment, inflation and general economic decline, lead Professor Hayek to the conclusion that the British labour market, and the British market economy as a whole, no longer tells the people of Britain where to use their resources because it has severely blunted the rewards for using them correctly and the penalties for using them wrongly.

Part V is a slightly edited version of an article in *The Times* of 10 October 1978 which describes the conditions of the British economy as Professor Hayek then saw it. His judgement in November 1980 is indicated in Part I.

This *Hobart Paper* sums up the teaching of a lifetime on the role of trade unions in a free society that Professor Hayek has patiently refined down the years, during many of which he was ignored or condemned, until the recent past when his thinking has begun to be seen as inconvenient but inescapable. In 1980 Professor Hayek's work stands unique.

Second Edition, 1984

In the 3½ years since the First Edition Parliament has taken the early steps to remove the legal power that enables British trade unions to damage the economy, often to the disadvantage of their members (and their families) as well as non-unionised employees. In a Postscript to this Second Edition,

Dr. Charles Hanson—who has made himself an authority on British trade union law—assesses those steps and argues for more.

The outdated notion that the trade unions are spokesmen for the underdog has inhibited British governments from removing the nearly 80-year-old legal privileges that have strengthened the unions' power to act as vested interests defending outdated occupations and restrictive practices in declining industries. Dr. Hanson indicates that the reforms so far are the beginning, and the end is not yet in sight. He specifically argues that more requires to be done urgently to remove immunities and introduce no-strike contracts in essential "public" (a euphemism for state or government) or private monopoly employment. Moreover, as the 1984 miners' strike has dramatised, the law on secondary picketing, which in practice has not been generally applied, requires further reform to include secondary strikes at the places of work of suppliers or customers of firms in dispute. These reforms, Dr. Hanson argues, would go far to meet Professor Hayek's critique of trade union legal privileges.

Dr. Hanson argues that privileges should also be removed from the professions. A further measure that is indispensable to complement legal reform is that of removing the power of "public" (state, government) employers to absorb increases in labour costs not earned by higher output. The power of labour combinations, among manual or professional workers, rests not only on legal power but ultimately on market power. Legal reform leaves untouched the power of trade unions or professional associations of coal miners or doctors, railwaymen or teachers, to enforce their demands on monopoly "public" employers in fuel and transport, education and medicine, in contrast to their opposite numbers in competitive private industry. Legal reform may therefore benefit the consumer of private goods and services but leave the taxpayer, who finances "public" (state, government) goods and services, to continue to suffer under the collusive acts of monopoly "public" employers and their employees' associations. Legal reform is not enough: it must be buttressed by dissolving the artificial coagulation of "public" market power by subjecting it to competition in the market.

The Second Edition is Professor Hayek's first publication in Britain since the Queen's Birthday Award of the dignity of Companion of Honour (CH) for his "services to the study of economics." This is the first public British honour since the Swedish award of the Nobel Prize 10 years ago, in 1974. It is a fitting recognition, at the age of 85, of the economist (and much else), British by choice rather than accident of birth, who has emerged as the world's leading exponent of classical English and Scottish political economy.

Hobart Paper 88
January 1981

H. G. Brennan and
J. M. Buchanan

Monopoly in Money and Inflation

A new form of government failure that economists are examining with increasing intensity is in the supply of money. For 200 years or more economists have generally supposed that one of the main functions of government was to provide the medium of exchange in which transactions in the market could be conducted. And even when the failure of government to maintain the value of money in the periods of inflation of the nineteenth and twentieth centuries was closely debated by economists, the task was assumed to be that of helping government to control the supply of money so that it would not debase its value. Economists thus attempted to devise methods of linking the value of money to a commodity such as gold that was as far as possible beyond the influence of government.

The focus of interest is now increasingly whether government will ever be able to provide a dependable means of exchange, and whether some other method of organising the supply of money may have to be evolved. In 1976 the Institute published a pioneering *Paper* by Professor F. A. Hayek in which he argued that the only way to ensure that the value of money was maintained would be to take it out of the control of government as the sole source and put it into the market where competing suppliers would be induced to maintain the value of their individual currency by limiting its supply. The *Paper* was entitled *Denationalisation of Money* because it is government that has "nationalised" money and so created a monopoly in its supply. Professor Hayek's argument was essentially against the *monopoly* control of money as such, whether by government or in a private banking system, and that it was competition in the supply of money that would prevent its debasement.

In Hobart Paper 88 Professors Geoffrey Brennan and James M. Buchanan take the argument further by refining the conditions in which government can best be deprived of the power to control money by monopoly. Like other papers from the fertile centre of learning in Blacksburg, Virginia, where they teach, and like other works of Professor Buchanan, Hobart Paper 88 extends the analysis beyond the stage it has reached so far not least by applying what in the USA is called "public choice" analysis and in Britain "the economics of politics,"[1] of which Professor Buchanan is a founding father. Most of the text should be understood by non-economists, who can skip the more technical discussion in Part II, especially Sections 7 and 8.

The *Hobart Paper* begins by doubting the realism of supposing that government can be left to control the supply of money without regard for its political interests. It rejects the notion that government will invariably use its power, in controlling money or anything else, to serve only the public interest. It argues that, consciously or unconsciously, we have supposed that government comprises benevolent despots whose motives and objectives did not have to be questioned since there was no conflict between the interests of the despots and the interests of the people.

This unrealistic, naïve, or romantic notion about the role of government, which made little allowance for the everyday political pressures in the working of party politics, reached its apogee in the teaching of Keynes, or, more correctly, in the teaching of the economists who claimed to interpret his teaching when he was no longer able to rebut their claims. The implied assumption of the Keynesians was that government could be left to provide the required medium of exchange by varying its supply in booms and slumps, creating or destroying it so as to maintain stability of demand, employment and income. The unreality of the supposition that government would or could be neutral in its control was demonstrated in Hobart Paper 78, *The Consequences of Mr. Keynes*, in which Professor Buchanan collaborated with an American colleague at Blacksburg, Professor R. E. Wagner, and a British economist now at the University of Birmingham, John Burton.

The present *Hobart Paper* discusses the reasons why the supposition is unrealistic and ends by considering methods of removing or minimising the power of government in the control of money. Professors Brennan and Buchanan discuss four main possible reforms: the issue by government of a fiat ("faith" or paper) money disciplined by a constitutional rule, a money issued by government but linked to a commodity to define its value, a money issued by government but disciplined by competition from privately-issued monies, and a free market in money with no government role at all. The authors favour constitutional discipline. Whatever method finally emerges from the discussion in the years ahead, the importance of the analysis is that it develops the process of considering how far government must be removed from supplying money, and how far it is possible by constitutional disciplines to prevent government from disrupting the supply of money and

1. J. M. Buchanan et al., *The Economics of Politics,* IEA Readings No. 18, IEA, 1978.

thereby the working of the economy as a whole. In the course of the discussion the authors touch on a conundrum now causing much anxiety in Britain: how to ensure that the authorities know and use the techniques that will effectively control the supply of money to master inflation. They say that a fiat money issued by government could be disciplined by constitutional rules defined either in terms of the *supply* of money or of the *value* of the unit of money. The former kind of rule has been proposed by Professor Friedman, who has argued that the supply of money should be related to the rate of economic growth. The second, proposed by economists of an earlier day, Irving Fisher and Henry Simons, argued that the monetary authority should keep the value of the monetary unit stable in terms of an index of prices. The advantage of the Friedman-type rule is that it is applied well before the increase in prices is due, although it may not be able to allow for unforeseen other influences on the course of prices. The advantage of the Fisher-Simons-type rule is that it can allow for unpredicted emergence of substitutes for money, such as credit cards, but it is more difficult to monitor since the adjustment takes place after the rise in prices and is too late.

It may be that in the 1980s, when there are more substitutes for money and, not least, when money is increasingly not used at all because barter is used to evade taxation, there will have to be more refined experimentation in the constitutional rules required to ensure that the monetary authority avoids or masters inflation.

Hobart Paper 89
June 1981

Colin Robinson and
Eileen Marshall

What Future for British Coal?

In the autumn of 1979 a major Public Inquiry, lasting for some six months, began into a proposal by the National Coal Board to mine coal in North East Leicestershire, principally in the Vale of Belvoir. It was recognised by both advocates and opponents that the first priority of the Inquiry was to establish whether or not there was a "need" for Belvoir coal. In the words of the NCB counsel's closing statement:

> We would unreservedly agree with Sir Frank Layfield (counsel for Leicestershire) when he said . . . "Economic need is the first factor to be considered."

The Inquiry, therefore, had to discuss and criticise the Board's plans for expanding coal output in Britain, as well as the specific proposal to sink three pits in and around the Vale of Belvoir.

Professor Colin Robinson appeared as a witness for Leicestershire County Council (which opposed the NCB's proposal) and argued that the NCB had failed to produce convincing evidence for its expansion plans. In general, he suggested, they were predominantly "supply determined," aiming at reaching quantities of output not specifically related to likely consumer demand given probable trends in the prices of coal and other fuels.

In Hobart Paper 89 Professor Robinson and Eileen Marshall analyse the prospects for the British coal industry, based originally on research carried out for the Belvoir Inquiry but brought up to date in the light of events since the Inquiry ended in the spring of 1980. The Paper discusses the market for coal in Britain, where it has been restricted by the government creation of virtual monopoly, and in the world market, which is more competitive. The analysis includes the most recent developments in February–March 1981 in which the use of the strike-threat by the miners' union induced the Government to yield to its demands. The *Hobart Paper* thus analyses competition and monopoly in the market both for coal and the labour that produces it, the consequences of nationalisation in Britain in a competitive world market, and the lessons that may have to be learned if a politically-created monopoly is not to resist the adaptation of industry to changing conditions of supply and demand.

Professor Robinson, a leading authority on the economics of the energy industry, and Eileen Marshall have produced a model *Hobart Paper* in applying the main elements of economic theory to an industry in which political bargaining has tended to obscure the opportunity costs of monopoly to other industries, to domestic consumers and to the economy as a whole. They trace the origins of the recent events for several decades in which the market for British coal has declined with technological innovation and rising living standards. In so doing they illustrate the power of market analysis to illuminate the changing structure and fortunes of the coal industry and of its employees at the coal face and above ground. Above all they demonstrate the damaging consequences of the nationalisation that, unlike the competitive production of coal in large producing countries overseas, has reduced the impact on British coal of changing market conditions that would have led it to make its adaptations more gradually and so avoided the discomfort and dislocations that now have to be made when the adaptations to changing conditions can no longer be postponed. Although the industry has been reduced in size as newer forms of fuel have emerged, the rate of adaptation has been determined not primarily by the decision of consumers choosing between coal and newer fuels but by the capacity of the producers to resist reforms and to slow them down to suit themselves.

The authors present an alarming portrayal of the ability of the National Coal Board, the National Union of Mineworkers and even the Department of Energy, which is supposed to safeguard the consumer interest above all, to use unrealistically optimistic forecasts of the demand for coal, based on low-quality economic argument, in order to induce government to allocate scarce resources to coal production that might have been used more efficiently elsewhere. And these romantic forecasts have also sadly raised false hopes among the miners, whom they were designed to protect. But that is the consequence of creating a monopoly in which the producer is judge and jury of his cause. The authors present their contrary estimate that the consumption of British coal will have dwindled by a further 11–40 per cent by the year 2000.

Professor Robinson and Eileen Marshall emphasise the distinction between the markets in British coal and for world coal. They argue that the higher costs of nationalised British coal contrast with the lower costs of privately produced coal in the USA, South Africa and Australia, and that this contrast largely accounts for the relatively poor outlook for British coal and the relatively bright outlook for overseas coal. Their conclusion is that there is little or no case for further protection of nationalised coal from the competition of cheaper and/or better coal from overseas, which would be to the advantage of the British steel, electricity and other industries, and of the householder.

The *Hobart Paper* raises disturbing fundamental issues in the conduct of British public policy. The claim made for nationalisation 35 years ago was that it would ensure that industry would be run for the good of the community as a whole. Little thought was given to the ability of nationalised industries to adapt themselves to adverse market conditions at home and overseas. The coal industry now illustrates the high price that is being paid for enabling nationalised industry to exploit the community by threatening government with local or general strike. Here, as elsewhere, there will have to be more attention paid to the economics of "public choice," which studies decisions made without the assistance of markets, and to the reforms in the British constitution to deny transient government the power to yield to vested interests at the expense of the general interest. It also indicates the neglected task of how to take out of government control and political preferment industries that do not have to be owned, financed or run by government, or its agencies, because they are not public goods and there are no large-scale economies to justify centralised control. The question is whether the adaptations would have been made with less traumatic upheaval if the industry had, as elsewhere, been in private ownership spending its own rather than taxpayers' money.

Professor Robinson and Eileen Marshall have written an authoritative, scholarly, clearly argued, and spirited analysis that will evoke respectful attention from a wide range of readers from teachers and students of economics to people in public life responsible for making or influencing policy. This *Hobart Paper* is a timely, persuasively argued and disturbing dissection of an industry that has caused British economy and society grievous anxiety and suffering for over half a century since the General Strike of 1926.

Hobart Paper 92
February 1982

Robert Miller and John B. Wood

What Price Unemployment?

Labour is one of the main factors of production that is sold in a market: it has a supply and demand, and both vary with its price. The demand for labour determines the degree of employment of the available labour force; and the extent to which the demand falls short of the total supply is regarded as the measure of "unemployment."

These fundamental concepts are being largely ignored in the current discussion of employment in Britain, and it is the purpose of this *Hobart Paper* by Robert Miller and John Wood to clarify the economic significance of the term, and to shed light on the current discussion by indicating the errors and misconceptions.

People are regarded as "employed" when they are producing goods or services that consumers want sufficiently to pay for. There are the special aspects of poverty, in which some people cannot pay for the goods or services they are judged as requiring; there are public goods that cannot be supplied in return for individual payment by consumers; there are periods of "recession" in which there is a general reduction in economic activity unrelated to individual industries and the demands for their products. But these three aspects do not disturb the central diagnosis of labour as a commodity or service sold in a market.

Recent concentration in Britain on "three million unemployed" is a dangerous and even mischievous over-simplification of truth. Much of British economic activity (much more than the small sector of 20 per cent comprising public goods) operates without close market measurement or disciplines. In these activities the consumer is unable to indicate whether he wants a product or service sufficiently to pay for it. There is no significant sense in which the labour used to produce it can be said to be employed or unemployed. The many in the so-called public services that produce education or medical care, fuel or transport, that the consumer has little voice in accepting or rejecting cannot be said to be "employed": they may be active and paid, but their employment does not necessarily produce valued products. The same is true of private industry that operates as a monopoly or is subsidised by the state. And that is also why the statistics of "full employment" in "non-market" socialist or communist states are hilarious fictions.

But the recorded figure of unemployment is in Britain misleading for many more reasons: some are voluntarily excluding themselves from registered employment—no-one in Britain, unlike the socialist states, has to work; many are kept out of work by the law that requires high minimum wages or redundancy pay or provides attractive social benefits in unemployment; many are kept out of work by trade unions—Professor Patrick Minford has calculated that not less than a million jobs are destroyed by union policy;[1] many unemployed are hard at work in or out of working hours and paid by cash or in kind in the "black economy" that Professor Edgar Feige estimates is more extensive than the official statistics allow.[2]

And "the three million unemployed" is wielded mischievously when used to imply that people not registered for work are suffering the hardship and privation of their grandfathers 50 years ago. Many more now have private savings; their social benefits are higher; and more are in families with other earners. Observers in the Press and broadcasting also confuse the public by implying that unemployment is necessarily harmful. Economic progress requires the creation of unemployment in order to make available labour for new and growing industries. To the economist this is a self-evident proposition. But no politician can say it lightly. National unemployment is, in January 1982, some 11 per cent of the labour force apparently available at current rates of pay. Disclosure that in some industries or towns the percentage is 20 is announced as though it were a calamity. Yet, if progress is to take place, the percentage must be higher the smaller the unit; in some families it may have to rise to 100 per cent. If this had not happened in the nineteenth century, and people had not moved from decaying to growing industries, there could have been no advance in the living standards we are enjoying in the twentieth century.

These and associated issues are analysed and discussed, and their implications for policy indicated, by the authors who, although members of the IEA staff, write in their personal capacities.

1. *Journal of Economic Affairs,* January 1982.
2. *Journal of Economic Affairs,* October 1981.

Hobart Paper 93
April 1982

Barry Bracewell-Milnes

Land and Heritage: The Public Interest in Personal Ownership

In Hobart Paper 93 Dr. Barry Bracewell-Milnes, an economist well versed in classical economics but with an independent mind that leads him to unconventional analyses and unorthodox conclusions, provides a refreshingly stimulating study of the economics of land ownership. He points to aspects of the subject and raises questions that might stimulate reconsideration of established approaches.

Dr. Bracewell-Milnes reviews the orthodox interpretation of land ownership, and finds it wanting. The pioneering flavour of his approach leads him to a closely reasoned discussion that requires correspondingly close attention to appreciate its significance. His independence of mind was demonstrated in 1973 when on grounds of principle he chose dismissal rather than resignation from his position as Economic Director of the Confederation of British Industry; his support for market-oriented rather than corporatist policies has been largely vindicated by subsequent developments.

In the course of his analysis Dr. Bracewell-Milnes makes some intriguing statements and reaches provocative conclusions: the personal ownership of land gives the owner a sense of satisfaction that does not always accompany the ownership of other assets: land as heritage is worth more to society when owned privately than collectively; the satisfaction of property rights in land becomes sterile when it is owned collectively, and so on. And the analysis leads the author to conclusions for public policy on taxation.

Whatever the argument on the approach that the personal ownership of land gives unique satisfaction both to the owners and to society in general, it is a direct challenge to the long-established view that the public interest was served only by the collective ownership of land through nationalisation. There was always a large often unstated assumption that "publicly-owned" land would be administered in the interest of the public. Perhaps experience of other forms of nationalisation has taught the lesson that, as in the railways, the mines, the schools and the hospitals, assets that are not appropriated to individuals are not husbanded because no individual can identify his interest. The reply to the argument for nationalisation was that only individual ownership would ensure individual care, protection and conservation. Dr. Bracewell-Milnes reinforces the objection to "public ownership" by a refined statement of the positive advantages both for the owner and for society.

For many years the words "private" and "public" have been misused or misunderstood. "Private" has been used to imply consequences contrary to the interest of the public. "Public" has been used to imply consequences necessarily favourable to the interest of the public. Post-war experience has confirmed the views of the classical economists, going back to David Hume and earlier, that the best interests of the public are served by private ownership. This *Paper* argues that the ownership should be not only private but personal. It could therefore, by extension, be read as a criticism not only of public ownership but also of non-personal ownership in large private organisations. Recent discussion on methods of re-creating personal interest in large organisations is a facet of the economics of personal ownership.

The Institute has to thank Professor Arthur Shenfield and other economists for reading early drafts and making observations that have been taken into account by the author in his final revisions.

Hobart Paper 94 *Steven Cheung*
April 1982

Will China Go "Capitalist"?

It might appear that the socialist or communist economies of Europe, Asia and Africa have decided that "government failure" is less damaging or more remediable than "market failure." At least, that would appear to be the inference from the continued existence of economies that seem to make little use of markets and yet appear to be able to produce tolerable living standards without them: at any rate, so far. Communism in Russia seems to be firmly established after 65 years since 1917 and in China for 33 years since 1949. But because both rest on coercion rather than on public consent, the inner strength of their economies, or their prospect of permanence, cannot be assumed. The interesting question is whether there are tendencies operating below the surface that will decide their strength and prospects.

For an analysis of these suppressed tendencies in China the Institute turned to a Chinese economist working in the open intellectual society of the USA at the University of Washington in Seattle, Washington State. In view of the Chinese cultural tradition in small trading, the individualism of the Chinese people, and the strength of the Chinese family, it seemed that the centralised communist economic system, resting on collective property ownership, was not likely to be stable or to last many more decades. Professor Cheung was therefore invited to analyse the working of the Chinese economy below the surface of its declarations or what is known about it in the Western world, and to assess the proposition that it may become a "capitalist" economy.

Hobart Paper 94 is the result. Professor Cheung goes deep into the economic theory of property rights and transaction costs to indicate the prospect that he puts into the form of a hypothesis or prediction: if the Chinese hold firm in their present policy intentions, they would eventually adopt a structure of property rights that resembles or works like that of a private enterprise system. His *Paper* is based on his work as an analytical economist (he is the author of Hobart Paper 82, *The Myth of Social Cost,* 1978), complemented by his recollections of China, in which he lived during World War II until the collapse of the Kuomintang in 1948, and which he visited in 1957 and again recently in 1979.

Symptoms of moves to a freer economy have been observed in China: the translations of the works of Adam Smith, Keynes and Friedman; the recognised spread and tolerance of real if small markets; the increasing knowledge of living standards enjoyed in the outside capitalist world; and the readiness to accept overseas investment and technology. This *Paper* was written in July 1981 and revised in November 1981, a highly confused period in China when these symptoms were coming into conflict with explicit governmental attempts to suppress "capitalistic" activities. Although conditions are equally unclear today and may remain so for a long time, the author holds firm in the judgements and predictions he offers here.

The central portion of the *Paper* is a sophisticated theoretical discussion that provides an explanation of his hypothesis not found in the writings of other observers of China. It is closely argued and repays close attention. But the *Paper* as a whole is clearly written in plain, non-technical English.

Observers may see a political struggle between the conservative communists who would foist communism on China as taught by Mao Tse-tung and the so-called "liberal" communists (another misuse of a noble word) who, under the leadership of Deng Xiaoping, would open up the communist economy, or who can see that it will be impossible to continue the economic centralisation if living standards are to be raised. But this battle reflects economic tendencies deeper than a personal or a political struggle for power. The analysis of these economic tendencies is the core of Professor Cheung's *Paper.*

Capitalism is likely to re-emerge earlier in China than in Russia, because it has been easier to suppress the Russian agricultural peasantry than the Chinese trader, and because Russia knew the benefits of capitalism for a shorter period to 1917 than did China to 1948. Yet the increasing knowledge of the outside world, the debilitating effect of the centralisation of decisions on investment, and the restlessness in the more advanced communist countries of Eastern Europe, not least Poland, Yugoslavia and Rumania, indicate that it may be only a decade or two before Russia goes the way of China.

Professor Cheung's analysis of trends in the advance of China from extreme communism to refined private enterprise is a stimulating text for students and teachers of economics and observers of the world politico-economic scene.

Hobart Paper 109
February 1988

William C. Mitchell

Government As It Is

Professor William Mitchell's study has been placed in the *Hobart Paper* series both because government itself is a service that can be subjected to economic analysis no less than food, clothing or housing, and because his analysis is very much concerned with government as it is in the real world and not as an ideal or a vision.

These two views of government as an economic activity like any other and as contending with real-world conditions are related. Government is an industry producing goods and services with scarce resources that could be used in other industries, or in other ways; it is therefore subject to economic "laws" both within its boundaries and in its relationships with other industries. The central economic question here is how far it uses its scarce resources efficiently as judged by their owners, the general population, for whom government can be regarded as acting in the capacity of trustees answerable to their "clients."

The second reason, that government must be judged by its performance in the real world, working with the same limitation of fallible people as in other industries, explains the title, which is derived from a pointed question asked 90 years ago by the renowned economist at Cambridge University, Alfred Marshall, long before it was diverted into an intellectual *cul-de-sac* by the followers of J. M. Keynes:

> "Do you mean government all wise, all just, all powerful or government as it now is?"

Although this distinction between ideal and actual government was in the minds of some early classical economists, it was largely forgotten, or consciously ignored, by scholars and social reformers since the late nineteenth century who, in their anxiety to devise remedies for the deficiencies and abuses attributed to industrialism, looked to government with its supposedly able political leaders, ample resources and unique duties to serve the general interest. Presumably Alfred Marshall's question of 1896 reflected the writings and advocacy of the scholars and social reformers of his day: notably, perhaps, T. H. Green, the philosopher who misled the Liberals, and the politically active socialists Sidney and Beatrice Webb, who confused the Labour instinct for voluntary self-help with state coercion. Despite the warning in 1887 of Lord Acton, the British jurist, that "Power tends to corrupt, and absolute power corrupts absolutely," many other scholars and social reformers in the past century must have supposed, or hoped, that government would be "all wise, all just, all powerful" in dealing with unemployment or inflation in the economy, inefficiency in industry and poverty among the people.

Their followers to this day in all schools of thought and all political parties, whether consciously or unconsciously, seem to suppose that government will have the outstanding political men (and women), the resources from taxation, and the good intentions to remove the remaining poverty and inequality, inefficiency in industry and the latest manifestations of inflation and unemployment in the late 20th century. The assumption is still, often explicitly in political party manifestos, that government will remove the various forms of "market failure." (And the implicit claim is that government action is the *only* available cure for "market failure.") The solution for "market failure," in short, is still widely thought to be government benevolence. This is the assumption, repeatedly falsified by history, that lies at the roots of our present discontents.

The study of the nature and function of government is the province of political science. The concentrated power that the state assembles in government can be used for evil as well as for good. Down the centuries philosophers have sought solutions to the dilemma. Plato's *Republic* envisaged a society ruled by the wisest. The claims to wisdom have understandably been plenty: the Jewish, the Catholic and the Protestant state would be run by priests who interpreted God's will (the Puritans in seventeenth century Massachusetts created a government in which only church members would share political power). Aristotle's *Politics* passed from ideals to reality and urged a democracy of ordinary men whose common sense would guarantee the weak a voice against the strong. As the city state was submerged by the larger national state, law was seen as the safeguard against its potential tyrannies. Hobbes envisaged individuals contracting with one another for self-preservation. Locke depicted a more equal contract between rulers and ruled. Rousseau's "social contract" said the general will gave a moral unity to the state (the idea that sparked the French Revolution). Hegel saw the state as the vehicle for the changing processes of history, which Marx, ignorant of the corruptibility of power, extended into an instrument for overturning society and solving all problems of oppression and injustice by removing the bourgeoisie.

In the real world "democracy" has taken varying forms. The British Parliament is a marriage of debate and representation. But do representatives debate the issues of importance to the people and reflect their opinions? Does representative government respect their preferences? Can representatives represent 80,000 or 100,000 voters with diverse requirements in education and medical care, even if they have arrived at a social "consensus" for defence? How have political scientists interpreted the activity of government? To economists, who see potentialities for good as well as for evil in the market, it has seemed that for several decades political scientists have seen the state and its government as instruments for good rather than evil. Yet for 30 to 35 years since the 1950s a new development in economics, described by its founders as "public choice," has studied the collective (non-market) decision-making of government and arrived at conclusions very different from those of the political scientists.

What then is political science teaching about "government as it is now"? Is "public choice" having any effect on the study of government by political scientists? And what is the inter-action between economists and political scientists? To enlighten economists interested in the study of markets we invited Professor Mitchell, an American political scientist, who for some years has taught that the economic study of government has relevant conclusions for the political study of government, to review the new approach of public choice and indicate its influence on the study of government and on the teaching of political science. He identifies six contributions: a better understanding of the real world behaviour of political institutions, a more systematic explanation ("theory") of the activity of "rent-seeking" interest groups in gaining political privileges, a new view of the power of government in managing the "political-business" cycle for electoral advantage, a more convincing explanation of the growth of government, a new "anatomy" and pathology of governmental failure, and a new approach to forestalling government failure by altering the constitutional rules governing political action.

In this IEA *Paper* Professor Mitchell is interpreting the thinking of economists to his own profession of political science, to many in which he says much of the approach, the analysis and the conclusions will be new. His Paper is also of interest to economists in showing where a political scientist thinks the economist's micro-economic approach is important for the macro-economic apparatus of the state. Where the political scientist speaks of "priorities" and "needs," the economist uses the tools of supply (of government and its services), demand, and price. People in the market spend their own money; people in politics spend other people's money. The politicians' intentions or plans are "wish-lists" that the political process cannot turn into responsible investment decisions because it divorces supply from demand and both from price.

The *Paper* is also intended mainly for university academics and for teachers of political science, philosophy, law, sociology and history. Yet readers whose interests lie in the working world of politics, industry, and the media will find that Professor Mitchell sheds light on their activities.

His key insight is that he sees the importance of price, and the consequences of its absence: *"no-one in politics knows the price of anything."* If so, government does not know what it is doing in allocating scarce resources to alternative uses. And appeals to "the public interest," "social justice," "fairness," or "need," which is all that remain to politicians as guides to government policy, are poor substitutes for price information, however imperfect, on relative scarcities.

The economics of pressure-group politics emphasised by Professor Mitchell will echo in British minds. The "rent-seekers" who lobby Parliament (and approach civil servants) were closely examined by British political scientist, Professor S. E. Finer, in a noted book in 1958, *Anonymous Empire: a Study of the Lobby in Britain.* But the public choice economists have dissected the rent-seekers more incisively than the political scientists by analysing the *individual* costs and benefits of the recipients and the sources of their subventions. Because politicians can grant enormous benefits to people who lobby government, it pays people to lobby government. Supply has created a demand. The benefits are generally concentrated on the relatively few—landowners, farmers, doctors, teachers, and others—at the expense of the relatively many. The large individual benefit to the few makes it profitable for them to invest sizeable sums in lobbying (and recruiting advisers formerly in politics or the civil service). But the many who pay for the benefit lose little as individuals, and therefore lack the inducement to oppose the rent-seekers.

This calculus of individual benefit and cost, moreover, produces a massive distortion in the economic system. The rent-seekers are characteristically producers, and the people who pay for the benefits producers extract from politicians are characteristically consumers. But they are the same people. Government has ironically induced the citizens of a democracy to put their immediate or short-term interests (as producers) before their own more fundamental long-term interests (as consumers). This producer-dominance is essentially the reason for the breakdown of the medieval mercantilist system: the technical inventions in the Industrial Revolution undermined the producers protected by mercantilist regulation. It is the reason why corporatist or syndicalist systems are economically weak and usually short-lived. And it is the reason why state socialist or communist systems are economically weak but can last as long as they are maintained by coercion. Rent-seeking lobbying as now operated by business[1] and union[2] interests, is encouraged by bloated democracies that run much more than they have to run, and can distribute privileges to the lobbies. Bloated democracy, like mercantilism, syndicalism and socialism, becomes myopic, opposed to change, protective, xenophobic. The economy in time slows down and seizes up, as periodically in the USSR. But that is also the ultimate effect of representative democratic government that allows itself to be importuned and distorted by the rent-seekers. Yet it is not the rent-seekers who are to blame; they are seeking benefits for their members. The fault lies with the economic and political system which makes it profitable to lobby government.

1. *The Guardian,* 8 January 1988, ominously reviews the activities of the lobbyists who, it claims wrongly, operate mainly for business. Its review contains not a word about the lobbying by trade unions (footnote 2 below).

2. *The Times Educational Supplement,* 8 January 1988, carries an article by David Hart, General Secretary of the National Association of Head Teachers, that "offers a diligent lobbyist's guide on how to get the Education Reform Bill amended where, and when, it matters. . . ."

Hobart Paper 111 *Norman P. Barry*
August 1988

The Invisible Hand in Economics and Politics

Like Professor William Mitchell's Hobart Paper 109, *Government As It Is,* written by an American political scientist, Professor Norman Barry, a British political scientist, examines in *Hobart Paper* 111 the political process of collective decision-making and contrasts it with the result of individual decision-making in the market process. Both authors go to the roots of the fundamental principles, still misunderstood or ignored by most British (and American) economists and political scientists, that explain the differences between the formation and consequences of individual and collective decision-making.

The two *Hobart Papers* complement each other. Professor Mitchell argues that conventional political science as still studied and taught to students fails to explain the political process, and therefore why it would have to be refined by the *economic* analysis of politics—its costs and benefits to individual voter/taxpayers rather than the indeterminate and pretentious debates on the generalised collective and unpriced "priorities" or "needs" that form the staple of "democratic" politics. Professor Barry now supplements this new kind of political science by contrasting the market as a continuing process with the conventional political study of society as an ideal goal or "end-state."

Both *Papers* are thus two more studies of the basic principles and structure of modern politico-economic society which have formed the bedrock of IEA analysis and prescription for reform in economic policy. In the years since 1960 some of the important "practical" IEA *Papers* have examined the production of specific goods and services and pointed to market solutions. Resale price maintenance has passed into history. Advertising is no longer denigrated on principle (and indeed is used by former detractors). Hire purchase has become as respectable as home mortgages (and both are supplied by former critics in the clearing banks). The restrictive professions are judged no more politically untouchable than the trade unions. Proposals for introducing choice into state services are being closely examined. And charging for government services (thus revealing them as not "public goods") is spreading. Yet the most essential IEA studies have been of the "theoretical" basic principle and structures of individual and collective behaviour.

Among the most notable, and effective in their long-term effects on changing minds, have been those on the cult of "growthmanship" at any price (Colin Clark), the false gods of "national plans" (John Brunner) and "incomes policies" (Samuel Brittan), the tiger of inflation (Friedrich Hayek), the false god of government spending as the cure for unemployment (Alan Walters, Milton Friedman), the pitfalls of "public choice" (J. M. Buchanan, Gordon Tullock), the delusions of "social cost" (Steven Cheung), the unique role and indispensability of the entrepreneur (Israel Kirzner), the political unreality of alternating budget deficits and surpluses (J. M. Buchanan, John Burton and Robert Wagner), the over-simplicities of the "mixed economy" (S. C. Littlechild), and many more.

Together the "theoretical" and "practical" studies have over 30 years shown the long-neglected strengths of the market process and the long-ignored weaknesses of the political process. And the demonstration has re-inforced the inclination of recent governments to implement policies hitherto misjudged as "politically impossible." The market is gradually being used (or not hindered) where it is superior to "politics." Desocialisation, renamed privatisation, has become commonplace in Britain, gradually accepted in all political parties, and has spread overseas. The market, formerly anathematised, is advocated without the risk of instant political suicide and instead embraced with prospect of electoral reward, not least from the newly-emancipated "working-classes," despite uninformed priestly displeasure.

The relationship between the "theoretical" and "practical" *Papers* has formed the kernel of IEA intellectual strategy. In the two-century battle of ideas between the four decisive schools of economic thought, personified by Adam Smith, Karl Marx, J. M. Keynes and Frederick Hayek, the fallacies have had to be demolished before better thinking was accepted. It was the intellectual "artillery" bombardment of "theory" that destroyed opposing fallacies before the "infantry" of proposals for practical reform could take demoralised opposing positions. The strategy of the military commander and the cricket captain inspired the parallels for the economic contest in the arguments for the state and the market.

This is the fundamental background to Professor Barry's *Paper.* He examines and contests the continuing critique of the market from the academic world that lags long behind both popular preference for the market-based "capitalist" system and its belated acceptance and advocacy by politicians in all parties since 1979. He deals mainly with the writings of Professor F. H. Hahn of Cambridge, A. K. Sen of Harvard, Gerard Debreu of California (Berkeley), and K. J. Arrow of Stanford. But there are still many other critics, and they will continue to influence a generation of students who will reflect fallacious teaching in their working lives into the twenty-first century. The latest example is the recent Marxist-overweighted successor to the celebrated 1890s *Palgrave Dictionary of Political Economy,* edited by economists at Cambridge, Harvard and Johns Hopkins Universities (J. Eatwell, M. Milgate, P. Newman, published by Macmillan, 1987). And the nostalgia for the teachings of Keynes is still echoed by older economists, like Professor James Tobin of Yale, in the remarkably balanced hour-long video written and presented by Professor Mark Blaug, *J. M. Keynes: Life, Ideas, Legacy* (IEA, 1988).

Professor Barry's *Hobart Paper* thus continues the intellectual debate between the state and the market since Adam Smith. There can by now be little doubt that, except among older economists won to Keynesian thinking in their youth, or younger economists who derive their distaste for liberal "capitalism" by contrasting it with an unrealisable vision of benevolent collectivism, the market has largely vanquished the state in argument and evidence. But the tasks of replacing the state and its supporting intellectual and vested interests will remain stubborn. Not the least task will be to break out of the vicious circle in which the political process progressively extends its writ. Politicians and bureaucrats have a natural professional interest in preserving their political province. "The invisible hand" that leads individuals in the market unintentionally to *serve* the public interest seems in politics to *thwart* the public interest. And even where politicians are influenced by new thinking, recent history since 1979 shows the power of vested interests, at least in the short run, to resist their new-found inclinations. Contemporary history reveals the stubborn paradox that politicians who wish to liberate the individual from the dominion of politics by enlarging choice in the market end after nine years by taking even more individual income and subjecting it to the precarious collective decision-making of politics. The conundrum remains to be solved by the study of the economics of "public choice."

Yet an encouraging exemplar is to be found not too far away in Europe. Once it was the social market economy of West Germany. Sweden maintains economic markets and political liberty but at the high price of individual enervation in a pervasive welfare state. The best lessons lie in Switzerland, which properly reduces its politicians to almost anonymous administrators of essentials of government. There is a long way to go.

These fundamental issues in the nature of politico-economic systems require to be analysed in largely abstract terms that are more easily absorbed by economists than by beginners in the subject or by non-economists accustomed to think in more concrete terms. Several such IEA *Papers* over the years have discussed the implications of macro-economic thinking for policy in the market economy (Professor L. M. Lachmann), the fallacies in the so-called Cambridge Revolution in economic thought (Professor Mark Blaug), and the replacement of state monopoly by private competition in the supply of money (Professor F. A. Hayek). There, and in other *Papers*, newcomers to economics were advised to read the text more than once to see the importance of the argument. Professor Barry's discussion is necessarily abstract and requires close reading, especially to follow the refinements in the reasoning, on which professional economists and political scientists may differ even where they broadly concur in the eventual implications for the choice between the state and the market.

The Institute presents Professor Barry's *Hobart Paper* as a timely contribution to the unabated intellectual battle on the roles of the state and the market that underlies the national and international controversies and events of our day.

This Preface is the last of my 250 written to put into context the work of some 300 IEA authors. I am especially glad to end with the *Hobart Papers* by Professors Mitchell and Barry because the outcome of the contest of the state and the market will turn on the degree to which the polity can be subjected to the economy. And both authors are political scientists whose analyses go to the roots of the economic debate.

In choosing authors for IEA Papers over 30 years, often with the assistance of the academic advisers, I sometimes felt like the manager of a cricket team putting the best players in to "bat" against the opposing sides. Historians will judge the effects of the long academic debate on public and political opinion, as seen in the intellectual and cultural revolution between the 1950s, when the market was anathema, and the 1980s, when it is being offered by every political party, old and new, and in the resurgence of Britain and the West against the decaying cult of the state in the East and the Third World.

PART II

Prefaces to Hobart Paperbacks

Hobart Paperback 1
May 1971

W. H. Hutt

Politically Impossible . . . ?

For over a decade the Institute has conceived studies of subjects it considered had been overlooked, or on which there was an imbalance of research and writing, commissioned the best available economists to work on them, and published their work in lengths varying from short papers to full-length books. It has often been asked to show how the policies emerging from these economic analyses could be put into practice, and why some had seemed to influence thinking in business and government while others seem to have been ignored.

What is within the competence and relevance of economists is to consider why economic prescription is adopted in some circumstances and neglected in others, why economists are heeded or ignored, when economic advice is fruitful and when it is abortive. How important are the possibly wide range of influences that bear on the formation of policy: from ideas to financial interest, with expediency, fashion and others between the extremes? The circumstances influencing or deciding the translation of analysis into action will be the object of a new series, named after the best-known Institute Papers, the *Hobart Paperbacks.* The length will typically be between that of a *Paper* and a book.

They will extend into political economy the economic analyses of the *Hobart Papers.* They will aim to maintain the authority for which the *Hobart Papers* have established a well-earned repute. Their authors are chosen for their optimum combination of these qualities. They will be asked not to avoid "difficult" issues, and to be unremitting in pursuing their analyses to their conclusions.

The new series reflects two further tendencies in opinion among economists. The late Professor A. C. Pigou taught that the object of any inquiry "may be either light or fruit, either knowledge for its own sake or knowledge for the sake of good things to which it leads. . . . In the sciences of human society be their appeal as bearers of light never so high, it is the promise of fruit and not of light that chiefly merits our regard." The English classical economists were regarded as concerned not with "economics" but with "political economy." They were interested in the politically-decided legal framework of society as well as with the economic relationships conducted within it. Hence the concern of the classical economists, from Adam Smith to John Stuart Mill and beyond, with the scope for individual activity in the national economy.

In the last third of the nineteenth century, roughly from Stanley Jevons onwards, through Alfred Marshall and Edwin Cannan, economics was regarded as austerely confined to economic relationships. A more recent school of economic thinking, originating amongst young American economists, J. M. Buchanan, Gordon Tullock, Anthony Downs and others, has applied economic analysis to the operation of political institutions, studying politicians as entrepreneurs aiming to maximize votes from their allocation of resources among competing electoral claims. The new political economy thus studies the economic system as a mechanism responding to the citizen as consumer in the market and as elector in the polling booth.

These are the broad spheres of study that the *Hobart Paperbacks* will seek to illuminate in terms of their significance for the British economy and for government and industry in particular. The first Hobart Paperback is a discussion of the fundamental relationship between the evolution of economic ideas and their translation into policy. What makes some economic thinking "politically possible" and other not?

This is the subject which Professor W. H. Hutt, a London-born economist who spent most of his life teaching in Cape Town and now writes in the USA, discusses with examples from Britain, America and South Africa. He has often been right during the past 40 years on many fundamental issues: labour, money, economic planning and others. He is too modest to say that he has been belatedly acknowledged long after a piece of writing considered at the time to be unrealistic. His *Theory of Collective Bargaining* contained in 1930 truths about the power of trade unions too little acknowledged until recent years. His *Economists and the Public,* 1936, told truths long before their time. His *Plan for Reconstruction,* 1943, indicated a way of liberalizing a centrally-directed economy by easing out the interests that had become entrenched in it. His rejection of Keynesian thought in *The Theory of Idle Resources,* 1939, has recently been acclaimed by Professor Axel Leijonhufvud as a *locus classicus* on a central weakness in Keynesianism.[1]

Professor Hutt develops his original suggestion that, since economists should not think or act like politicians but should not preclude their judgement from being heeded by politicians, they should present their conclu-

1. *Keynes and the Classics,* Occasional Paper 30, IEA, 1969.

sions and advice in two stages. The former in its undiluted form should be the best that economics can teach, the latter in the "second best" form diluted by political judgement. It could then be seen that the failure to act on economic advice is that of the politicians, who may sacrifice the best that economics can teach by misjudgement of what is "politically possible."

This assessment of an absorbing review of economic thinking, economists' advice and politics since the 1930s may also be regarded as coming long before its time. Whatever Professor Hutt writes is the work of an independent scholar, uninhibited about whether his opinion will be found palatable or not. His new work should begin a new argument among economists on the form in which they should make their judgements to those who could profit from them. Whether he is heeded in the short run or the long run, his work will have been vindicated.

The Institute wishes to thank Professor G. C. Allen, Emeritus Professor of Political Economy, University of London, and Professor A. A. Shenfield, Visiting Professor of Economics, Rockford College, Illinois, for observations on an early draft that Professor Hutt has borne in mind in his final revisions.

Hobart Paperback 2
May 1971

Samuel Brittan

Government and the Market Economy

The Preface to the first *Hobart Paperback* by Professor W. H. Hutt, *Politically Impossible . . . ?*, explained the purpose of the new series: to discuss, in the spirit of what was once called "political economy,"[1] the influences which affect the translation of economic ideas into practical policy and the nature of economic activity in public affairs. Professor Hutt examined the notion that some (or many) ideas are not adopted because they are considered "politically impossible."

The second *Hobart Paperback*, by Mr. Samuel Brittan, moves closer to the formation of policy. Subsequent *Paperbacks* will take a more theoretical or empirical form according to the specialisms of the authors.

Mr. Brittan reviews the economics of the Government's policies since June 1970 and asks a question that should intrigue economists as well as politicians: how far can they be said to reflect the prescriptions emerging from the thinking of what in Britain is referred to as classical or new-classical economics and of the economists whom Mr. Brittan calls "economic liberals." The importance of this question is not whether government policy can be judged right or wrong in the thinking of "economic liberals" in Mr. Brittan's sense, but whether it is intellectually consistent, and, if not, why some policies seem to make for a more "liberal" economy and why others seem to undermine it. Mr. Brittan writes as one of the leading economic journalists of his day who most effectively bridges the gulf between the observer of practical economic and financial affairs and the thinker with the depth of the academic. Although his *Paperback* is based on a lecture originally addressed to a meeting of civil servants, it was amplified before his award of the prize for the Harold Wincott Foundation Journalist of the Year. It therefore reflects the latest stage in Mr. Brittan's thinking on economics and economic policy which may seem to outsiders to have been evolving since or before he served as an adviser in the Department of Economic Affairs.

He finds that in several directions government economic policy has strengthened the market element in the economy but in others has weakened

1. Professor T. W. Hutchison, *Markets and the Franchise*, Occasional Paper 10, IEA, 1966.

it and in yet others has been more or less neutral. His discussion of current policy, couched in terms of principles, is stimulating and uncompromising so that other economists who broadly share his approach may not accept his interpretation of particular policies. His argument on general principles will command substantial assent in much of the ground he covers from "economic liberals"—and perhaps increasingly from economists in general: his review of monopoly policy, his appraisal of state welfare, his examination of the housing market, the increasing role for income supplements and a reverse income tax, and the general determination to require industry to cover its costs rather than expect the public to subsidize it through taxation. His discussion of technical machinery—his plea for the restoration of the Consumer Council or an analogous body, his belief that a modified IRC would have been a "lesser evil" than other kinds of interventions still practised, his qualified blessing for the National Economic Development Council in the absence of a full parliamentary scrutiny of economic policy, and, not least, his carefully-worded case for a "temporary" freeze (a year)—may produce as much disagreement as agreement among economists in general and "economic liberals" in particular.

In this cogent essay perhaps the argument most open to dispute is that for a freeze. It may seem tempting to advocate a moratorium on the freely working movement of labour prices, but academic economists, particularly "economic liberals," who look back in British economic history and across the seas to other countries in more recent times will mostly take longer to convince. The more sophisticated advocates, who urge it as a "second best" and would prefer to avoid it if other policies could be made effective, must not be confused with those who give a freeze an ardent welcome as a potent part of a directed and controlled economy. The most plausible ground on which the more sophisticated, such as Mr. Brittan, make their case is that inflation has passed from being the result of monetary expansion in producing demand pull to being the consequence of labour monopoly in provoking cost push. And they would claim that a reform in the trade union law will take too long to remove the unions' privileged powers in the labour market.

But the objections remain formidable. They are not only the administrative complexities of making a freeze work with logical consistency. They are not only the unknown consequences for the price of labour when the freeze has ended, when the clamp is released from the valve, which most of its advocates tend to evade, although Mr. Brittan does at least discuss this aspect. The objections to a freeze are, most of all, its harmful effects in diverting attention away from the fundamental causes of inflation and the unpleasant, unpopular but just as fundamental cures for it. A critic would stress that policy must be concerned not only with the removal of labour (or capital) monopoly but also with the incidence of taxation (and social insurance) in the labour market which prevents real wages from rising, or may even reduce them, in a period of rising money wages. At the more recent heights of taxation on incomes, when little value is attached to "social wages" and employees from managing director to messenger look only at their "take-home" pay, high taxation is not necessarily deflationary, as Keynesians have long maintained, but may have become inflationary. And lower taxation requires reduced government expenditure, which conservative-minded politicians in both parties usually think, not always with convincing reason, "politically impossible."

Mr. Brittan ends his essay with a gentle admonition to his fellow economists, in journalism as well as in academia, to remember that "market forces and the price mechanism . . . are after all their stock in trade; otherwise they become merely statisticians dealing in figures of dubious validity." This proposition suggests two aspects of importance for the light and fruit that economics can yield in its application to policy. First, economists, and perhaps economic journalists, may have allowed their reservations about the abuse of prices and markets to become an aversion to prices and markets *per se.* Second, in the concentration on macro-economic developments in economic theory and applied economics, their concern with totals and people in the mass, economists, and again economic journalists, may have tended to lose sight of the significance of micro-economic analysis and its applications to people as individuals, responding to changing prices as consumers.

The *Hobart Paperbacks* are intended to extend into political economy the economic analysis of the Hobart *Papers* that have established a well-earned repute. Their authors will be chosen for their optimum combination of these qualities.

Hobart Paperback 4
January 1972

F. A. Hayek and Sudha R. Shenoy

A Tiger by the Tail

The purpose of the *Hobart Paperbacks* is to discuss, in the spirit of what was once called "political economy,"[1] the influences which affect the translation of economic ideas into practical policy and the economics of government activity. In the first *Paperback* Professor W. H. Hutt examined the notion that some ideas are not adopted because they are considered to be "politically impossible."

The translation of economic thinking into government action is perhaps nowhere more vividly illustrated than in the work of John Maynard Keynes. He was the most influential economist of our times: his ideas have influenced governments of all philosophic flavours more than any other economist. Yet it is not clear that his work will survive longer than that of some of his contemporaries. Perhaps no economist more than Adam Smith has had both early influence on government policy and enduring influence on the thinking of economists of succeeding generations. The extent to which economic ideas are adopted by government does not necessarily reflect their contribution to fundamental economic truths. The reasons for their adoption may range from respect for the new insights they show on the working of the economy to political expediency.

The powerful intellect of J. M. Keynes, his persuasive writing, and his capacity to formulate economic theory for government action not only made him the dominant economist, but also muted the doubts that some economists had about him from *The General Theory of Employment, Interest and Money,* published in 1936, and even earlier. Even though Keynes warned as early as 1945 that his followers had gone "sour and silly," and he seemed to be retreating in 1946 from his supposed demolition of "Classical" economic thought, his teachings have continued to dominate not only economic thinking in government but also economic teaching.

There may be debate for years to come on what Keynes really meant. Some economists never accepted the Keynesian system. They included not only A. C. Pigou, D. H. Robertson and others at Cambridge, but also the lesser-known but tenacious W. H. Hutt who, in his *Economists and the Pub-*

1. Professor T. W. Hutchison, *Markets and the Franchise,* Occasional Paper 10, IEA, 1966.

lic, published soon after *The General Theory*, warned against its inflationary implications.

The outstanding critic who was never persuaded by Keynes's analysis is F. A. Hayek, the Austrian scholar, who was teaching at the London School of Economics in 1936, and who has kept his British passport despite teaching posts in America, Germany and now in his native Austria.

Long before *The General Theory* Professor Hayek wrote a critique of Keynes's 1930 *Treatise on Money*. In the last 40 years he has written periodic criticisms of the Keynesian system, although at one stage he withdrew from the debate on monetary policy because he considered that Keynes, and the Keynesians, were not discussing the aspects that seemed to him fundamental.

The present *Hobart Paperback* comprises 17 extracts from his writings and lectures, two from Keynes and one from F. D. Graham of Princeton University. They were assembled and are introduced by Miss Sudha Shenoy, an Indian economist who has studied mainly in Britain. Together with a new essay written in July 1971 these extracts form an introduction to Professor Hayek's writings to which economists may wish to return.

Professor Hayek's writings prompt the reflection that the work of an economist should not be judged by the notice taken of him by politicians or even by other academics of his day. Why was Keynes so influential in his time and Hayek's (and other economists') reservations widely ignored? Why has Keynes dominated economic teaching for so long? How far is Keynesianism responsible for the acquiescence in post-war inflation? Are the doubts of many economists about Keynes now to be reflected in government thinking? Is taxation, as Keynes taught, still regarded as deflationary, or is it at last being seen that high tax rates and large deductions from earnings are inflationary? Has the Keynesian emphasis on macro-economics distracted attention from the structure of relative prices and costs that emerge from micro-economics?

This *Paperback* is offered as a contribution to the reconsideration of Keynesianism in the 1970s for teachers and students of economics, for policymakers in government, for the civil servants who guide or misguide them, and for journalists who are sometimes more concerned with the fashionable than with the fundamental in economic thinking.

Second Edition, 1978

The First Edition of *A Tiger by the Tail* reminded economists that for 40 years Professor Hayek's critique of Keynesian economics had been consistent, persistent and, in the end, vindicated. The extracts collated by Miss Sudha Shenoy comprised a graphic introduction to Professor Hayek's longer works since his early differences with Keynes.

The First Edition was published in 1972 and was re-printed in 1973. Since the First Edition the doubts about the Keynesian analysis by economists who followed Keynes have been increasing, and the readiness to listen to Professor Hayek's critique has accordingly grown. His work in general was, belatedly, recognised in the award of the Nobel Prize in 1974. And in 1975 *The Times,* which had not been Hayekian since the 1930s, paid Professor Hayek, in an oblique reference to *A Tiger by the Tail,* the tribute of identifying him as the economist above all who had accurately diagnosed the progression of inflation and its dangers to the economy:

> As Professor Friedrich Hayek has argued ever since his pre-war disputes with Keynes, the price of maintaining full employment by more and more inflationary public finance is not only accelerating inflation but also a progressive diversion of economic resources into activities favoured by or dependent on inflation. If inflation is to be checked, that structural distortion has to be reversed, which must be painful.[2]

Nothing written by the neo-Keynesians has refuted this diagnosis; and it is now the common currency not only of an increasing number of economists but of economic commentators in the press in Britain, America and Europe.

As the continuing demand from readers for *A Tiger by the Tail* has occasioned a further reprinting, the original text has been made into a new edition by adding three pieces of writing in the mid-1940s in which Professor Hayek anticipated developments in economic affairs and policies 30 years and more later. As in the First Edition, they are introduced by Miss Shenoy, who also writes on the significance for business decisions of the distinction between average and relative prices and on the secondary role of money supply.

The analysis is still relevant since governments in all countries that have allowed the tiger out of its cage are still pursuing its tail.

2. *The Times,* 4 January, 1975.

Hobart Paperback 5
September 1973

William A. Niskanen

Bureaucracy: Servant or Master?
Lessons from America

The purpose of the *Hobart Paperbacks* is to discuss, in the spirit of what was once called "political economy," primarily the influences which affect the translation of economic ideas into practical policy and secondarily the economics of government activity. In the first *Paperback* Professor W. H. Hutt examined the notion that some ideas are not adopted because they are considered to be "politically impossible."

In this *Hobart Paperback* Professor William A. Niskanen of the University of California examines an influence on policy largely left untouched by economic analysis. This neglect is surprising since it would seem natural for the economist to wonder whether the translation of ideas into policy is influenced by the machinery of government and the people who man it, and, if so, how far. There is a common romantic "public servant" attitude to the civil service as hard working, on the whole efficient, but above all incorruptible: it may derive from the intriguing supposition that to make a man a public official is to change his character and transform him into a public benefactor. There is also the opposite view of a Machiavellian bureaucracy perpetuating its power by "managing" or thwarting politicians and at the expense of the people. If history seems to provide examples to support both views, neither adequately explains the working or power of the "bureaucrats" who run the machinery of government in twentieth-century Britain. British bureaucrats cannot convincingly be sanctified as altruists nor pilloried as predators.

In revealing lectures delivered at Harvard in 1970 while he was a Minister, Mr. R. H. S. Crossman, a former academic political scientist at Oxford, who wrote a distinguished introduction to a new edition of Bagehot's *The English Constitution,* discussed the awesome power of the British civil service to influence Ministers and the formation of policy, yet exonerated it from culpability and blames politicians for submitting to its power. In this *Hobart Paperback,* Professor Niskanen, an economist who has spent five years as a public official with Robert McNamara and George Schultz under Presidents Kennedy, Johnson and Nixon in Washington, attempts to analyse the bureaucracy as economists have long analysed the firm. He asks what determines its size, how its output or efficiency is to be measured, what it attempts to maximise (its "maximand"), and so on.

His analysis implies no political or philosophical value judgements; he is concerned to dissect the bureaucracy with more surgical technical tools of the economist than are used by the political scientist or the sociologist. He defines a bureau as a non-profit organisation (which may be governmental or private) that is financed, wholly or partly, by a periodic grant. He examines its power as a competitor and a monopoly, its "product," the incentives and motives of the bureaucrat, and the relationship between a bureau and its sponsor as that of a "bilateral monopoly": a seller with no alternative customer confronted by a customer with no alternative supplier. From this economic "model" much of the analysis and the conclusions follow.

Professor Niskanen's main finding is that bureaucracies tend to be too large. The technical analysis is outlined in an Appendix (a short, simplified statement of a longer theoretical, mathematical explanation in his study, *Bureaucracy and Representative Government*). Non-economists who find the Appendix too technical should be able to follow the verbal discussion of its inferences in Chapter II.

This main conclusion leads Professor Niskanen to discuss three methods of correcting the excessive size of bureaucracies: first, re-construction of their internal working by competition or by quasi-profit incentives to bureaucrats to maximise the surplus of budgets over costs, second, the development of market alternatives to government agencies, and third, political reorganisation to make bureaucracies more sensitive to the ultimate consumer, or "public opinion."

Professor Niskanen's examples are based on the American machinery of government and the American economy. How far are administrative machinery, human nature, political motive, economic analysis, different or comparable in other Western countries? To consider whether Professor Niskanen's analysis and conclusions are more widely applicable to the British machinery of government and the British economy, the Institute invited four commentaries: from two former Ministers, Mr. Douglas Houghton, Minister for the co-ordination of the social services, 1966–67, and Mr. Nicholas Ridley, Under Secretary of State at the Department of Trade and Industry, 1970–72; and two former civil servants, Professor Maurice Kogan, formerly at the Department of Education and Science, 1953–67, and Mr. Ian Senior, formerly at the Post Office, 1962–67.

From his long experience as an official and a Minister, Mr. Houghton argues that little can be learned from America because of the differing conditions for which the British have evolved domestic solutions. Professor Kogan thinks that Professor Niskanen has raised interesting questions. Mr. Senior generally approves of the analysis but would sharpen the solutions. Mr. Ridley commends the diagnosis and argues for early reform. We thank them for their informed contributions.

In view of the large and still growing proportion of the British economy that is supervised, regulated or run by government officials, the British bureaucracy no less than the private sector should be subjected to close economic analysis. Whether half of the British economy should be conducted by government, or more, or less, both the government sector and the private sector would be more efficient if the bureaucracy is made as good as it can be.

The scholarly study of bureaucracy has been almost monopolised by political scientists and sociologists: from Max Weber to C. Northcote Parkinson. Apart from a 30-year-old work by Ludwig von Mises, *Bureaucracy* (1944), there are only two book-size studies by economists: Professor Gordon Tullock's *The Politics of Bureaucracy* (1965) and Professor Anthony Downs's *Inside Bureaucracy* (1967). Professor Niskanen's analysis now takes the economic examination of the machinery of government further by applying, *inter alia,* the relatively new American development of "the economics of politics," a subject almost entirely neglected by British economists. Whatever the views formed of his analysis and his conclusions, Professor Niskanen has opened up a subject which deserves more attention in Britain than it has so far received from economists, politicians, observers of government, and the general public. Is the British bureaucracy efficient? Does it serve the government of the day, the people at large, or itself?—and in what proportions? Is the framework within which it operates best designed to enable it to achieve what it sets out to do?

The increasing power of the British bureaucracy and the increasing interest by the public in its activities are reflected in the readiness of the Head of the Civil Service, Sir William Armstrong, to discuss its power and problems in public. Concern for local "bureaucracy" is also reflected in the Redcliffe-Maud committee on conflicts of interest in local government. Whatever may emerge from an official examination of bureaucracy it would seem timely to study it more closely, yet in a severely objective manner.

The Institute offers Professor Niskanen's Paperback as an original, stimulating and rigorously analytical essay by an independent thinker that should be widely studied in Britain.

Hobart Paperback 6
October 1974

Mark Blaug

The Cambridge Revolution: Success or Failure?

The unifying theme and purpose of the *Hobart Paperbacks* has been the relationship between economic thinking and policy, or more specifically the circumstances in which economic ideas are evolved, and which decide whether or not they affect the making of policy. So far *Paperbacks* by Professor W. H. Hutt, Mr. Samuel Brittan, Professor W. A. Niskanen and a compilation of the works of Professor F. A. Hayek have dealt with aspects of this general theme.

The next in the series delves deeply into the origins of a school of economic thinking and the disputations between its main exponents and economists of other schools of thought. The author, Professor Mark Blaug of the University of London, author of a work on the history of economic theory,[1] writes a searching and penetrating analysis of the evolution of thought of perhaps the most radical British school of economics in recent decades. Since the time of Alfred Marshall, and through the influence of A. C. Pigou, D. H. Robertson and J. M. Keynes, Cambridge has been probably the most influential school of economic thinking in the world. Since Keynes, and mainly through the work of Professor Joan Robinson, Professor Lord Kaldor (perhaps the best known to the British public), Professor Lord Kahn and Mr. Piero Sraffa, "Cambridge economists" have continued to exert a dominant influence on the evolution of economic theory, the teaching of economics in British and overseas universities, and not least on the formation of economic policy in Britain and the British Commonwealth. It is, therefore, of close interest to the layman as well as to the student of economics, to know what the Cambridge economists are saying in the 1970s.

The teaching of economics at Cambridge in recent years seems to have been dominated mainly by a small number of senior economists, whose work has woven together elements of the nineteenth-century doctrines of David Ricardo and Karl Marx with the twentieth-century thinking of Keynes and Kalecki into a fabric known as Cambridge theories of value and distribution. It is these economists who have for some years engaged in a

1. *Economic Theory in Retrospect*, Heinemann, 1968.

tenacious intellectual encounter with a group of economists at the other Cambridge—in Massachusetts at the Massachusetts Institute of Technology—namely Professors Paul A. Samuelson, Robert M. Solow and others who broadly follow the mainstream of neo-classical theory emanating from the classical economics of Walras and Marshall.

In this *Paperback*, Professor Blaug engages in a far-ranging dissection of the Cambridge (UK) school of economics in the attempt to appraise its contribution, or lack of it, to the evolution of economic ideas. Ostensibly, the Cambridge theories are directed at basic issues of policy on the degree to which wages and profits in mixed economies are capable of being influenced by government intervention. Professor Blaug concludes that much of Cambridge thinking is insufficiently in touch with the real world to be relevant for policy-making. This is one of the outstanding puzzles about the Cambridge theories. Not everyone will agree with Professor Blaug's explanation of how the results of Cambridge thinking have come to depart so widely from its intentions. But his explanation will stimulate new insights into the relationship between economic theory and economic policy.

Professor Blaug has produced the ideal text for students: he examines the thinking of the main participants in the debate but also refers repeatedly to the reactions of leading economists around the world. In the course of the analysis he discusses the leading progenitors of the Cambridge school and the neo-classical school, and relates the contemporary discussion to the history and general development of economic thought. Here the reader will find some of the nineteenth- and twentieth-century masters of the subject: Wicksell, Böhm-Bawerk, Pareto, Irving Fisher, J. B. Clark, Hicks, Leontief, Pasinetti, Houthakker, Walters, Arrow, Hahn and others, in addition to those named above. Professor Blaug's *Paperback* is a text especially designed for students that clarifies the thinking of contemporary economists and also makes an original contribution to the continuing debate between the Cambridge and neo-classical schools of thought.

Hobart Paperback 9 *Gordon Tullock*
July 1976

The Vote Motive

The *Hobart Paperbacks* were devised as a series of studies of medium length between *Papers* and books in which economists would analyse the relationship between economic thinking and policy, and in particular consider the circumstances which encouraged or inhibited the transformation of one into the other.

The first in the series, the "theme" volume, was written in 1971 by Professor W. H. Hutt, under the title *Politically Impossible . . . ?* Subsequent numbers have analysed the early economic policies of the 1970–74 Government (Samuel Brittan), the Austrian neo-classical thinking of Professor F. A. Hayek from 1931 to 1972, the economics of bureaucracy (Professor W. A. Niskanen), and the Cambridge School of economics (Professor Mark Blaug). The next in the series extends its range and introduces what is for British economic teaching, political debate, and press discussion virtually a new subject.

British universities seem to have ignored a development in the application of economic theory to the activity of government that has been refined in the USA for over 15 years. Although some British economists are interested in it there seem to be no formal university teaching courses, nor established teaching posts. The development goes under various names: the Theory of Public Choice; the Economics of Democracy; and others. It is perhaps best understood if it is thought of as the economics of politics. This is the essence of Hobart Paperback No. 9, in which Professor Gordon Tullock, one of the founders of this theoretical development of economics with Professor J. M. Buchanan, originally at the University of Virginia, outlines its main propositions.

The economics of politics is concerned not with the product of government (defence, welfare, etc.) but with its functions, which it analyses in much the same way as it analyses the structure of industry—the way it is organised, the inducements, pressures, incentives and sanctions that influence the people who run it, its general objectives and in particular its "maximand," the quantity it attempts to maximise, the goal it wants to optimise. Government is thus analysed as a piece of machinery, like the market, that people could use to achieve their purposes. It analyses the motives and activities of politicians, civil servants, government officials, etc., as people with personal interests that may or may not coincide with the interest of the general public they are supposed to serve. It is an analysis of how people behave in the world as it is, not how they should behave; it is behaviourist or positive economic theory of what is, not normative economic theory of what it should be.

The theory is in its early stages and is still being refined. Economists, political theorists and other social scientists it has attracted have not yet reached settled conclusions. But even at this stage it has yielded insights that illuminate the work of politicians and government and should attract more attention in British universities, among people concerned with government policy, and not least among politicians and government officials themselves.

Professor Tullock writes with a disarming, witty prose-style that makes his text reasonably easy to follow although closely argued. At some points he uses charts which readers who prefer to follow the argument in words can omit, at least on a first reading.

So far the conclusions for the efficiency of voting systems, the effects of the policies in a political system with two or more parties, the relative efficiencies and imperfections of government and market, the role of competition in making bureaucracies more sensitive to consumer preferences, the function of log-rolling (explicit and implicit) and others would seem to shed new light on the working of government and party politics.

The conventional approach to the bureaucracy has been to see it peopled by sea-green incorruptibles concerned only with serving the public interest. The theory of public choice traces the motives of public officials to the consequences of their activities. The theory also seems to offer intriguing advice for politicians on how policies in two-party and multi-party systems are best devised to maximise the support of the electorate. Not least revealing is Professor Tullock's discussion of log-rolling in representative government, even when it is implicit as in Cabinet compromises or party manifesto formulae agreed by party leaders without reference to rank-and-file supporters. Cabinet "leaks" may be a development in this process.

A main conclusion that emerges from Professor Tullock's analysis is that majority decisions are not as good for maximising the public interest as decisions based on majorities nearer two-thirds. Such a principle would reshape the British and US political systems, which tend to be based on simple majorities, although Professor Tullock says that the analysis upon which it is based is becoming accepted doctrine in the study of public finance in the USA.

Much of the analysis may strike the reader as cynical in its severely austere examination of political activity designed to maximise electoral support. But it would seem much more realistic than the common and conventional attitude that draws a distinction between the self-interest of men in industry and the selfless service of men in government.

There may be a reluctance to accept the realism, perhaps because it is disturbing to see public men and public officials analysed as serving their self-interests. But it is an error to suppose that men who serve their self-interests are necessarily in conflict with the public interest. It is an error to suppose that men in industry who maximise profit or that men in government who pursue the motive to maintaining power are necessarily doing so at the expense of the public. What matters for scientific analysis is whether self-interest in industry or government coincides with or conflicts with the public interest. The theory of public choice is designed to discover the circumstances in which there is coincidence or conflict, and the institutions that could increase the prospect of harmony. The theory supposes that men in both industry and government are moved by the same primary motive. This basic assumption leads to more realistic conclusions than the assumptions of earlier economic theories that there was a difference between motives in industry and in government.

To restate Professor Tullock's central theme and illustrate it from developments in the British economy we invited Dr. Morris Perlman of the London School of Economics, one of the few academics we know who is interested in the subject, to write a short commentary for the elucidation of British readers. He has done so with telling examples and several telling phrases. We hope it will help to open up the subject to British readers—professional economists and non-economists—who did not know of it.

Some of Dr. Perlman's exposition and examples may reinforce the impression of cynicism. The reason may be that we have come to think of politicians and public officials as in a class of their own, apart from the rest of us mere mortals. But he explains that the theory is capable of shedding light on the activities and consequences of government where former economic approaches were much less enlightening. Here perhaps the central example is the difficulty of explaining a wide range of government activities in terms of the economic concepts of "public goods" or "externalities."

Examples from Britain in recent years seem to show that government policy cannot be explained in conventional economic terms without considering the political returns to government in the form of electoral popularity and the prospects of keeping or returning to office. It may seem oversimplified to explain government policy on suburban fares (Labour) or agricultural subsidies (Conservative) in terms of the judgement made by politicians on their effects on General Elections or by-elections. But that is the real world that economics has to examine and explain. The appalling Concorde blunder, which no doubt politicians of all parties will explain away in order to save face, cannot be understood without a theory of the economics of politics and a theory of the economics of bureaucracy.

Some may think there is danger in exposing the activities of people in public life to the rigorous analysis that people in industry have long endured. There would certainly seem to be an element of cant in politicians who explain every policy as efforts to serve "the public interest" without referring to the personal or political benefits to themselves.

The real reasons for government policy are rarely stated with the candour that would enable the public to understand them. Politicians seem to be playing out a public charade in which everything is explained by question-begging terms like "fair," "reasonable," "adequate," "just," and similar. The ultimate benefits to the public from developing the economics of politics may be that, by helping the public to understand politics and the bureaucracy (national and local) better, it would be enabled to make more rational choices between politicians, parties and policies, and to distinguish the functions that must be left to government and those that are better performed in the market.

An intriguing implication of the theory is not only that it guides party leaders in formulating policies to maximise votes in a given electoral system. By implication it also shows statesmen what changes in party alignment they may have to envisage to make desirable policies more possible. That may have been what Peel did in the 1840s; it may be what is now necessary to introduce policies that would be welcomed by the populace but that seem unlikely given the present arrangement of parties with conflicting wings. For 200 years economists have studied and examined the activities, achievements and "imperfections" of the market. The Institute is grateful to Professor Tullock and Dr. Perlman for combining from opposite sides of the Atlantic to provide British readers with a text that helps to explain, and should intensify interest in, the activities, achievements and "imperfections" of government.

Hobart Paperback 11 *T. W. Hutchison*
June 1977

Keynes v. the Keynesians

The *Hobart Paperbacks* were devised as a series of studies of medium length between *Papers* and books in which economists would analyse the relationship between economic thinking and policy, and in particular consider the circumstances which encouraged or inhibited the transformation of one into the other.

The first in the series, the "theme" volume, was written in 1971 by Professor W. H. Hutt, under the title *Politically Impossible . . . ?* Subsequent numbers have analysed the early economic policies of the 1970–74 Government (Samuel Brittan), the Austrian neo-classical thinking of Professor F. A. Hayek from 1931 to 1972, the economics of bureaucracy (Professor W. A. Niskanen), the Cambridge School of economics (Professor Mark Blaug) and the theory and practice of collective bargaining (Professor Hutt), the theory of public choice and the extent to which economic policy cannot be understood without allowing for the political motivations of government (Professor Gordon Tullock and Dr. Morris Perlman). The present in the series develops the theme of the impact of economic ideas on policy and the influence of economists on the thinking of government and politicians.

It would be common ground among economists of all schools and politicians in many countries that the economist who exerted more influence than any other on world economic thinking and public policy in the last 40 years was John Maynard Keynes. He lived only 10 years after his *General Theory of Employment, Interest and Money,* published in 1936, but his impact on minds and action has continued almost undiminished until at least the last few years. What Keynes said, or meant, is still disputed, and he is quoted in support by economists and politicians who differ among themselves.

Not least, Keynesian thinking is still closely followed by the Treasury in its advice to Ministers and by the National Institute of Economic and Social Research, the largely government-financed organisation whose generally supposed second opinions seem to be based on different subjective judgements but essentially similar short-run forecasting techniques. Economic advisers drawn from the universities have also, until recently, reflected Keynesian thinking, and one of them, Mr. Michael Stewart, has recently defended it as correct but thwarted by the electoral tactics of political parties in reversing their predecessor's policies,[1] as in income and price control.

In this *Hobart Paperback* Professor T. W. Hutchison, author of several works on the history of economic thought, tests the interpretations of Keynes in the light of his writings and utterances within a few years of 1936. He defends Keynes both against several critics and then against former colleagues and students at the University of Cambridge who claim to be, or who are regarded as, Keynesians in their interpretations, development and applications of his system of thought.

Professor Hutchison argues that Keynes would not have supported their interpretation of five major aspects of economic policy: the nature of full employment, the methods of ensuring economic growth, the relative importance of price stability and other economic aims such as full employment, the control of inflation by incomes policies, and the desirability of public expenditure. And from this view he maintains that Keynes's name and repute have been used to support policies not justified by his writings.

To indicate the reaction of Cambridge economists, leading exponents of Keynesian economics were invited to comment on Professor Hutchison's text. Lord Kahn and Professor Sir Austin Robinson responded, and Professor Hutchison was given the right of reply.

The reader of this short *Hobart Paperback* will find in it an intriguing assembly of extracts from Keynesian writings and of the interpretations placed on them by economists who have exerted a continuing and substantial influence on British economic thought and policy for three decades. Keynesian thinking has come under increasing criticism in recent years, and it has been argued by Professor Axel Leijonhufvud that there is a difference between Keynesian economics and the economics of Keynes.[2] The five issues listed above and others are central to the discussion and formation of economic policy in 1977, over 30 years after Keynes's death, and will continue to be so for years to come. If anyone doubted Keynes's celebrated dictum about the influence of ideas and thought on policy,[2] his work and life are testimony to its strength. No doubt economists will debate for many years what Keynes said, and what he meant. This *Hobart Paperback* is intended as a contribution to that debate.

We have the sad duty of recording our gratitude to the late Professor Harry Johnson who read Professor Hutchison's text and offered comments

1. *The Jekyll & Hyde Years: Politics & Economic Policy since 1946*, J. M. Dent, 1977.
2. Quoted by Professor Hutchison, p. 35, fn. 1.

which embodied possibly his last economic judgement before his final illness in February. The Institute hopes to find a more lasting memorial by which to express its gratitude for Harry Johnson's services to it since he was made an Adviser in 1974 and for his advice on several texts. We should also like to thank Professors Milton Friedman and F. A. Hayek for reading Professor Hutchison's text and for their comments on it.

Professor Hutchison's study and the Comments by Lord Kahn and Sir Austin Robinson reveal the views of the most influential British applied political economist in the twentieth century so far. Since the exchange also sheds light not only on what Keynes said but also on what he meant, it is of interest to students of the history of economic thought. Not least, since Keynes's influence on economic policy has continued long after his life, the text is of even more immediate interest to British employers and employees, taxpayers and tax-spenders, voters and politicians, consumers and producers, public men and interpreters of economic thought in the press and television.

Hobart Paperback 19
October 1984

S. R. Dennison

Choice in Education

The *Hobart Paperbacks* were designed to discuss, in the spirit of what was once called "political economy," the influences which affect the translation of economic ideas into practical policy. In the realm of policy initiated or applied by government these influences are essentially the content of the economics of "public choice," as it is generally described in the USA, or the economics of politics, as it tends to be described in Britain. They are the economics of government, of democracy, of bureaucracy, of party politics, of the activity by pressure groups to influence government, and generally of the motivations and consequences of people in politics.

These influences are vividly apparent in the historical development of education in Britain. The notion that the thinking of scholars and their proposals for the organisation of education by politicians, officials and teachers will be scrupulously translated into policy and action for the sole good of children and students receives little support from the last 100 years. What has emerged is a structure of schools that has been conditioned largely by the interests of producers rather than of consumers, public officials appointed by government rather than parents.

In *Hobart Paperback* No. 19 Professor S. R. Dennison reviews the ideas for the organisation of education urged by economists, politicians and sociologists, and finds that the results are far different from the intentions; he concludes, indeed, that on many issues the results are the opposite of the intentions. Professor Dennison is uniquely qualified to attempt his appraisal by his rare combination of qualifications during his working life. He has been university Vice-Chancellor (and Vice-Chairman of the Committee of Vice-Chancellors); a Professor of Economics; a member of the University Grants Committee; Chairman of a Grammar school; and an Examiner in Economics at all stages from university degrees to A-levels. The experience he acquired and the judgements he formed in these varied activities emerge in this IEA Paper.

Professor Dennison writes primarily as an economist who is sceptical of the arguments used not only in recent years but also over the decades in favour of shifting the control of education from families and parents to politicians and officials. He subjects the main arguments to a spirited and robust scrutiny. His conclusion that most of them are faulty or perverse leads him to compile a combative but authoritative text that has been absent from the literature of the economics and the political economy of education for too long.

He examines the arguments of the political parties and groups of educationists. He joins issue on detail or on principle with academics and practitioners—Professor Mark Blaug, Dr. John Rae, Headmaster of Westminster School, Professor A. H. Halsey, Professor Tessa Blackstone, Professor David Donnison. He finds much of the argument faulted by circular reasoning, fallacious economic analysis, intellectual confusion, dogmatic assertion without argument or evidence; and he questions the statistics variously as circular, manipulated or based on solecism. His general conclusion is that the arguments for increasing state control of education are to varying degrees false, supported by questionable evidence, and rejected by the experience of history. He argues that the experiments in increasing state control, not least in the theory underlying the comprehensive school, have largely failed and have little prospect of succeeding. He ends with proposals that would make the state system more accountable to parents and, more fundamentally, for strengthening education independent of the state.

For 50 years or more large claims have been made for state control or regulation of economic life generally that it would be more efficient, more equitable, and more "democratic" than economic activity in the market. Impressive hypotheses have been built on the assumption that "public men," "public employees" using "public funds," would faithfully serve the "public interest." The argument has been applied to medical care, housing, pensions, fuel, transport, steel, local government in general, and not least to education. There is now increasing scepticism, doubt, and anxiety by the former advocates of the beneficence of the state. The rebuttal of the questionable arguments examined here by Professor Dennison should find a readier hearing now than for many years, not least in the ruling Conservative Government and Party that undertook to move the focus of influence from government to the family, from the producer to the consumer, but has so far failed, except in minor stratagems that do little for the citizen as parent, especially for the inarticulate and the uninfluential, for whom a voice on Boards of Governors is an irrelevance.

Professor Dennison's re-appraisal of the argument and the evidence will be instinctively resisted by people who benefit from the political control of education and/or who see their interest as producers paramount over their interests as consumers. But in the prevailing change in attitudes to the role of the state in economic, political, civic, and cultural life in general, the Institute publishes Professor Dennison's authoritative, closely argued and challenging analysis in the confident expectation that it will further stimulate the agonising re-appraisal of the role of the state in education.

PART III

Prefaces to IEA Readings

IEA Readings 9
September 1972

R. M. Hartwell, G. E. Mingay, Rhodes Boyson, Norman McCord, C. G. Hanson, A. W. Coats, W. H. Chaloner, W. O. Henderson, J. M. Jefferson

The Long Debate on Poverty

This book is about poverty rather than about history. But since the nature and extent of poverty and the cures for it are the subject of prolonged debate among economists as well as sociologists, and since the origins of present-day poverty are commonly traced to the Industrial Revolution which is thought to have exacerbated it, economists must know what the historians have discovered.

For long, many historians and economists—G. R. Porter, T. B. Macaulay, J. S. Mill, J. E. Cairnes, Alfred Marshall—held that poverty and social distress were ameliorated in the late eighteenth and early nineteenth centuries by industrialisation. The almost opposite view, drawn from the works of Arnold Toynbee, and apparently confirmed by that of Sidney and Beatrice Webb, J. L. and Barbara Hammond, and later historians of social conditions like Professor E. J. Hobsbawm of Birkbeck College,[1] and Mr. E. P. Thompson, formerly of the University of Warwick,[2] has contested this interpretation and argued that the poverty of nineteenth century Britain was more acute than it had been in earlier periods. More recently their view has been challenged, *inter alia,* by historians who considered there had been an improvement in living standards in the early and middle nineteenth century, or that, except for a few occupations like hand-loom weaving and tailoring, if there had been a decline for a time it had been caused largely by the Napoleonic Wars rather than by industrialisation and early "capitalism."

The view that industrialism raised living standards was re-asserted powerfully in modern form (with statistical evidence and economic argument) by Sir John Clapham in the 1920s. It was broadly supported in the more literary work of Dorothy George, Dorothy Marshall, and Dr. Ivy Pinchbeck, and in several lesser-known works on aspects of social or working condi-

1. *Labouring Men, Studies in the History of Labour,* Weidenfeld and Nicolson, 1964; *Industry and Empire: An Economic History of Britain since 1750,* Weidenfeld and Nicolson, 1986, and Penguin Books, 1969.

2. *The Making of the English Working Class* (1963), Pelican Edition, Penguin Books, 1968.

tions, as in Professor W. H. Hutt's study of the Factory Acts and factory conditions.[3] It has been substantially confirmed by the recent research of younger historians and economists interested in the history of poverty. Although widely known to historians and to students in the learned journals, it does not seem to have received as much attention by teachers and students of history, or by writers of works intended for general readers, as the view that industrialisation depressed living standards or exacerbated poverty. There is still a prevalent impression that the poverty of modern times originated in or was the consequence of early nineteenth-century developments. It continues in school and university textbooks, and in some of the Open University, as the better authenticated interpretation of nineteenth-century social history. And many non-academics seem to believe that the famous novels of the early and mid-nineteenth century were faithful descriptions of their times.

The significance of this historical debate for economists concerned with social policy in the 1970s is that contemporary thinking on the treatment of poverty often seems to be thrown back a century and a half and argued in terms of the economic and social changes accompanying the Industrial Revolution. It would seem that some protagonists, or their popularisers have, perhaps unintentionally, used history to strengthen the case they make in diagnosing the causes of poverty and specifying remedies.

To clarify the contribution made to the debate on poverty by more recent researches, this volume has assembled new essays on the significant economic and social developments in the century and a half after 1760. Part I comprises an essay by Dr. R. M. Hartwell of Oxford who, as an economist with a special interest in history, discusses the changing nature and extent of poverty down the centuries and its forms in the nineteenth century. Part II consists of four essays on more specialised studies, industries or regions. Professor G. E. Mingay of Kent discusses the transformation of agriculture. Dr. Rhodes Boyson writes on the life of the Lancashire factory worker, and Dr. Norman McCord of the University of Newcastle on the relief of poverty as exemplified in Newcastle and Durham. Dr. C. G. Hanson, also of Newcastle, outlines the development of self-provision before the coming of the Welfare State. Part III assesses contemporary writings and Professor A. W. Coats analyses the views of the classical economists on industrialisation and poverty. Dr. W. O. Henderson and Dr. W. H. Chaloner of the University of Manchester re-appraise the description by Friedrich Engels of the "hungry

3. "The Factory System of the 19th Century," *Economica*, March 1926.

forties." Mr. Michael Jefferson, an economist and a student of the early and mid-nineteenth-century social novel, writes an original assessment of the degree to which it accurately portrayed the conditions of its times. His interpretation would seem broadly expressed by Lord David Cecil:

> . . . to read these books for information is not to read them with the purpose that their authors intended. Art is not like mathematics or philosophy. It is a subjective, sensual and highly personal activity in which facts and ideas are the servants of fancy and feeling; and the artist's first aim is not truth but delight.[4]

The long debate on poverty and the effects of industrialisation will continue for decades. It may be that the debate is concerned with the wrong issue. Certainly there will be more contributions from outside the ranks of the historians offering different interpretations. The distinguished economist, Sir John Hicks, wrote recently:

> There is no doubt at all that industrialism, in the end, has been highly favourable to the real wage of labour. Real wages have risen enormously, in all industrialised countries, over the last century; and it is surely evident that, without the increase in productive power that is due to industrialisation, the rise in real wages could not possibly have occurred. The important question is why it was so long delayed. There is no doubt at all that it was delayed; whether there was a small rise, or an actual fall, in the general level of real wages in England between (say) 1780 and 1840 leaves that issue untouched. It is the lag of wages behind industrialisation which . . . has to be explained.[5]

Perhaps the debate to which the historians should address themselves is why economic growth did not raise living standards more quickly. Professor Hicks argues that the change from the casual employment of pre-industrialisation to the regular employment brought by the factory system enabled the workers in the new industries to "combine" to strengthen their bargaining power. It would again appear to be not so much combination *per se* as industrialisation and its regularity of employment that indirectly and ultimately brought higher living standards and the prospect of increasing release from the poverty of the pre-industrial age.

This assembly of essays attempts to provide for economists, historians,

4. "The Art of Reading," in *English Critical Essays,* Oxford University Press, 1958, p. 182.
5. *A Theory of Economic History,* Oxford University Press, 1969, p. 148.

students of social policy and the general reader a conspectus of the age of the Industrial Revolution to help them judge how far the poverty of the twentieth century is a legacy of the nineteenth, or whether it was dramatised and publicised in the replacement of the eighteenth-century domestic system by the nineteenth-century industrial system financed by "capitalism."

The authors write as individual scholars, with varying expertise, research and emphases to their essays, but the volume as a whole forms a corrective to the imbalance still widespread in historical teaching that modern poverty has its roots in the advent of industrialisation. As such it should be especially valuable to teachers of the economics of welfare policy in the present day as well as to students of social history.

IEA Readings 12
August 1973

Armen Alchian, William Allen, Gordon Tullock, Anthony Culyer, Thomas Ireland, David Johnson, Michael Cooper, James Koch, Marilyn J. Ireland, A. J. Salsbury

The Economics of Charity

The *IEA Readings* are intended to assemble varying approaches to a subject by economists. This *Readings* assembles essays analysing the economics of "giving" (Part I) and discussions of its application to a commodity rarely discussed by economists (or other social scientists), blood (Part II).

Readings No. 12 has evolved from a *Hobart Paper* in 1968 by two young economists, M. H. Cooper and A. J. Culyer at the University of Exeter, entitled *The Price of Blood.* Its origin was a case of a shortage of blood which led to the question whether the British system of voluntary giving by blood donors was sufficient to ensure the supply of blood that could be made available for saving life. Point was given to the inquiry by the view of an influential social administrator, the late Professor R. M. Titmuss, that there was no shortage of blood in Britain.[1] Cooper and Culyer concluded their analysis with the view that there might be a case for supplementing the voluntary donor system by pricing.

In 1971 the Cooper/Culyer thesis was contested by Titmuss in *The Gift Relationship,* which received widespread attention. He widened the discussion to the economics and ethics of giving in general and the efficiency with which blood was given or sold in several countries, mainly in the USA. His main conclusion was, in broadly ethical terms, that giving was good and selling was selfish or sordid, and that selling blood had led to undesirable consequences, especially in the USA.

The Gift Relationship was widely reviewed and approved by academics and the general press, at least for its moral fervour. More recent reflection by economists has produced critical appraisal. Professors Simon Rottenburg[2]

1. *Choice and "the Welfare State,"* Fabian Tract 370, 1967, reprinted in *Commitment to Welfare,* Allen and Unwin, 1968.

2. "The Production and Exchange of Used Body Parts," in *Toward Liberty: Essays in Honour of Ludwig von Mises,* Vol. II, Institute for Humane Studies, Menlo Park, California, 1971.

and Kenneth Arrow[3] have published major criticisms of the Titmuss analysis, and Professor Nathan Glazer,[4] in sympathetic vein, was doubtful about much of the reasoning.

Although it is difficult to separate the economics of giving from the ethics, it is of central importance for economists. This *Readings* suggests four inferences. It is over-simple to distinguish between giving as good and selling as not good. Professors Armen Alchian and William R. Allen, authors of perhaps the most penetrating introductory economic textbook in the English language,[5] outline elements in the pure theory of giving.

Philanthropy does not conflict with economic theory, which can be applied to giving as well as to selling. Professor Gordon Tullock, in a characteristically incisive discussion of "The Charity of the Uncharitable," analyses the less evident motives for giving. Mr. Anthony J. Culyer, a rising young economist at the University of York and author of a new work of social policy,[6] inquires searchingly into the meaning of the concepts used by economists and sociologists and concludes with new insights. And Professors Thomas Ireland and David Johnson, young American economists who have developed the theory of philanthropy, review the outlines of their findings.

These five essays offer an attempt to analyse the economics of giving, and they emerge with conclusions more refined and less apparent than is common in sociological writing. Giving is not to be separated easily into a category on a higher moral plane than selling, which is normally part of a process of exchange in which both parties benefit; giving can create a sense of indebtedness in the recipient,[7] and it can foment an attitude of dependence.[8] In particular collective giving, as in the Welfare State or in aid to other countries,[9] can do short-term good at the expense of long-term harm by weaken-

3. "Gifts and Exchanges," in *Philosophy and Public Affairs,* Princeton University Press, Summer 1972.

4. "Blood," in *The Public Interest,* Summer 1971.

5. *University Economics,* Wadsworth Publishing Company, Belmont, California, 1972 (3rd edn.); in the UK, Prentice-Hall International, Hemel Hempstead, Herts.

6. *The Economics of Social Policy,* Martin Robertson, London, 1973.

7. Professor Thomas Szasz has argued that paying gives the power to reject undesired medical treatment. (BBC broadcast, 2 October, 1972)

8. The late F. A. Harper (Institute of Humane Studies, California) once quoted a paraphrase of a saying by the Talmudic scholar Moses Maimonides: "The noblest charity is to prevent a man from accepting charity, and the best alms are to show and enable a man to dispense with alms."

9. P. T. Bauer, "Foreign Aid: An Instrument for Progress?," in Barbara Ward and P. T. Bauer, *Two Views on Aid to Developing Countries,* Occasional Paper 9, IEA, 1966, and *Dissent on Development,* Weidenfeld and Nicolson, 1971.

ing the capacity to build independence. Much of the economics of giving has been developed in the USA: hence most of the authors in Part I are American economists who are showing that economics can be applied to maximise the utility of giving no less than that of selling.

Second, if the obscurantist distinction between giving and selling can be removed from the discussion, it is possible to consider, as Cooper and Culyer argued in 1968 and amplify in Part II, how far payment can be added to expand the supply of blood to save life. This approach is reinforced by two shorter discussions: Professors Ireland and James Koch attempt a hypothetical supply curve of blood with a range of prices; Professor Johnson contrasts the British and American methods of assembling volunteer and paid blood.

Third, the Titmuss argument was that blood provided at a price by "professional" blood suppliers created a larger risk of infection than did blood given by voluntary donors. This charge raised technical issues beyond the competence of economists, and a British doctor and an American lawyer were invited to contribute essays on these aspects to a special section, "Technical Evidence." If there were no method of testing blood for infection, the proposition would weaken the case for generating supplies by payment. But there appear to be technical developments in testing blood which reduce or remove the risk: the medical contribution by Dr. A. J. Salsbury and the legal essay by Professor Marilyn J. Ireland suggests that the Titmuss hypothesis may be partly or wholly refuted. In that event, the medical/legal reason for distinguishing between volunteer and paid blood may be removed.

Fourth, the implication that a society which makes use of markets and pricing is in a sense more materialistic and less humane than one that does not appears questionable. Professor David Johnson's essay analyses three kinds of markets: the private market, for long the staple of economic analysis, the political market, made familiar by Professors J. M. Buchanan and Gordon Tullock and other economists in America, and the charity market, the newest addition, in which economists analyse the economics of giving and receiving in much the same way as they have long analysed the economics of buying and selling. Professors Thomas Ireland and Johnson have developed the economics of charity by working on the foundations laid by Buchanan and Tullock and others in America.

The Keynesian concentration on the macro-economics of national totals—income, expenditure, production, wages, costs and other aggregates and their derivatives—in large part explains the relative neglect of the potential use of markets and pricing techniques in solving economic problems.

It is because the study of markets has continued to interest economists more in the USA than in Britain that the fruitful developments in the economics of giving and in the possible application of pricing to unfamiliar commodities or services have been more prominent there. In Britain the Institute has furthered the application of pricing analysis not only to blood but also to water, fire-fighting services, refuse collection, animal semen, telephones, broadcasting, roads, car parking, and, not least, welfare services, many or most of which are neglected by economists reared in the macroeconomic tradition.

This *Readings* introduces new economic thinking to British readers and takes further its application to the use of pricing for increasing the supply of blood. Some of the contributions, notably those by Messrs. Cooper and Culyer, were first written in 1971 (revised before publication). The collection will be of interest primarily to teachers and students of economics but also to sociologists, social administrators and others concerned with the economics and ethics of giving in general and to surgeons, physicians and others anxious about the shortage of blood.

The Institute offers this *Readings* as an illustration of the potential of market analysis in an activity not normally thought to be the province of the economist.

IEA Readings 18
September 1978

James Buchanan, C. K. Rowley, Albert Breton, Jack Wiseman, Bruno Frey, A. T. Peacock, Jo Grimond, W. A. Niskanen, Martin Ricketts

The Economics of Politics

The IEA Readings have been devised to refine the market in economic thinking by presenting varying approaches to a single theme in one volume. They are intended primarily for teachers and students of economics but are edited to help non-economists in industry and government who want to know what light economics can shed on the activities with which they are concerned.

Several Readings have been based on Seminars. Hitherto the audiences have comprised mostly non-economists in industry, government, the media who have heard papers by economic specialists in the subject. The economic theory of "public choice," the machinery by which people with widely differing preferences make decisions on the production and distribution of goods and services they share jointly—government, bureaucracy, politics, democracy—originated and has been largely developed in the USA. It has been spreading to other countries.

To present its main elements, the Seminar was arranged primarily for university and other teachers of economics and other social sciences. The list of participants includes academics (in several faculties) and non-academic people in government, industry and the media especially interested in the subject.

The Institute was fortunate in being able to persuade one of the Founding Fathers of the new theory, Professor J. M. Buchanan, who has been an adviser of the Institute since 1967, to deliver the opening lecture in order to indicate the origins and developments of the theory and to act as the keynote address for the Seminar. His lecture was heard by an audience of about 200 which included laymen interested in the general principles rather than in the detailed analyses and applications discussed in the Seminar.

Professor Buchanan's lecture is a masterly conspectus of the historical evolution of the new theory of public choice or "economics of politics." He performed the difficult task of compressing into some 5,500 words a rapidly growing school of economic thinking. Even where he used shorthand technical language the main elements were clear.

At the Seminar elements of the economics of politics were expounded and developed in the subject: two from overseas, Professor Albert Breton of Canada and Professor Bruno Frey of Switzerland, and Professors C. K. Rowley, A. T. Peacock and Jack Wiseman of Britain.

Their papers showed new insights into the working of government and its instrument, bureaucracy, of the politics of government and of representative democracy in general. It would seem that in some respects they are able to explain the working of political democracy with more illumination than the political scientists have done.

To indicate how far the new theory of politics has been found illuminating in other social sciences the panel assembled five shorter discussions, by Professor Nevil Johnson, an authority on political institutions, Mr. Ken Judge, an unorthodox thinker in social administration, M. Henri Lepage, who reviewed developments in France, Mr. Robert Grant, a specialist in business, and Mr. Paul Whiteley, who teaches politics.

The *Readings* also contains two additional essays. The first is by W. A. Niskanen, formerly Professor of Economics at the University of California at Berkeley, who was unable to attend the Seminar. He has contributed the text of a lecture on bureaucracy in government and business, delivered to the American Association for the Advancement of Science. The second essay, by Martin Ricketts of the University College at Buckingham, on the thinking of Adam Smith relevant to the subject, was awarded the first prize in the 1976 IEA Adam Smith essay competition.

Important aspects of the subject were also raised in the Question and Discussion sessions following each paper, notably by Professor Stanislav Andreski, who teaches sociology at the University of London, Mr. John Burton of Kingston Polytechnic, Mr. Douglas Eden who teaches history and politics at Middlesex Polytechnic, Mr. Christopher Goodrich, then a Ph.D. student at the London School of Economics, Mr. Roy Houghton, senior lecturer in economics at the University of Sheffield, Professor George Jones, a specialist in government at the London School of Economics, Professor Stephen C. Littlechild of the University of Birmingham, Professor Brian Loasby of the University of Stirling, Professor J. E. Meade, Professor David Myddelton of the Cranfield Institute of Technology, Dr. Morris Perlman of the London School of Economics, Mr. Ian Senior of the Economists Advisory Group, and Professor Tom Wilson of the University of Glasgow.

The literature on the new economics of politics or public choice (sometimes also referred to as "the new political economy") is in Britain so sparse, specialist, or inaccessible in the technical journals, that this *Readings* should be seen as a uniquely authoritative review of the subject for academics who are stimulated by and wish to teach it, for people in the activities of government and politics which it analyses, and not least for the general public which benefits or suffers from the activities of government. It should thus form an ideal text for teaching and for study by lay readers.

The Institute is grateful to the six main lecturers, to the five panellists, and to the Rt. Hon. Jo Grimond who opened the Seminar with informed observations on the new theory as seen by the practising public man. It also wishes to thank Lord Robbins and Professor Max Hartwell who chaired the morning and afternoon sessions for the liberal discipline they exercised over the proceedings.

IEA Readings 45
October 1996

E. G. West, David Green, Martin Ricketts,
Michael Beenstock, Charles Hanson,
George Yarrow, Dennis O'Keeffe, Nigel Ashford

Reprivatising Welfare: After the Lost Century

> "History is not merely what happened; it is what happened in the context of what might have happened."
>
> Hugh Trevor-Roper, Regius Professor of History, University of Oxford

The welfare state has been the subject of exhaustive discussion and debate between economists, sociologists and political scientists. Doubts have emerged on whether the original egalitarian purposes of its founders can be sustained when there is growing rejection of the high taxes required to pay for them and rising incomes enable more people to buy better services in the market. The original hopes were broadly, in the four main services, high and rising standards in education, the best medical care for all (a utopian but politically tempting vision), housing at low rents for people with low incomes, pensions to maintain standards of living in retirement for all.

Such hopes have been disappointed and the defects are becoming increasingly apparent. The political process has a short electoral time-scale: government responds to current dissatisfactions, well founded or not. It is resigned to placate the organised interests of managements and trade unions of employees. And the contest between the political parties inflates the system: the anxiety of the party in power to display its compassion for the "deprived" prompts its claims to spend more on the welfare state than the party in Opposition.

The parties may differ at House of Commons question-time or in the debates between former Ministers in the House of Lords, but there is tacit conspiracy to maintain the welfare state for its party-political advantages. It is still a powerful way to win votes.

There are no confessions from Prime Ministers, or from academic supporters, no expressions of remorse, no apologies for continuing the long procession of flawed state institutions. Yet they continue to deny the people the direct control and influence that parents, prospective patients, tenants, and prospective pensioners could be exerting over the schools, the hospitals, the homes, the provisions for income after a life of work.

The Institute's Work on the Welfare State

When, in 1963, the Institute began its revolutionary inquiries into the economics of the welfare state by introducing the central instrument of economic analysis, the pricing mechanism created by the device of a voucher to cover school fees and health insurance, its authors questioned opinion polling that had shown massive—around 80 per cent—public support for "free" welfare since the last war. The pioneering introduction of pricing was recognised by Professor Mark Blaug, the historian of economic thought, who emphasised its importance for social scientists. His verdict should have warned the academics and the scholars:

> Economists will recognise immediately that the (IEA) enquiry in effect elicited information about the slope of the demand schedule.[1]

The findings were a fundamental corrective to the misleading opinion polling since the 1950s. The introduction of pricing showed that people were just as rational about paying for state education and medical care as they were about private goods and services. To adapt Milton Friedman's dictum, "There's no such thing as a free lunch," research published by the Institute demonstrated that "There's no such thing as demand without a price." The priced surveys[2] revealed that preferences between state and private services varied with their prices. But sociologists, opinion pollsters, and politicians went on ignoring the price factor in public services and preferences.

The Institute persisted in inquiries into "free" state welfare services. In 1964 *Education for Democrats,* by Professors Alan Peacock and Jack Wiseman, analysed the economics of a free market in schooling paid for by vouchers to create the choices excluded by state education. It persuaded a young economist, who blossomed into Professor E. G. West, the leading authority on the genesis of British education, to examine its origins. His *Education and the State* in 1965, with its evidence of wide and growing self-help

1. *Education: A Framework for Choice,* IEA Readings No. 1, London: Institute of Economic Affairs, 1967.

2. *Choice in Welfare,* IEA, 1963, 1965, 1970, 1978, 1987.

by the common people in the 1860s and earlier, provoked disbelief by historians.

The *Choice in Welfare* surveys in 1965 and 1970[3] had confirmed the 1963 findings. They were followed in 1972 by an examination of the extent and causes of nineteenth-century "social deprivation." *The Long Debate on Poverty,*[4] written by nine historians, similarly caused shock-waves among academics who had long portrayed the welfare state as the indispensable saviour of the working classes. The historians revealed a very different interpretation of the nineteenth century from the fiction of Dickens, the Brontes, Blake, Shelley, Southey, Wordsworth, Carlyle, Cobbet and other nineteenth-century writers.

The defects of the welfare state were creating increasing anxiety in the 1970s. Not least was the false claim that it was redistributing income from the rich to the poor. An academic sociologist had offered the Institute a scholarly account that revealed then little-known defects. In 1982 Dr. David Green's *The Welfare State: For Rich or for Poor?* argued that it redistributed income to the rich from the poor.

Five years later, Professor Julian Le Grand and Dr. R. Goodin revealed that much the same defect was apparent in the USA and Australia. This is a reversal of the claims for the welfare state.

The myth continues that the welfare state is the only way to rescue the poor from the consequences of their poverty. Historians continue to ignore the evidence that the working classes were building their own welfare "states" long before the Fabians began their outdated teachings in 1884 and the Webbs continued it with Beveridge and Titmuss at the London School of Economics they founded in 1895.

The persistent failure of conventional historians to examine the relevant issues prompted the Institute to publish a Symposium on "Welfare: The Lost Century" in the October 1994 issue of its journal, *Economic Affairs,* and then to produce this set of *Readings* as a much expanded version of that Symposium. It is time to supplement the meandering debate on the welfare state by a judgement in the light of private payments—as they were developing before the state replaced them by taxes.

3. *Choice in Welfare, 1965, . . . Choice in Welfare, 1970,* Third Report into Knowledge and Preferences in Education, Health Services and Pensions, IEA, 1971.

4. *The Long Debate on Poverty: Essays on Industrialisation and the "Condition of England,"* IEA Readings No. 9, 1972.

The Case for the "Counter-Factual"

This is the historical method of the "counter-factual," the study of the history not only of the events that occurred, the institutions that were built, but the more revealing study of why they displaced others that were developing with distinct advantages. The richer history of the "counter-factual" is put simply in the quotation from Professor Lord Dacre (Hugh Trevor-Roper).

The parallel in economic theory is Wieser's "law of cost" formulated by a founder of the Austrian school of economics, Friedrich von Wieser, (1851–1926), that the value of anything is not, as Karl Marx had taught, measured by the value of the labour used in its production, but by the alternatives foregone, the values of the goods and services sacrificed in order to produce it. The cost of the welfare state is thus judged by the value of the welfare services that had been emerging in the market but were suppressed by the state. The fundamental "cost" of the welfare state is the schools, the hospitals, the homes, the pensions, the insurance against unemployment and the other welfare services that were developing privately in the nineteenth century but were almost displaced by the state, the culprit that prevented the people from building for its families the services and institutions that experience and experiment showed best suited their circumstances and preferences.

To pursue the counter-factual approach, eight economists, political scientists, sociologists, philosophers and historians were invited "to demonstrate a new way of thinking about the theory and practice of welfare policies." Their responses constitute the 10 chapters in this volume.

Five essays cover the main services. Professor E. G. West, formerly of the University of Kent, later of Carleton University in Ottawa, Canada, confirms from further evidence the findings of his 1965 study, *Education and the State,* that there had been substantial development of schooling in Britain long before the state first provided schools in 1870. The evidence had been largely neglected by historians who had not studied the antecedents of state-provided education. The question is how private schools would have developed if they had not been gradually replaced by the "free" (tax-financed) state schools.

Dr. David Green presents parallel evidence for medical care and insurance against ill-health. The state had jumped on "galloping horses" that would have raced ahead if they had not been put out to grass.

Professor Martin Ricketts of Buckingham University describes the market for housing as it has been distorted by government policies on town planning, rent restrictions and other regulations, and how it could be expected to emerge if the distortions were removed. He concludes that well-intentioned legislation on housing has on balance harmed the lower-income people they were designed to help. A further aspect of the market for housing is that home ownership among the so-called "artisan classes" was emerging as early as the 1880s in the industrial towns of England.[5] The early forms of unemployment insurance and the scope for their future expansion in the light of original researches[6] into insurance costs for varying kinds of unemployment are analysed by Professor Michael Beenstock, of the City University Business School. In his view, insurance for unemployment need no longer be controlled by government.

The sixth essay reviews the extent and variety of saving for retirement and other purposes that were expanding from the late nineteenth century and have lately been urged by government because it will be unable to provide the state pensions it has long promised by "national insurance."

Dr. Charles Hanson of Newcastle University examines the institutions established by working-class people to provide income in sickness and old age. And George Yarrow of the University of Oxford analyses the achievement of a main device, the Friendly Societies, and their potential if government now in the 1990s and the new century replaced its discrimination against them by opportunities to resume and expand the services they originally developed, some over the long decades.

The principles underlying the contrasting supply of welfare by the single mechanisms of the state and in the diverse mechanisms of the market are discussed in two essays. Dr. Dennis O'Keeffe argues the economic/sociological merits of "giving" in its broadest sense in the two systems. Dr. Nigel Ashford indicates the political steps required to pass from one system to the other.

Readers are left to draw conclusions from this journey of scholarly insights by the authors into the services that might now be educating the young, nursing the sick, housing families, and maintaining the retired in their years after a life of earning: all without the political pressures from the self-serving state.

5. A. Seldon, *Wither the Welfare State,* Occasional Paper 60, London: Institute of Economic Affairs, 1981.

6. Michael Beenstock and Valerie Brasse, *Insurance for Unemployment,* London: Allen & Unwin for IEA, 1986; Michael Beenstock and Associates, *Work, Welfare and Taxation,* London: Allen & Unwin, 1987.

Liberating People from the Welfare State

In our day there are tentative attempts to liberate the people from the political state and to return to them the choices and freedoms, the sense of family responsibilities and cohesion, and the resulting direct influence their forebears were learning to exert on welfare services.

Politicians in all parties are recognising for the first time that their power to continue welfare services as a virtual state monopoly for most people is waning. It is seen most clearly in the growing acceptance by the Opposition of the modest hesitant moves by the Government to create choices in all four main welfare services: the voucher system for nursery schools, a choice between state and private schools; the "internal market" in the National Health Service; the sale of local authority housing to its tenants; and, most markedly so far, the encouragement of private saving for retirement.

The Austrian school of economists—from Eugen von Böhm-Bawerk in 1914 to the naturalised British Friedrich Hayek in our day—has long taught that the political power of government operates within the ultimately stronger powers of the market. Four tendencies will undermine the state: rising incomes, advancing technology, escape to welfare services in Europe, and the rejection of British taxes to pay for private schooling and health services.

Rising incomes will enable more people to escape from inadequate state schools and find ways, by insurance or extended fees, to pay for private schooling. They will insure with competing suppliers to pay for private medicine, not least to avoid the time-wasting queuing and the long waiting for hospital treatment. Few of the children accustomed to the comforts of air travel to holidays in Spain and beyond will return to live with the petty restrictions imposed on their parents' Council homes. And few will be content to retire on the increasingly precarious state pension.

Reprivatising Welfare: After the Lost Century shows that after 100 years, government is being forced to yield its control over welfare to the market. Welfare was being provided by the market from the late nineteenth century (and earlier), long before it was almost suppressed by government in "the welfare state." Welfare is being "reprivatised."

In the late twentieth century the market forces of supply (mainly advancing technology) and demand (especially rising incomes) are now at last replacing government. The early private services are returning after "the Lost

Century"—in much advanced form but with the same advantages of the market in restoring the power of the consumer to escape from the politician.

The book uses the history of "the Lost Century" to contrast the disadvantages of state welfare of the past against the advantages of the market welfare of the future.

We have to thank Professor Michael Beenstock for his analysis of the "Lost Century" used in the title.

Socialism Has No Future

The capitalist system is mankind's best hope because it works with the grain of human nature; socialism rests on coercion.

The Conservatives have introduced more socialism—state control of economic life—than has Labour. And the Conservative Party to this day has senior politicians who think that socialism is noxious except when run by Conservatives.

The socialists have had their master craftsmen in empty advertising—from George Bernard Shaw, H. G. Wells, the Webbs and the Coles down to the Castles, the Benns and the Heffers.

Socialism is a dream that has misled Britain since the Fabians. I had hoped that the incantation "production for use, not for profit" had long succumbed to experience. Where is there such a socialist society? Whose "use"?

Socialism has never validated its claims to ensure justice or equality, or to abolish poverty and conflict. The advertisers of socialism have promised to replace a capitalism whose faults we know by a socialism whose faults they deny. They have never had evidence from history to support them. All they can offer is to replace a system that uses individual liberty to produce communal affluence by a system that subjects individual liberty to centralized coercion.

The defects of capitalism—wide differences in income, monopoly, alienation, tardy treatment of "social" costs—are corrigible because they are not inherent. Capitalism has not removed them but continually refines its solutions. The defects of socialism—ignorance of public wants, inefficiency, conflict, coercion, corruption, monopoly and secrecy—are incorrigible because they are endemic.

We have frittered our resources in nationalisation of fuel and transport, bureaucratisation of education, medical care and welfare, and municipalisation of services that have no business in local government. Nor are unemployment or inflation the products of capitalism. They are even worse, but disguised, in socialism.

There is no escape in even more socialism. Big government, centralisation, high taxation are the causes of inflation, unemployment, slow growth, avoidable poverty, not the cures. More of this medicine would debilitate the economic patient still further.

For a century socialism has been the opium of the intellectuals and the public they misled. They have distracted us long enough from the task of removing the removable faults of a system that combines prodigious productivity with life-long liberty.

China will go capitalist. Soviet Russia will not survive the century. Labour as we know it will never rule again. Socialism is an irrelevance.

Yours faithfully,
Arthur Seldon

INDEX

INDEX TO THE COLLECTED WORKS OF ARTHUR SELDON

The text for this book is set in Minion; the display type is Meta Plus Book. Both are relatively new faces, chosen to reflect Seldon's influence on and activity in contemporary social and economic thought. Minion was designed by Robert Slimbach for Adobe in 1990. In spirit and intent it derives from the Garamond tradition. Meta, designed by Erik Spiekermann in 1993, with open spacing for legibility at small sizes, has grown into an extended family and is now widely used.

Printed on paper that is acid-free and meets the requirements of the American National Standard for Permanence of Paper for Printed Library Materials, z39.48-1992. ♾

Book design by Barbara Williams, BW&A Books, Inc., Durham, North Carolina
Typography by Graphic Composition, Inc., Athens, Georgia
Printed and bound by Edwards Brothers, Inc., Ann Arbor, Michigan